YIELDING GENDER

YIELDING GENDER

Feminism, deconstruction and the
history of philosophy

Penelope Deutscher

London and New York

First published 1997
by Routledge
11 New Fetter Lane, London EC4P 4EE

Simultaneously published in the USA and Canada
by Routledge
29 West 35th Street, New York, NY 10001

Typeset in Palatino by Keystroke, Jacaranda Lodge, Wolverhampton
Printed and bound in Great Britain by Hartnolls Ltd, Bodmin, Cornwall

British Library Cataloguing in Publication Data
A catalogue record for this book is available from the British Library

Library of Congress Cataloging in Publication Data
Deutscher, Penelope,
Yielding gender : Feminism, deconstruction and the history of
philosophy / Penelope Deutscher.
Includes bibliographical references and index.
(pbk. : alk. paper)
1. Feminist theory. 2. Deconstruction. 3. Philosophy, modern.
I. Title.
HQ1190.D49   1997
305.42′01–dc21   97–7477

ISBN 0–415–13944–9 (hbk)
0–415–13945–7 (pbk)

CONTENTS

ACKNOWLEDGEMENTS

Earlier versions of some material appear as the following publications: 'The Evanescence of Masculinity: Deferral in Saint Augustine's *Confessions* and Some Thoughts on its Bearing on the Sex/Gender Debate', *Australian Feminist Studies* 15 (1992); "The Only Diabolical Thing About Women . . .": Luce Irigaray on Divinity', *Hypatia* 9:4 (1994); 'French Feminist Philosophers on French Public Policy: Michèle Le Dœuff and Luce Irigaray', *Australian Journal of French Studies* 34:1 (1997), and 'Operative Différance: Recent Queer, Gender, and Postcolonial Theory', *Journal of Political Philosophy* 4:4 (1996).

I particularly acknowledge Genevieve Lloyd for her supervision of the doctoral thesis which formed the basis for part of this work; and three other inspiring teachers: Moira Gatens, Elizabeth Grosz and Sarah Kofman.

Thanks to all those at the Australian National University (and elsewhere) who were good about my ghostly presence as I finished this book while teaching. I've been very fortunate to work with a supportive Head of Department, Paul Thom, and with the much-valued Bev Shallcross and Reta Gear.

I'm especially grateful to the following friends and family who sustained me throughout 1996. Love and thanks to Michael, who made the martinis, and to Pepita, the spy-girl, who sent surprise gifts in the mail. Liz has been an amazing and dear colleague, Rosanne plotted her arguments with me and listened to me plot mine, and Rico gave acute readings and vigorous conversation. The extraordinary talents of Jennifer and Jane included their extraordinary talent for friendship at the end of the phone; and my mother and father were constantly encouraging.

A final thanks to Valerie Hazel for her efficient indexing work, and to the staff associated with U.K. Routledge (in particular Adrian Driscoll, Tony Bruce, Barbara Duke and Pauline Marsh) whose combination of professionalism and consultation was deeply appreciated.

INTRODUCTION

FEMINIST PHILOSOPHY AND CONSTITUTIVE INSTABILITY

Gender has never been a stable matter. It has been argued that the meanings of 'female' and 'woman' are troubled and unfixed. In the history of philosophy the meanings of 'female' and 'woman' abound with ambiguity, self-contradiction and paradoxical argument. Gender relies on incoherence of definition. As a cultural effect, as a textual effect and as an effect in a phallocentric history of philosophy, gender is rendered by its internal instability.

The politics of this argument have been discussed at length in debates about deconstruction and deconstructive feminism. Some commentators have staved off deconstruction's misinterpretation as nihilist by emphasising the stabilising role of constitutive instability. Some have emphasised the destabilising role of constitutive instability, so as to argue that gender is troubled. Does gender's instability sustain or subvert its hegemony? Or is this a misleading disjunctive? A better position is offered by Judith Butler and Eve Sedgwick: constitutive instability is simultaneously destabilising and stabilising.

Debates of this type which have circulated around deconstruction and deconstructive feminism are discussed in the first half of this book. They influence the readings of St Augustine, Rousseau and Beauvoir subsequently presented. Rather than looking 'behind', attempting to explain, simply criticising, or attempting to stabilise textual instability, I analyse instability as constitutive of phallocentrism in the history of philosophy.

As an introduction to questions of methodology I frame this work by considering two emblematically different feminist interpretations of the history of philosophy, Lloyd's *The Man of Reason* and Green's *The Woman of Reason*. In both works, the argument is put, or accepted, that reason has been historically associated with masculinity. Both feminist philosophers understand such associations as unstable. Yet they do not interpret the pivotal role played by instability in sustaining the masculine connotations of reason. For Lloyd, the masculine connotations of reason occur despite their instability. For Green, they are diminished by instability. I shall

1

argue that the masculine connotations of reason are mobilised by their instability, and I shall stress that deconstruction, and deconstructive feminisms, have offered strategies for a more complex analysis of constitutive instability.

Since Lloyd and Green are known for their subtle and sympathetic readings of Derrida in other areas, it is striking that deconstructive feminism figures in the work of both philosophers as a spectre to be resisted. Both associate deconstructive feminism with feminism of difference, understood as an anti-humanist genre which rejects reason because of its masculine connotations and remetaphorises women as 'different' rather than equally rational. For this reason, Lloyd and Green seek to distance themselves from deconstructive feminism. Distracted by the issues of rationality versus refigured femininity, humanism versus anti-humanism, they do not interpret deconstruction and deconstructive feminism in the terms most relevant to their own projects: in terms of contributions to the feminist interpretation of history of philosophy.

THE MAN OF REASON

Thirteen years have elapsed since the publication of a small, highly influential work by Australian feminist philosopher Genevieve Lloyd: *The Man of Reason* (1984). It has become a given within feminist philosophy that over the course of intellectual history, going back to ancient Greek thought, reason has been imbued with the symbolic connotations of masculinity. This claim needed little more defence than the citation of the more lurid passages in the history of ideas, such as Bacon's presentation of nature as akin to a maiden bound in wedlock to a masculine inquirer (Lloyd 1984: 11–12). But Lloyd's argument involved more ingenious interpretations. For example, one does not find in the work of Descartes either literal or figurative textual elements which thematise women or femininity. Still, Lloyd argues, Descartes conceived reason as a transcendence of the sensuous. While he does not give feminine connotations to the sensuous, such connotations were conventional before and after his own work. Thus, 'there are aspects of Descartes' thought which – however unintentionally – provided a basis for a sexual division of mental labour whose influence is still very much with us' (Lloyd 1984: 49).

If *The Man of Reason* was a controversial work, its core argument that reason had, indirectly or directly, been associated with masculinity was not contentious. Instead, to some the work was controversial because Lloyd seemed, in focusing on metaphorical elements of philosophy, to be concentrating on the more trivial or incidental elements of the history of philosophy, and so to be distorting that history. Another genre of criticism arose because 'the claim that Reason is "male" . . . inevitably conjure[d] up the idea that what is true or reasonable for men might be not at all so

2

for women' (Lloyd 1984: viii). Some readers took Lloyd's argument to be that reason was intrinsically masculine, leading to suggestions 'as one bewildered male philosopher thought – that such laws as *modus ponens* did not apply to female reasoners' (Lloyd 1993a: xv). The work was controversial for other readers again because of the possible implication (deplored by Lloyd) that reason should be rejected by feminists because of its masculine connotations. In rejecting this implication, Lloyd expressed reservations in 1984 about feminist affirmations of femininity and devaluations of rational ideals. By 1993, this caution had translated into specific reservations about feminist deconstruction, some versions of which, on Lloyd's account, 'see the future as lying in the affirmation of a new feminine' (Lloyd 1993a: ix).

I want to interpret in tandem with *The Man of Reason* a recent work by another Australian philosopher, Karen Green, *The Woman of Reason* (1993). Like *The Man of Reason*, it is structured in terms of a chronological review of perspectives on women and femininity in the history of philosophy. Both works offer sections on figures such as Plato and Aristotle, Rousseau, Hegel, Sartre and Beauvoir. Like *The Man of Reason* it acknowledges that femininity has been placed in sharp opposition to the masculine, and associated with the irrational, the sensible and the private sphere. And both works express strong doubts about anti-humanism, deconstruction and feminism of difference. Germane to my own project is the conflict between the titles of the works. *The Man* and *The Woman of Reason* deploy different types of methodology and orientation in feminist reinterpretation of the history of philosophy, a discussion of which will clarify the impetus for my own approach.

THE WOMAN OF REASON

Reviewing Green's discussion of philosophers to whom there is devoted an equivalent section in *The Man of Reason*, one finds that whereas Lloyd emphasises phallocentrism and misogyny in canonical philosophers, Green shows how misogyny or phallocentrism is mitigated in those same philosophers. Their discussions of the Greek philosophers, Rousseau and Beauvoir can be compared.

First, Lloyd discusses the way in which Plato and Aristotle associate knowledge with 'the extrusion of what was symbolically associated with the feminine' (Lloyd 1984: 4). For Green, although Plato does view women as weaker in all areas than men, he also offers some ideas about the ideal society (for example, on issues such as childcare) which are 'like' those of 'many feminist writers'. Aristotle may have offered a justification for patriarchy, but Green also reminds us that 'many of the things that Aristotle has to say in criticism of Plato are likely to strike a chord with women' (Green 1995: 4–5).

Second, Lloyd emphasises the Rousseau for whom, despite women's natural closeness to nature, 'it is men who make Rousseau's journey from corrupted Reason to Nature' so that their closeness to nature is 'an achievement of Reason' (Lloyd 1984: 64). In a complicated fashion, women are marginalised in Rousseau's work, excluded from the public sphere, and from reason. By contrast, while Green acknowledges 'the deep sexism of some of [Rousseau's] remarks', she goes on to emphasise the Rousseau whose 'views on women begin to look more complex and sophisticated than has been emphasised by earlier feminists' (Green 1995: 65). Green's Rousseau is another canonical figure who, despite his notorious misogyny, actually offers some views which accord with (Green's reading of) contemporary feminism – such as his valuation of love, compassion and sympathy, and the importance he accords women's influence in society.

Third, Lloyd's Sartre and Beauvoir are figures who retain negative connotations of femininity as that which is transcended in the affirmation of human freedom (Lloyd 1984: 101). By contrast, despite acknowledging Beauvoir's devaluation of feminine embodiment, Green values that aspect of Beauvoir's project which contributes to humanist epistemology. She acknowledges the anti-female moralism in both Sartrian and Beauvoirian theory. Yet, as in her approach to the misogyny of previous philosophers, Green deems Beauvoir's work more complex than is generally appreciated.

Green serves as representative of one kind of approach taken by the feminist philosopher who argues that the misogyny of the history of philosophy is unstable, woven with contradiction. For Green, this is a history more *complex and complicated* than is generally appreciated by feminist commentators. Individual philosophers become in her eyes figures we might appreciate as more complex, containing more valuable elements, than has previously been understood. Green seems to suppose that contradiction *diminishes* misogyny.

For example, though emphasising that Beauvoir's work is fissured with contradiction and anti-feminist tendencies (Green 1995: 132–5), Green locates elements in her work which have value from a feminist perspective:

> there are a number of deeply conflicting strands within de Beauvoir's thought which need to be straightened out if we are to see our way to grounding a reasonable discussion of these matters. I will argue that the most fruitful strand in de Beauvoir's thought is one which suggests accepting the actual historical writings of women as providing a basis for developing such an understanding. This strategy also provides us with the opportunity of articulating a distinctive feminist humanism.
>
> (Green 1995: 128–9)

4

An intermittent refrain in *The Woman of Reason* is that accounts of woman and femininity in the history of philosophy have been more unstable, complex, contradictory or ambivalent than feminists have tended to avow. However, for Green this means reinterpreting Beauvoir, like Plato, Aristotle and Rousseau, as complex figures who do have some elements to offer a feminist humanism despite their misogyny.

The methodological orientations of Lloyd and Green are very different. Where Lloyd interprets concepts of reason and knowledge in the history of philosophy, Green focuses on theories of political and social organisation. Where Lloyd focuses on the masculine connotations of reason, Green reviews the history of philosophy for those elements it might have to contribute to a humanist feminism. However, the key point on which I wish to compare Green and Lloyd is their different approach to the analysis of a philosopher's 'complexity'.

An example can be seen in a comparison of their discussions of Rousseau. Both theorists emphasise the complexity of Rousseau's thought about the role of women. Both point out that women are not simply devalued in Rousseau's thought. While women are excluded from reason, reason is not simply valued. Rousseau is suspicious of reason and values nature, to which women are said to be closer. Rather than devaluing women, Rousseau values women highly as closer to nature. Nevertheless, his misogyny is well known. He is notorious as the philosopher who declared that woman is made specially to please man (Rousseau 1991: 358). So both Lloyd and Green agree that Rousseau's is not a 'simple' misogyny.

How these two feminist commentators analyse the complexity of Rousseau's misogyny can therefore be contrasted. Lloyd emphasises that *despite the complexity*, Rousseau does exclude women from a reason which is associated with the masculine, and (so long as it is in proximity to nature) valued. Green implies that Rousseau's anti-feminism is *mitigated* by its complexity. I shall focus further on this 'mitigation' refrain in Green's work, and then return to the 'despite' refrain in Lloyd's work.

For Green, Rousseau may be sex-biased, but Rousseau should also be seen as a philosopher who values care, empathy and love. How is the complexity of a philosopher's misogyny analysed in the following passage?

> Before completely condemning Rousseau on the basis of these passages quoted . . . it is worthwhile considering his justification for these views in greater detail. For although he believes that women should be different from men and should not aspire to 'masculine virtues', he also ascribes a very important place to them in society, and for each derogatory quotation a more flattering counterpart could be supplied.
>
> (Green 1995: 70)

The fact that 'for each derogatory quotation a more flattering counterpart' is available seems to suggest that there is more for feminists to salvage in Rousseau than is suggested by the derogatory elements alone. Apparently, the flattering counterparts diminish the sting of the derogatory elements. This is a common approach in the analysis of contradictory tendencies in texts, and one which will be revisited – and criticised – in the discussions of Augustine, Rousseau and Beauvoir presented in the second half of the book.

The key point is not *whether* the images and accounts of women in the history of philosophy are unstable, complex and contradictory. Most commentators would, with different emphasis, agree that this is the case. The key issue is what strategies are favoured by the feminist commentator in analysing such instability. Is instability emphasised or de-emphasised? Is it understood as troubling to, as disruptive of or as consolidating of phallocentrism? Is it understood as playing an important textual role? The second half of this work discusses this issue, offering some critical metacommentary on feminist interpretation of history of philosophy.

Rereading *The Man of Reason*, one finds that it often does bear witness, in its various entries on canonical philosophers, to the ambivalence, complexity or contradictory nature of associations between masculinity and reason. One encounters comments such as:

> it is important to be aware that the 'exclusion' of the feminine has not been a straightforward repudiation. Subtle accommodations have been incorporated into the social organization of sexual division – based on, or rationalized by, philosophical thought – which allow 'feminine' traits and activities to be both preserved and downgraded.
>
> (Lloyd 1984: 105)

In 1993, this tenor is even stronger in Lloyd's work:

> The idea of the sexless soul coexists with the maleness of reason, despite the appearance of tension . . . These unstable and contradictory alignments of reason with the male–female distinction reach back into the conceptualization of reason in the Western philosophical tradition.
>
> (Lloyd 1993b: 77)

Most of Lloyd's entries on canonical philosophers make passing reference to such contradiction and tension. Nevertheless, it is noteworthy that the presence of contradictory tendencies is not strongly thematised in *The Man of Reason*.

To take an example which will allow a comparison with Green, Lloyd's discussion of Rousseau recognises the complexity of his concurrent devaluation and valuation of reason. Lloyd nevertheless comes to a definitive conclusion about Rousseau's texts: they do, in fact, contribute to the exclusion of women from reason. One hears a kind of 'nevertheless' tone in Lloyd's concluding comment on Rousseau: 'but it is men who make Rousseau's journey from corrupted Reason to Nature'. Although she acknowledges the complexity, the multiple lines of Rousseauist argument, it is as if Lloyd takes Rousseau's misogyny to be effected 'despite' its instability, rather than because of it. This is an equally common approach to the analysis of textual instability which will also be further discussed and questioned in the second half of this work.

STABILISING TENDENCIES

Despite their recognition of unstable textual elements relating to women and femininity in the history of philosophy, Lloyd and Green are both exemplary of a critical tendency which averts an interpretation of how instability sustains phallocentrism. For Green, we should read the derogatory quotations with the more flattering counterparts, supposing that the one palliates the other. But perhaps it is the flattery which enables the derogatory content? Green's approach towards textual instability can be named subtractive. One contradictory tendency in a philosophical account is understood as lessening the other. The critic subtracts the one from the other, with the outcome that a contradictory text is stabilised into an overriding tenor: in this case, a mitigated misogyny. In fact, Lloyd also stabilises those unstable elements into an overriding tenor of the text. She locates the real import of an unstable text: consolidation of the masculine connotations of reason. Although this may be the real import of a text, I still suggest that the interpretation is unnecessarily stabilising since it does not analyse the way in which masculinism is rendered by instability. Effectively, *The Man of Reason* often segregates the masculinism of reason from textual instability since although the former is understood as occurring *with* the latter, it is often understood as occurring *despite* the latter, rather than *because* of the latter. *The Woman of Reason* presents itself as attentive to textual complexity, but stabilises that complexity where a sexist philosopher's inconsistent narrative is interpreted as a palliated narrative.

One of my own methodological givens is that contradictions and tensions do *not* mitigate. They sustain phallocentric accounts of women and femininity. I shall argue that, in different ways, many feminist commentators render unstable accounts of women and femininity in the history of philosophy unnecessarily consistent or stable, and produce unnecessarily consistent narratives about unstable texts. Feminist philosophy also needs to focus on contradictory textual tendencies, rather than looking between or beyond them to the 'real meaning' of a confused philosophical argument, or looking behind them, as when critics think such tendencies are trivial, or attempt to explain or account for them. In the second half of this book, I review the methodologies drawn upon in feminist interpretation of three figures: Rousseau, Augustine and Beauvoir. I focus critically on the different strategies typically used to analyse the contradictory, unstable tendencies in canonical accounts of women and femininity. I offer alternative readings focusing on the way in which contradiction, tension and instability sustain phallocentric accounts of women and femininity.

FEMINISM AND DECONSTRUCTION

In these works by Lloyd and Green deconstructive feminism represents a direction neither wishes to follow. For Green, deconstruction represents an undesirable anti-humanism. For Lloyd, deconstruction represents a genre of feminism she resists: a feminism of difference which revalues or reinvents the feminine, rather than defending women's rationality. For Green also, deconstructive feminism is conflated with feminism of difference. Both Green and Lloyd are wary that feminism of difference consolidates conventional associations of women with irrationality. It seems this genre of feminist rereading of history of philosophy might also be characterised by its tendency to associate deconstructive feminism with feminism of difference. This is a phenomenon also evident in Moira Gatens' *Feminism and Philosophy* and in Andrea Nye's *Philosophy and Feminism*. Because of this conflation, the question of what deconstructive feminism might have to offer feminist rereadings of history of philosophy is cluttered by the debate between 'feminisms of equality' and 'feminisms of difference'.

Since Green's feminism retains humanist ideals, it is at pains to distance itself from a deconstructive feminism which she understands as 'anti-humanist'. Since Lloyd is not anti-rationalist, she takes pains to distance herself from a deconstructive feminism often understood as 'anti-rationalist'. Two tendencies are evident. First, deconstructive feminism is reduced to the debate between feminism of equality and feminism of difference. Both Green and Lloyd offer feminist interpretations of the history of philosophy. Yet, intriguingly, they fail to identify deconstructive feminism as a resource of methodologies for feminist interpretations of the history of philosophy. They reinforce stereotypes about deconstructive feminism, feminism of difference or French feminism which state that the prime concern of this genre of feminism is to remetaphorise sexual difference.

My approach is other where, in chapter 3, I discuss 'three French feminists' in terms of their contributions to feminist interpretation of the history of philosophy, expanding the ways in which French feminist philosophers have been discussed. I introduce one French feminist, Luce

Irigaray, who thematises the remetaphorisation of sexual difference, and two who do not: Michèle Le Dœuff and Sarah Kofman. Rather than discussing these theorists in terms of this issue, I analyse the varied methodologies they deploy in the interpretation of the history of philosophy. While different from each other, they each offer analyses of the role of textual instability in canonical, phallocentric accounts of the history of philosophy. We should be wary of the reduction of deconstructive feminism to the affirmation of a new feminine:

> the final chapter strikes a cautionary note about the affirmation of 'the feminine'. Although I might express that caution differently, it seems no less appropriate in the present, as feminists try to think through the 'deconstruction' of the male–female distinction. Deconstructive strategies can assist our understanding of the symbolic content of 'male' and 'female' . . . But their upshot needs careful attention.
> Some versions of feminist deconstruction of the male–female distinction see the future as lying in the affirmation of a new feminine.
>
> (Lloyd 1993a: ix)

This reduction averts the potentially fecund encounter between different domains of interpretation of the history of philosophy. Though there is an aspect of deconstruction much closer to their interests, namely deconstructive readings of the history of philosophy, deconstruction and deconstructive feminism only make an appearance in the work of Lloyd and Green on the topic of sexual difference. This is a symptom of the very stylised ways in which deconstruction has been coded by different domains of anglophone commentary, an issue discussed in chapter 2.

All the while, in the domain of contemporary post-structuralist, late 1980s gender and sexuality theory, deconstruction has had a different kind of impact in the work of theorists such as Judith Butler and Eve Sedgwick. Deconstruction is differently represented by Butler and Sedgwick and their work offers a very different rehearsal of debates about constitutive instability. Butler's *Gender Trouble* analyses the instability between concepts of sex and gender, and the instability at the heart of naturalised gender identity. Sedgwick's *Epistemology of the Closet* analyses the instability of definitions of homosexual identity, and of distinctions between same-sex male–male desire identified as 'homosexual' and same-sex male–male desire which diffuses through homosocial masculine culture. A juxtaposition of these different contexts allows us to ask certain questions. What different kinds of methodological work have been effected by something named as deconstruction in these contexts? How is this related to the different ways in which deconstruction has been styled in these different contexts? Furthermore, what different approaches to the analysis of constitutive instability have arisen in these different contexts?

What happens when the 'man of reason' meets 'gender trouble'? The different treatment of deconstructibility and the analysis of instability in recent feminist material on gender performativity will be used to shed light on the analysis of gender in the texts of the history of philosophy. Working at the point of such intersections, this book analyses arguments that gender is unstable, and analyses unstable arguments in the history of philosophy about the role and nature of women.

1

GENDER TROUBLE/ CONSTITUTIVE TROUBLE

To understand these conceptual relations as irresolvably unstable is not, however, to understand them as inefficacious or innocuous.

(Eve Kosofsky Sedgwick)

In a conversation published in the journal *differences*, Gayle Rubin concludes by laughing a little at her interviewer, Judith Butler. Rubin has just offered some long comments about sadomasochist imagery, to which Butler responds:

I'd like to bring us back to gender.

And so Rubin teases her:

You would! . . . I think I will leave any further comments on gender to you, in your capacity as the reigning 'Queen' of Gender!

(Butler with Rubin 1994: 97)

Judith Butler's rapid ascent to 'reigning Queen of Gender' began with the publication of her book *Gender Trouble* (1990). Although *Gender Trouble* had nothing to do with ideals of dissolving gender distinctions, Butler's book is sometimes taken as an expression of the times when gender is purportedly in trouble. Characterised as the book which spoke for subverting gender distinctions, it has been a book for a time which spans mainstream Western ideals of taking 'playful' attitudes to gender stereotypes and the popularisation of the radical concept of queer. This term has been used to evoke a gay pride which refuses identity politics. In the words of Eve Sedgwick, it could be thought of as 'the open mesh of possibilities, gaps, overlaps, dissonances and resonances, lapses and excesses of meaning when the constituent elements of anyone's gender, of anyone's sexuality aren't made (or *can't be* made) to signify monolithically' (Sedgwick 1993b: 8). In this sense, Monique Wittig's depiction of homosexuality as radically different and exterior to heterosexuality would not be queer. In *Gender Trouble*, Butler refuses what she describes as Wittig's radical disjunction between heterosexuality and homosexuality

11

as 'simply not true': 'there are structures of psychic homosexuality within heterosexual relations, and structures of psychic heterosexuality within gay and lesbian sexuality and relations' (Butler 1990: 121).

If the 1970s saw a brief popularisation of 'unisex', perhaps the 1990s may be thought of as witnessing a brief celebration of fragmented, unstable identities. Rather than men and women being the same as each other ('unisex'), a man or a woman, homosexual or heterosexual, is not even 'same' to him or herself ('queer'). Because libidinal desire for the opposite sex is often inscribed with libidinal identification with the same sex, and libidinal desire for the same sex often inscribed with libidinal identification with the opposite sex, the boundaries between homosexuality and heterosexuality would not be thought of as stable. As a destabilisation of identity politics, the icon for queer might be the woman who desires and has sexual relations with a man 'as' a gay man, or the gay sadomasochistically oriented man who might have 'more in common' with the sadomasochistically oriented heterosexual woman than a non-sadomasochistically oriented gay man, 'lesbian-identified men or lesbians who sleep with men' (Sedgwick 1993b: 8), or the transsexual who affirms an identity as 'transsexual', in the space of the 'trans', or 'in-between' rather than as leaping a binary divide between male and female (Stone 1991: 299). Not unisex, then, but fragmentations of binary, uniform concepts of gender and sexuality, whereby a gay man *might* identify with a gay woman, not in a politics of 'we are all the same', but in a politics of 'we are all different to ourselves'.

Consider how Sedgwick begins her book *Tendencies*, with a conjuring of 'queer times':

> At the 1992 gay pride parade in New York City, there was a handsome, intensely muscular man in full leather regalia, sporting on his distended chest a T-shirt that read, KEEP YOUR HANDS OFF MY UTERUS . . . FAGGOT and BIG FAG were the T-shirt legends self-applied by many, many women; DYKE and the more topical LICK BUSH by many, many men . . . And everywhere at the march, on women and on men, there were T-shirts that said simply: QUEER. It was a QUEER time . . . On the scene of national gay/lesbian activism, in the *Village Voice*, in the 'zines, on the streets and even in some classrooms, I suppose this must be called the moment of Queer.
>
> (Sedgwick 1993b: xi–xii)

THE POLITICS OF INSTABILITY

I begin with two theorists, Judith Butler and Eve Sedgwick, who have been taken as icons for the ideal of a general shaking up of gender categories. One thing uniting Butler and Sedgwick is the way in which they have found themselves widely associated with the very approaches to gender and sexuality from which they seek to distance themselves. Neither Sedgwick nor Butler argues that gender does not 'matter', that it is in this sense 'in trouble'. Both argue that gender categories have the strongest grip on contemporary culture. But they are two of the theorists most associated with the concept of queer, which frequently serves as a stand-in term for the simple ideal of shaking up categories of gender and sexuality.

For queer has been confusable with a rhetoric of gender bending or a celebration of gender confusion or transgression, 'the lure of an existence without limit' (Martin 1993: 123). It has even been associated with ideals of sexual and gender libertarianism, in what Biddy Martin has called an anti-normative radicalism and romantic celebration of queerness. In the celebration of a general gender dislodging and the affirmation of multiplicities and pluralities of desires and identifications, there is sometimes the promise of living 'post-gender', or some implication that gender no longer *matters*. Neither Butler nor Sedgwick has argued that gender does not matter, though both have wanted to invalidate the fictions of natural, original, discrete or stable gender categories. Both have insisted that one cannot get 'outside' what one deconstructs. To think that gender does not matter is to confuse deconstructibility with the fantasy of being able to get 'outside' that which is deconstructible. Neither Sedgwick nor Butler adopts the fantasy that one can dispense with the normative, or move to a post-gendered 'existence without limit'.

The idea that gender is in trouble intersects with the idea that feminism has become less relevant. The critique of gender can suggest an unnecessary preoccupation with gender. Does feminist analysis reinforce through its categories of analysis gender categories rendered irrelevant by a concept of 'post-gender'? I have seen enthusiastic students explain that as they don't believe in gender any more, they can't see the need to go on analysing it or to theorise its subversion. We are living in a culture of gender fluidity, so why the retrograde obsession with gender categories? Maybe one can expose the instability of gender categories. But is there a continued need to do so? And doesn't doing so overly validate the gender binarisms whose transcendence or dissolution is vaunted? As Martin writes:

> Some queer theory ... has embraced the notion that gender is infinitely changeable and/or irrelevant to the far greater mobility of our desires ... In this view, gender ... becomes voluntary and fictional in the strongest sense.
>
> (Martin 1993: 122)

But examples of sexual oppression, inequity and violence are hardly far from hand. In this sense, it is not difficult to rebut the fantasy that gender

13

is irrelevant, voluntary or fictional, or that one can will oneself outside the normative.

Most interesting in all this is what the idea of 'instability' is taken to mean, when gender is seen as a retrograde fiction. To many, the fact that gender categories can be analysed as 'unstable' and 'confused' means that gender is irrelevant or invalid. At work is a telling interpretation of the function of those instabilities, ambiguities, gaps, overlaps, dissonances, lapses and excesses of meaning inherent in gender categories. The supposition is that the trouble internal to gender categories destabilises those categories to break their grip. The supposition is that the 'trouble' causes a breakdown of gender norms. But if exposing gender as 'troubled' breaks the grip of gender normativity and transposes us into the post-gender era, why hasn't 'post-gender' happened earlier? For as Eve Sedgwick points out in the 'Axiomatic' to *Epistemology of the Closet*, 'there is reason to believe that the oppressive sexual system of the past hundred years was if anything born and bred . . . in the briar patch of the most notorious and repeated decenterings and exposures' (Sedgwick 1990: 10–11). If demonstrating the irresolvable instability of gender categories disables gender normativity, why have not all the various decenterings and exposures of gender categories of times past already done their job? Gender may be deconstructible, but the grip of gender normativity is not thereby undone:

> A deconstructive analysis of such definitional knots, however necessary, [is not] at all sufficient to disable them.
>
> (Sedgwick 1990: 10)

In her 'Axiomatic', Eve Sedgwick refers to a 'definitional crisis' of masculinity (Sedgwick 1990: 20). Judith Butler has referred to the 'constitutive ambiguity' of sex (Butler with Rubin 1994: 6). Both Butler and Sedgwick have discussed the definitional ambiguities, the crises in signification of sex, gender and sexuality. Butler and Sedgwick became associated with queer politics, and queer in turn with the optimism that categories of sex, gender and sexuality are voluntary fictions. Butler and Sedgwick do talk about gender in terms of 'crisis' and 'ambiguity'. This language may have reinforced the perception that a queer politics simply discards definitional categories.

It is important, then, that the one refers to the '*constitutive* ambiguity of "sex"' (Butler 1994b: 6, my italic), the other to 'the *operations* of . . . incoherence of definition' (Sedgwick 1990: 11, my italic). Operation, constitution – what do such terms suggest, if not the commitment of these theorists to analysing sex and gender as constituted, and produced, as operative, not as irrelevant or fictional? Furthermore, there is a suggestion implied in such phrases about how these theorists think we should understand the work of ambiguity and incoherence of definition. When

14

Butler uses a phrase like 'the constitutive ambiguity of sex', she is not just emphasising that the categories of sex are ambiguous; she is also making an assertion about the way in which she thinks ambiguity can perform. Ambiguity can be constitutive. Butler is implying here that incoherence of definition produces discursive 'operations': gender effects. The categories of sex may be analysable as 'self-contradictory', to use Sedgwick's phase. But what Sedgwick proposes in her 'Axiomatic' is that self-contradictory discursive fields of force do have 'performative effects' (Sedgwick 1990: 9).

Yet this rhetoric about demonstrating the internal 'trouble' (ambiguity, incoherence, excess) of sex, gender and sexuality categories was translated into a rhetoric of undertaking to actively trouble gender. This was a rhetoric in which Butler appeared at times complicit. She does suggest in the preface to *Gender Trouble* that exposing internal instability can serve as a means for us to ask 'What [is the] best way to trouble the gender categories that support gender hierarchy?' (Butler 1990: viii). Thus the issue of internally troubled categories is interconnected by Butler with the idea of 'causing trouble' to gender. But readers have sometimes translated this into a concept of gender having been 'troubled' (decentred and exposed as troubled) to the extent that only a diehard would maintain gender as a category of analysis. What is identifiable in Butler and Sedgwick as a rhetoric of gender instability in terms of 'operation', 'performative effects' and 'constitution' has been read as a rhetoric of deconstitution and dissolution of gender.

This is an understanding of 'trouble' particularly inappropriate to the early projects of Butler and Sedgwick. I have already suggested that it relies on drawing a long line from the site a critic might designate as deconstructible to optimism about its abandonment. Of course, showing gender to be a deconstructible category may mean resisting its naturalisation and normalisation. But there is a world of difference between this and the optimism that gender categories, because they are deconstructible, are discardable fictions.

When Sedgwick speaks of a 'definitional crisis', she does not mean that gender and sexuality are in crisis; she means that the idea that there is coherence of definition is in crisis. To suppose that gender is in crisis because its coherence of definition is in crisis is to suppose that gender normativity's good operation relies on its coherence of definition. When Butler and Sedgwick use phrases like 'constitutive ambiguity' and the 'performative effects of incoherence of definition', they are implying the very opposite. They are implying that gender and heterosexual normativity operate on the strength of the ambiguity of their definition, not of their coherence. So there is no reason to think that exposing gender as founded in incoherence contributes to the dissolving of gender. That definitional trouble is lurking in the heart of the categories sex, gender and

15

sexuality may seem to indicate a greater possibility for the discarding of those terms. But Butler and Sedgwick presuppose a contrary succession of ideas.

To return to Sedgwick's 'Axiomatic'. When Sedgwick discusses incoherence of definition, she immediately refers not to the invalidity or discardability of categories incoherently defined, but instead to the 'material or rhetorical leverage', the 'profit', generated by that incoherence of definition. Sedgwick suggests that incoherence, far from contributing to a crisis in the apparatuses of gender and sexuality, *substitutes* for a crisis. Can crisis in definition substitute for, rather than contribute to, crisis in gender and sexuality norms? Can crisis in definition be analysed, not so much as 'causing trouble', but as constitutive, or operative? Janet Halley, in an article on classification of homosexual identity in United States federal equal protection law, is one critic who seems to think so.

Halley offers close analysis of the incoherence of categories of homosexual identity appealed to in a series of homophobic judgements in recent American case law. She discusses two much-analysed cases: *Bowers* v. *Hardwick* and *Padula* v. *Webster*. In *Bowers* v. *Hardwick*, the point of law was whether homosexual sodomy was protected under the constitutional right to privacy. In *Padula* v. *Webster*, the question was whether the constitutional right to equal protection under the law excluded employment discrimination against homosexuals. In both cases, the rulings were negative.

Halley focuses on the confusion of the definitions of sexual identity in question. What interests her is the incoherence of legal representations of 'homosexual identity'. On the one hand, American legal judgements have described homosexuality as non-volitional, an inherent abnormality. But on the other hand homophobic judgements are also made on the basis of the claim that contact with homosexuals could be dangerous for those who are putatively non-homosexual:

> A key rationale for anti-homosexual discrimination, then, is anxiety about the ambiguity of heterosexual interactions, about a potential for mutability that undermines heterosexual identity. Lest the change actually take place, 'known' homosexuals must be segregated.
>
> (Halley 1991: 367)

A comparison can be drawn here between the approaches of Halley and Sedgwick. Halley analyses the internal incoherence of identity definition. She locates 'definitional crisis', in Sedgwick's terms.[1] In that sense, Halley could be said to 'destabilise' the references to homosexual identity through exposing their incoherence. Halley suggests that hetero-sexual masculinity is being fictionalised as entirely 'other' to the spectre of homosexual masculinity as a congenital abnormality. But, inconsistently

16

and subverting this, homosexuality is also being represented as having
the potential to contaminate heterosexual males.

Halley is analysing the incoherence of the identities named as homosexual in that homophobic legislation. What does she take as the function
of such incoherence? We tend to associate incoherence or inconsistency
of terms with a dysfunctional argument, with embarrassing exposure of
flaws, leading to troubling reconsideration of that which is so exposed. If
one exposes incoherence or inconsistency of terms in a philosophical
argument, or a politician's argument, one poses a source of embarrassment. We might not have high hopes for embarrassing a politician. But
the philosopher, at least, might have to rethink his or her terms. It is a
subversive, troubling thing to do to a philosopher's argument to expose
its incoherence or inconsistency of terms, to expose the contradiction or
to deconstruct the position.

So Halley's interpretation allows us to ask whether deconstruction
should always be thought of in the same way. Incoherence of definition
in American law might not amount to 'internal trouble' – to rendering its
application ineffective – though we might still refer to an internally
troubled definition or internal instability of terms. For example, Janet
Halley argues that it is the very instability of definition concerning homosexual identity which is crucial to the 'coercive power' of homophobic
law. So it would be misleading to refer to the instability of definition as
'internal trouble' for the operation or power of the law. 'Internal trouble'
might seem to imply internal corrosion or breakdown. Halley suggests
something more akin to internal *'reinforcement'*:

> Read together, these cases ['*Bowers* v. *Hardwick* and *Padula* v.
> *Webster*] suggest that sodomy is currently misread in a discursive
> dynamic that not only generates the official version of homosexual
> identity but also constitutes a 'heterosexual' class *whose occlusion and*
> *instability are crucial to its coercive power.*
>
> (Halley 1991: 353, my italic)

Sedgwick makes some clear statements on this point. She notes
how critics have sometimes seen as subversive (*troubling*) the practice of
revealing the internal instability, incoherence or destabilisation of binary
pairs of identity terms like 'heterosexuality/homosexuality'. 'Locating
instability' is sometimes described as 'destabilising' the identity effects
in question. Deconstruction has often been styled as a strategy for
destabilising dichotomous oppositions. Sedgwick cites one critic, Harold
Beaver, for whom 'the whole sexual system is fundamentally decentred
and exposed' by locating the inconsistency and internal instability
of definitional terms relating to sexuality (Beaver 1981: 116).

Sedgwick herself is an avowedly deconstructive critic. She thinks it
crucial to reveal definitional crisis, but she does not overplay what such a

deconstruction represents in terms of subversion. Though she argues that the binary opposition between homosocial heterosexuality and homosexuality is internally unstable, she does not suppose that instability renders the opposition dysfunctional. On the contrary, the instability is the *condition of possibility* of the effectiveness of homophobia:

> To understand these conceptual relations as irresolvably unstable is not, however, to understand them as inefficacious or innocuous. . .
> To the contrary, a deconstructive understanding of these binarisms makes it possible to identify them as sites that are *peculiarly* densely charged with lasting potential for powerful manipulation – through precisely the mechanisms of self-contradictory definition.
>
> (Sedgwick 1990: 10)

So for Sedgwick deconstruction lacks the connotations of disruption. To deconstruct is not *in that sense* to 'trouble' dichotomous oppositions. Sedgwick agrees that binary oppositions relating to sexuality and gender are incoherent, but doubts that they are internally troubled in some *useful* way – in some way which might contribute to a dissolution of those terms or to the advent of some utopia of 'free play of meaning and sex', as Roland Barthes envisaged it (Barthes 1977: 133, cited in Sedgwick 1990: 10).

Remarking on the 'always already' internally unstable and incoherent status of binary oppositions related to sexuality and gender, we can now add to Sedgwick's comment:

> a deconstructive analysis of such definitional knots, however necessary, [is not] at all sufficient to destabilise them.

Her rejoinder:

> Quite the opposite: I would suggest that an understanding of their irresolvable instability has been continually available.
>
> (Sedgwick 1990: 10)

Thus Sedgwick labels her own strategy 'deconstructive' but avoids two claims that are typically associated with deconstruction: first, that the internal instability of binarisms has a self-corrosive efficacy or internally subversive effect, and second, that the deconstructive critic's exposure of that internal instability has a corrosive efficacy. Instead, she insists, the most incoherent binarisms survive and *thrive* on their own internal incoherence. It is exactly that kind of suggestion which Halley also makes when she proposes that the incoherence of American law and the instability of its definitional categories relating to homosexuality are crucial to its homophobic coercive power. Halley does not think that the incoherence of 'heterosexual identity' is a 'problem' (in that sense, *troubling*) for the homophobic law which seems most to rely on the idea

18

of a coherent 'heterosexual identity'. The problem is that incoherence of definition is *untroubling* to homophobic law.

Here the definition of homosexual identity crucial to homophobic law is 'unstable', but homophobic law is not 'destabilised' by the contradictory nature of definition at its heart, if 'destabilised' is taken to mean contributing to the liberation from the 'binary prison', to borrow again Barthes's extravagant formulation. On Halley's interpretation, homophobia is 'stabilised' or at least enabled by the instability at its heart.

At issue, then, is the analysis of internal instability in a given site of identity, definition or category. How do instability and the location of instability become connected with issues of subversion? What is the connection between this series of ideas: arguing that there is 'trouble' at the heart of gender; taking on as a strategy or project the 'troubling' of gender; and asking whether the 'trouble' which can be located at the heart of gender categories can trouble the life of the category? One must, in fact, form a theory of how 'trouble' (instability, ambiguity, incoherence of definition) has stabilising effects. Does 'trouble' necessarily trouble? Or is it more troubling that some of the trouble at the heart of gender categories seems to be so untroubling, to be capable, in fact, of upholding the status quo? What is troubling is the fact that gender and homophobia operate with great efficacy on the basis of their internal trouble.

The interconnection of this series of issues in Judith Butler's work is well known. This work has provoked considerable debate on issues of subversion, and has led to, in the words of Sedgwick, 'some of the uses scholars are trying to make of performativity as they think they are understanding it from Judith Butler's and other related recent work: straining their eyes to ascertain whether particular performances (e.g. of drag) are really *parodic and subversive* (e.g. of gender essentialism) or just *uphold the status quo*' (Sedgwick 1993a: 15).

Here, Sedgwick rightly rejects the suggestion that a given performance should be thought of as having 'either' the status of 'subversive' 'or' the status of 'upholding the status quo'. Implied in the straining of eyes is that a given performance must be one or the other. Most likely, it is both. Implied also is that 'upholding the status quo' and 'subverting' are themselves uncontested categories. Yet, how can we identify a 'subversion'? What form does it have to take, what effects must it have, to count? Is it always so easy to identify the 'status quo', as opposed to that which disrupts 'the status quo'? Can one pinpoint a performance as upholding the status quo – or the contrary? I want to examine these concepts of 'instability' and 'subversion' as they first became associated in Butler's *Gender Trouble*.

JUDITH BUTLER'S *GENDER TROUBLE*

At one point in *Gender Trouble*, in the context of an otherwise sympathetic reading, Judith Butler distances herself from one aspect of Gayle Rubin's influential 'The Traffic of Women'. Rubin takes as her political ideal 'that the law can be effectively overthrown and that the cultural interpretation of differently sexed bodies can proceed, ideally, without reference to gender disparity' (Butler 1990: 75). Butler asks:

> What leads her to the conclusion that gender is merely a function of compulsory heterosexuality and that without that compulsory status, the field of bodies would no longer be marked in gendered terms? Clearly, Rubin had already envisioned an alternative sexual world.
>
> (Butler 1990: 75)

Butler's wariness about imagined alternative sexual worlds is partly based on her suspicion of fictions about an original 'authentic' state of the human – the fiction of 'original' non-gendered bodies which are then 'culturally constrained' into gendered bodies. Butler also resists critiques of the gender system whose ideal is transcending that system.

It is true that in the conclusion and through *Gender Trouble*, Butler does offer speculative comments on the issues of parody and subversion in terms of which her work has been so persistently discussed. But the book is actually structured around core chapters of exposition on the work of a series of contemporary French theorists: Lacan, Kristeva, Foucault, Wittig. An introductory chapter discusses the sex/gender debate in feminism, the work of French feminist theorists Beauvoir and Irigaray, the problem of concepts of women's identity, and whether such concepts are necessary for feminist political action. Only in her conclusion does Butler return to the latter.

The reader turning to *Gender Trouble* for a discussion of parody and subversion will encounter central sections which review structuralism, Lévi-Strauss on kinship structures and the incest taboo, Lacan's account of the necessary failure of the sexed subject before paternal law, and criticism of the heterosexual and masculinist observational point and historical invariance of the Lacanian concept of the phallus (Butler 1990: 49). Butler reviews Freud on the Oedipus complex, psychoanalytic accounts of gender identification and melancholia, and feminist deployments of psychoanalysis, and offers a Foucauldian analysis of the repressive hypothesis grounding the 'causal' order relied on in much psychoanalytic theory. She offers a critical review of Kristeva's subversion of Lacan's model of subjectivity, arguing that it over-naturalises the maternal body without challenging the hegemony of the paternal law, and reviews Foucault's account of sex as constructed identity-effect before moving to a critical discussion of Wittig's attempt to describe bodies and sexualities 'without recourse to sex' (Butler 1990: 113). Butler argues that Wittig had recourse to 'the traditional discourse of the philosophical pursuit of presence' (Butler 1990: 118), then discusses Mary Douglas, concepts of abjection and the connection between bodily boundaries, binary distinctions between inner and outer and the constitution of subjectivity. The book reads less as a manifesto for gender trouble, more as an overview of key figures in contemporary French theory.

However, the book does not offer neutral exposition, and readers were responding appropriately to the way in which it was constructed and framed. In particular, the core expository material is framed so that Butler retells the work of contemporary structuralist and post-structuralist theory in terms of her own thematics. She creates a genealogy of theorists who, in her recounting, offer accounts of gender formation and identification as grounded in complexity and dissonance. Yet, often, this will not be the major theme of the theorist under discussion. Butler cuts and pastes a scrapbook of moments in the work of theorists which come closest to her concepts of dissonance and instability.

For example, Butler offers an expository chapter critical of Lacan targeting a nostalgia for a lost, phantasmatic 'plenitude' or *jouissance*. Nevertheless, she lifts from the exposition of psychoanalysis Lacan's suggestion that gender should be thought of as unstable. She suggests that Lacan offers an account of the subject as necessarily, inevitably 'failing' in gender identification, since Lacanian sexual identity is grounded in ideal phantasms which one never succeeds in even approximating. Criticism of Lacan is based on the way in which he sets up a romanticised pathos of necessary failure – which Butler likens to the tone of religious tragedy (Butler 1990: 56). But the critique is still intertwined with Butler's focus on the key element in Lacan's work: the account of gender identity as unstable, as a phantasm with which a self can never entirely coincide. Thus, she concludes the section on Lacan and psychoanalysis:

> The foregoing analyses of Lacan, [Joan] Rivière and Freud's *The Ego and the Id* offer competing versions of how gender identifications work – indeed, of whether they can be said to 'work' at all. Can gender complexity and dissonance be accounted for by the multiplication and convergence of a variety of culturally dissonant identifications? Or is all identification constructed through the exclusion of a sexuality that puts those identifications into question?
>
> (Butler 1990: 66)

A great deal is going on here. Butler has offered a sustained critique of Freud and Lacan, criticising everything from the lingering heterosexual bias in the model of psychosexual development and desire to the 'repressive hypothesis' which supposes that incestuous heterosexual desire precedes the paternal law which forbids it. She would, rather, emphasise the extent to which that law incites and produces repressed desire. Yet in the above passage, Butler is also pointing out that the analyses of Lacan, Rivière and Freud offer first, an account of gender identification as unstable and troubled, as 'complex and dissonant'. Second, Butler suggests that these theorists offer one way of understanding the complexity of gender. Rather than dividing up the population into two bifurcated sexes, we would understand the population in terms of the convergence of a range of multiple, different kinds of identifications with masculinity and femininity:

> multiple identifications can constitute a nonhierarchical configuration of shifting and overlapping identifications that call into question the primacy of any univocal gender attribution.
>
> (Butler 1990: 66)

And third, we might also glean from the same psychoanalytic account an account of *all* gender identification as unstable because based on the exclusion of an 'othered' sexuality. For example, acceptable heterosexual desire is premised, via the psychoanalytic account, on the repression and unacceptability of incestuous and homosexual desire:

> The excluded term is an excluded sexuality that contests the self-grounding pretensions of the subject as well as its claims to know the source and object of its desire.
>
> (Butler 1990: 66)

Butler concludes her discussion of psychoanalysis by synthesising it with a Foucauldian critique of the repressive hypothesis. She would expand psychoanalysis by having it recognise the extent to which paternal law not only represses incestuous desire, but incites that desire, claiming that it produces '*both* sanctioned heterosexuality and transgressive homosexuality', and the illusion of a sexuality before the law which is itself the creation of the law (Butler 1990: 74). She will criticise the supposition of 'one' unified paternal law, its effects restricted to the repressive. Nevertheless, Butler has also used a provisional occupation of a psychoanalytic model of subjectivity to introduce a certain model of gender:

> The alternative perspective on identification that emerges from psychoanalytic theory suggests that multiple and coexisting identifications produce conflicts, convergences, and innovative dissonances within gender configurations which contest the fixity of masculine and feminine placements with respect to the paternal law. In effect, the possibility of multiple identifications . . . suggests that the Law is not deterministic and that 'the' law may not even be singular.
>
> (Butler 1990: 67)

Butler works both with and against the grain of psychoanalysis. It is psychoanalysis which claims there is a singular, determining law. But it is also psychoanalysis itself which tells us of multiple, dissonant gender configurations and identifications, suggesting that we should rethink the concept of paternal law as either unified or singular.

In the second set of readings, Butler offers an exposition of the succession of ideas in Kristeva, Foucault and Wittig. In the first set of readings, Butler's critical readings of French theory have been intertwined with a retelling of that theory containing materials for an account of gender as unstable. The second core of readings develop this project. Again, the central work involves critical readings of French theory. But this time, rather than presenting the theorists as also offering an account of the instability of gender, Butler assesses them as challenging to, or *subverting*, accounts of gender. Another way of putting this: Butler introduces the language of the 'subversion of gender', and assesses the theorists in terms of the success of their accounts of subversion. The chapter is entitled 'Subversive Body Acts'. This presupposes what is meant by subversion. That question turned out to be crucial in the subsequent interpretation and use of Butler's work.

Thus, a transition occurs from issues of instability to issues of subversion. In the first set of readings, Butler discusses, via psychoanalytic theory, senses in which gender identity may be said to be *unstable*. But in the second set of readings, she has moved to attempts by theorists to 'destabilise' gender, or to theorise how gender is rendered unstable. But she moots the issue of how satisfactory an account of the subversion of gender (as distinct from the internal *instability* of gender) may be derived from each theorist under consideration.

For example, Butler offers a series of criticisms of Kristeva. Kristeva 'does not seriously challenge the structuralist assumption that the prohibitive paternal law is foundational to culture itself' and accepts the account of heterosexuality as 'prerequisite to kinship and to culture' (Butler 1990: 86, 87). She is critical of Kristeva, as of other psychoanalytic theorists, for focusing only on the prohibitive nature of paternal law. Kristeva fails to consider what desires might be incited or generated by paternal law as purportedly 'natural' drives of a female body (Butler 1990: 93). Butler also objects to Kristeva's figuring of a pre-cultural bodily realm (Butler 1990: 80).

However, Butler also criticises Kristeva on the grounds of the adequacy of her account of subversion. For example, where Kristeva locates in the 'semiotic' or 'prediscursive libidinal economy' a feminine site of subversion of paternal law, Butler argues that the account is inadequate. Kristeva retains an account of the semiotic as subordinate to the Symbolic (Butler 1990: 80). The Symbolic may be disrupted by the semiotic, on Kristeva's account, but the paternal law is still conceived as 'stable' – it continues to be reproduced.

Butler's assessment of Kristeva is based on how 'effective' a concept of 'subversion' is offered by the Kristevan theory of the semiotic (Butler 1990: 80). Presumably, an 'effective subversion' would disrupt the reproduction of the hegemony of the paternal law. For, as Butler states her objection:

> Even if we accept Kristeva's theory of primary drives, it is unclear that the subversive effects of such drives can serve, via the semiotic, as anything more than a temporary and futile disruption of the hegemony of the paternal law.
>
> (Butler 1990: 81)

Butler assesses Kristeva's account in terms of political strategy and names that strategy as failed because of the temporary nature of the disruptions Kristeva can envisage:

> In the end, it seems that Kristeva offers us a strategy of subversion that can never become a sustained political practice.
>
> (Butler 1990: 81)

Again, later, Butler questions Kristeva's foreclosure of the 'possibility of subversion as an effective or realisable cultural practice'. Here we assume that subversion is being named by Butler precisely as that kind of dissonance or destabilisation which one could identify as an effective or realisable cultural practice. Butler taxes Kristeva precisely on the question of locating a certain disruptive potential in maternal drives, without specifying what subversion means:

> Although she clearly sees subversive and disruptive potential in those semiotic expressions that challenge the hegemony of the paternal law, it is less clear in what precisely this subversion consists.
>
> (Butler 1990: 89)

Butler omits, nevertheless, to clarify what subversion means in her own usage.

In the reading of Foucault which links the material on Kristeva and Wittig, we see similar concerns expressed, in relation to Foucault's discussion of hermaphrodite Herculine Barbin. Butler assesses Foucault as offering a certain emancipatory ideal (Butler 1990: 94) which is problematic as a model of subversion. Whatever falls outside binary models of gender is romanticised as 'the happy limbo of a non-identity' (Butler 1990: 94, citing Foucault 1980: xiii). Butler resists the Foucault who, inconsistently, seeks to locate what is outside the law. She responds that the subversive should always be seen as neither prior nor exterior to the law, but produced by it. Where we locate what we want to name as 'subversive' – in this case, Herculine's apparent 'happy limbo' – we need not assume that we have located an 'outside' to the law:

24

Herculine's pleasures and desires are in no way the bucolic innocence that thrives and proliferates prior to the imposition of a juridical law. Neither does s/he fully fall outside the signifying economy of masculinity. S/he is 'outside' the law, but the law maintains this 'outside' within itself.

(Butler 1990: 106)

Last, in her discussion of Monique Wittig's *Les Guérillères* and *The Lesbian Body* Butler makes a series of similar criticisms focused on the issue of subversion. Butler discusses Wittig's ideal of the lesbian as transcending man/woman oppositions, and her position that one cannot destabilise the binary sexual system from within. Rather than a project of immanent subversion, Wittig takes as necessary the political project of overthrowing the whole sexual system by reshaping grammar and linguistic usage, for example. Wittig is criticised by Butler for an inadequate model of subversion. Wittig exaggerates the unity and integrity of heterosexual power, presuming that only radical revolution constitutes a viable subversion (Butler 1990: 121). Though homosexuality sometimes parodies or repeats or resignifies heterosexuality in ways which one might think are subversive, Wittig cannot successfully rely on the subversive power of 'parody'. According to her position, the only way in which one can subvert the heterosexual matrix is from a position utterly outside that matrix. Butler argues that Wittig's position fails to recognise the small, fleeting subversions of the heterosexual matrix which occur from within that matrix (Butler 1990: 121). Wittig posits a heterosexuality more coherent than it really is. On Butler's reading it is because Wittig excludes the analysis of the heterosexual matrix as *unstable*, *dis*unified, *not* integral that her concept of subversion is unsatisfactory; subversion becomes what can be effected only from a radically utopian position 'outside' culture. As with her critique of Foucault, Butler resists this, wanting to locate subversion within the sexual system, law and culture.

Butler discusses concepts of gender as 'unstable' and then shifts ground to concepts of destabilising gender, finally bringing the issues together. For Butler, it is an account of the former which enables an effective account of the latter. Destabilisation occurs not only from exterior positions. We should be primed to recognise the destabilising work of internal instability.

I have suggested already that the link between instability and subversion is not evident. Sometimes instability in a given site of sexual or gender category has effects which are anything but destabilising. An example is Janet Halley's suggestion that homophobic legal judgements are enabled, not disrupted, by the incoherence and ambiguity of their definitions of homosexuality.

Now, when Butler resists Gayle Rubin's politics of 'alternative sexual worlds' it is partly because of her desire to affirm the resistance which

25

occurs within the 'given sexual system'. Her criticism of Wittig is similarly that too uniform and stable a concept of heterosexuality emerges if subversion is attributed only to that which is radically exterior to heterosexuality. Wittig and Rubin might agree with Butler that gender norms should be seen as unstable, but they might not agree with the attempt to use the language of internal subversion to describe internal instability or dissonance. This is precisely because what they *mean* by subversion is a radically different sexual system, and not the internal dissonance and instability inherent in heterosexuality. Butler herself makes the point that heterosexuality continues to be normalised and is a 'compulsory system', so that locating internal instability may not identify something the critic wants to name as 'subversion'. 'Subversion', after all, has the connotations of overthrowing, overturning, upsetting, effecting destruction.

Butler's slide, in *Gender Trouble*, from discussion of the 'internal instability' of gender identification to the subversion of gender is appropriate, because she means by subversion no more than internal instability. But when she criticises others for the inadequacy of their concepts of subversion, she refers not only to the concept of the internally unstable, but to the concept of political strategy.

For example, the critique of Foucault and Wittig is based on the fact that they focus on destabilisation proceeding from forces exterior to what is destabilised. Thus they underemphasise the possibilities of internal destabilisation. But the critique of Kristeva is different. Although Kristeva theorises internal instability (in this case, the semiotic within the symbolic), the kind of subversion offered by the semiotic is a 'strategy of subversion that can never become a sustained political practice'; it can be nothing more than a 'temporary and futile disruption of the hegemony of the paternal law' (Butler 1990: 81). It would seem that the only satisfactory subversion in Butler's view is that which permanently and irrevocably disrupts, a conclusion which Butler elsewhere resists.

In fact, Butler was arguing that heterosexuality and the binary sex system are both compulsory and yet permanently unstable. Unstable because of their perpetual need for reiteration and re-enactment, because parody lies at the heart of 'natural' gender. Could the criticism which Butler makes of Kristeva be levelled at Butler herself, since the internal subversion constituted by the parody at the heart of gender norms can never become a sustained political practice and is no more than a 'temporary and futile disruption of the hegemony of the paternal law' (Butler 1990: 81)? In fact, the criticism fails because Butler is not discussing subversion as political strategy, but rather as something which lies at the heart of all reproducibility. Thus, she is close to Janet Halley's position. Where Halley argues that homophobia is strengthened and enabled by its own internal instability (incoherence of definition), Butler will argue that gender norms are enabled by their own internal instability, by the necessity of reproducibility and parody. The difference, though, is that whereas for Halley the enabling function of instability is nothing but insidious, for Butler the enabling function of parody retains some kind of *promise* as subversive. Parody shows that gender norms are not stable. Parody opens up, she will say, the possibility for new configurations of gender. This is the crucial difference between the way in which two critics think of internal instability as 'constitutive'. Halley makes no connection between instability and any of the typical connotations of subversion, whereas Butler does sometimes make those connections. She sometimes undermines that association too – as when she criticises Wittig for being so preoccupied with subversion from without that she overlooks small internal instabilities. But then she sometimes reinforces the association; she associates understanding gender as internally unstable, and opening up the way for new configurations of bodies.

FROM INSTABILITY TO SUBVERSION

Although exposition constitutes the core of *Gender Trouble*, it is not in terms of the two series of readings of psychoanalytic theory and of Kristeva, Foucault and Wittig that the book first become well known. First and foremost, Butler's position is associated with two main ideas: the contribution she made to the 'sex/gender' debate, and her ideas about gender parody, gender performance and gender performativity.

The sex/gender debate belongs to the period in feminist theory when gender behaviour was understood as 'culturally constructed'. Gender was distinguished from 'sex', understood as the 'biological' fact of being man or woman. Emphasising the cultural constructedness of 'gender' was an important move in feminism, because it denaturalised stereotypes of masculine and feminine behaviour. But Butler argued that feminists wrongly took the categories of 'sex' or 'biology' to be extra-discursive, or 'pre-cultural'. Gender appears to be the behaviour arising from the fact of biological sex. Feminists had argued that gender behaviour arose not as an effect of biological sex but from the effects of cultural construction. However, they had not challenged the concept of biological sex as tabula rasa to be then written on by culture. Butler argued that where sex appeared to be the cause and gender behaviour the effect, the very 'originality' and 'prior-ness' of sex was itself the effect – of cultural convention which posits the pre-cultural biological given. Butler argues that gender naturalisation relies on 'distinctions between the natural and the artificial, depth and surface, inner and outer'. Although sex appeared as inner and gender behaviour as outer, *both* sex and gender 'can be shown as productions that create the effect of the natural, the original and the inevitable' (Butler 1990: viii).

So *Gender Trouble* was taken up partly as a critique of sex as a category of originality. The other aspect of the book for which Butler became well known was the emphasis on gender performativity. Butler emphasises the retrospective time involved in the naturalisation of sex and gender as categories. The performance of gender in which all subjects participate is perform*ative*: producing the effect of an interior core of gender identity, and generating as a cultural effect the inner sexed identity that it purports to express, or be the effect of. Arguing that 'gender reality is created through sustained social performances' (Butler 1990: 141) (although not by agents separable from or preceding those performances),[2] Butler destabilises the opposition between natural and artificial gender perform-ance. Indeed, gender could be thought of as a kind of drag, as a variation on drag.

Thus concluding her material on Monique Wittig, Butler moves towards the concept of gender as drag. She cites Esther Newton's *Mother Camp*, in which Parker Tyler offers reflections on Garbo:

> Garbo 'got in drag' whenever she took some heavy glamour part, whenever she melted in or out of a man's arms, whenever she simply let that heavenly-flexed neck . . . bear the weight of her thrown-back head . . . How resplendent seems the art of acting! It is all impersonation, whether the sex underneath is true or not.
>
> (cited in Butler 1990: 128)

Following this lead, Butler took drag gender performance to be the emblem of all gender:

> *In imitating gender, drag implicitly reveals the imitative structure of gender itself.*
>
> (Butler 1990: 137)

Or, as she stated in 1993, 'To claim that all gender is like drag, or is drag, is to suggest that "imitation" is at the heart of the *heterosexual* project and its gender binarisms, that drag is not a secondary imitation that presupposes a prior and original gender' (Butler 1993: 125).

Such a comment is not intended to suggest that there is anything particularly subversive about literal drag itself. Butler was suggesting that gender could be thought of as a form of drag insofar as it involved the re-enactment, repetition or 'performance' of gender norms. We tend not to think of an individual's gender behaviour in these terms, because we tend to think of it as normal and natural. For this reason, for Butler, or Parker Tyler, to suggest that all gender could be thought of as a form of drag is 'subversive'. But, if *all* gender performance could be thought of in these terms, drag itself would not be subversive. For if gender could be thought of as a form of drag, this would suggest that all gender could be thought of as particularly subversive.

Certainly, Butler suggests that all gender is 'unstable', requiring re-enactment, repetition, performance. But she does not want to suggest that all gender is subversive in the sense that its constitutive instability *disables* gender effects. She is suggesting quite the reverse. The constitutive instability of gender (the element of re-enactment, repetition, performance) *enables* gender effects.

However, Butler was taken up as a particular advocate of *drag* performance and of deliberate parodies of gender. She was understood as arguing that drag was particularly subversive. This was an interpretation from which she later had to distance herself:

> Although many readers understood *Gender Trouble* to be arguing for the proliferation of drag performances as a way of subverting dominant gender norms, I want to underscore that there is no necessary relation between drag and subversion.
>
> (Butler 1993: 125)[3]

Yet it is clear how the confusion arises from the book. We have seen that Butler repeatedly associates imitation and repetition of norms with 'subversion'. This is a theme intermittently introduced through the core two expository chapters of *Gender Trouble*. The real question was the sense in which 'subversion' was being used, and Butler herself sometimes uses the term interchangeably with 'instability'.

When, at the conclusion of the Kristeva/Foucault/ Wittig chapter, Butler moved to a series of references to drag and to parody, the reader was primed to collapse this with the concept of 'the subversive' or 'subversion' which Butler had intermittently introduced through the book. Parody and subversion became conflated as issues. Butler rightly protested that her references to literal drag were very few in *Gender Trouble*. Given their actual rarity, she must have been startled by readers who took *Gender Trouble* as 'arguing for the proliferation of drag performances as a way of subverting dominant gender norms' (Butler 1993: 125).

What probably provoked the interpretation was not the frequency of Butler's references to literal drag, but the way in which the concurrent issues of gender parody and subversion had been persistently introduced. When, in the last pages of the book, Butler did finally refer to literal drag, it must have seemed that that was what the book was leading up to. The fact that drag is also evoked in the preface must have strengthened the impression. Butler opens with a reference to *Female Trouble* and John Waters, 'whose impersonation of women implicitly suggests that gender is a kind of persistent impersonation that passes as the real' (Butler 1990: viii) and whose performance is named by Butler as *destabilising* the very distinctions between the natural and the artificial through which gender operates. Drag is not much discussed in the book, yet the book is framed by it.

29

If her readers return to the detail and genre of exposition in the core chapters, they have no reason to expect Butler to see subversion in drag more than in any gender performance. But they will have seen the term 'subversion' used regularly by that point. They will have seen Butler's criticism of the subversive potential of Kristeva's concept of the semiotic: that it can never become a 'sustained political practice', never anything more than a 'temporary and futile disruption'. One is very likely to ask – if *not* drag, if not deliberate parody, then what is subversive, what *is* the political practice?

So Butler brought upon herself the unanticipated interpretation. She shifts from the issue of the instability of gender (chapter 2) to the issue of the subversion of gender (chapter 3), without a discussion of what counted as subversion. And all the theorists presented in chapter 3 were taxed precisely for the unsatisfactory nature of their accounts of gender subversion. In addition to the critique of Kristeva, the critique of Foucault occurs at the point where against the tenor of his own arguments, Foucault seems to locate the subversive as that which is outside the law. The critique of Wittig occurs at the point where subversion becomes that which can only be effected from a radically utopian position 'outside' culture.

Subversion is thus an ever-present refrain in *Gender Trouble* from the question with which chapter 2 concludes, of what critical strategies and sources of subversion appear as the consequence of psychoanalytic accounts; to her discussion of the meaning *or subversive possibilities* of identification (Butler 1990: 66); to her promise: 'I will suggest a way to reconceptualize the relation between drives, language, and patriarchal prerogative which might serve a more effective *strategy of subversion*' (Butler 1990: 81, my italic), and so on. Often the issues of parody and subversion had simply been placed together as if naturally. At one point, for example, Butler comments that in the gay and lesbian community there are subversive and parodic convergences, which feminist psychoanalytic accounts tend to overlook (Butler 1990: 66). At another, in the name of rejecting the ideal of a wholesale transcendence of power/ heterosexuality she speaks about the '*subversive and parodic* redeployment of power' in gay and lesbian practice (Butler 1990: 124, my italic).

So, while the references to drag were few, the allusions to parody were intermittent. The term lurks in statements about the parodic contexts in which 'the natural' is thematised within gay and lesbian cultures, and most confusingly in the conclusion, where Butler did indeed seem to be the apologist for drag *as subversive*:

> there is a subversive laughter in the pastiche-effect of parodic practices . . . The parodic repetition of gender exposes as well the illusion of gender identity as an intractable depth and inner substance.
>
> (Butler 1990: 146)

It is for these reasons that the reader might suppose that when chapter 3 concludes with some comments on drag, and is then followed with a conclusion entitled 'From Parody to Politics', drag gender parody is the politics of parody around which Butler has wanted to invoke the term 'subversive'. Yet, in fact, it is not. The crucial term grounding Butler's use of the term 'subversive' is not 'drag' but *instability*. If the terms 'parody' and 'subversive' had hovered around the whole exposition, no less had the term 'instability'.

Butler did not mean to promote or recommend strategies of parody, but to reanalyse the heterosexual binary system as 'an intrinsic comedy', 'a constant parody of itself' (Butler 1990: 122). Far from arguing that drag was truly subversive, she *never* speculated, in *Gender Trouble*, on what was truly subversive. What she did think was that the *possibilities* of subversion were opened up by the instability of the gender system. One of her objections to Lacan was that the analysis of paternal law as all-encompassing left no room for subversion; the objection to Wittig was that if one saw subversion only in that which entirely transcended power relations, one would never see subversion. What Butler means is instability, but she herself has hitched together instability and subversion.

Whenever Butler makes any gesture towards possibilities of subversion, these are systematically linked to the gender system itself as unstable, paradoxical, troubled. Via Wittig she had claimed that one can never identify with heterosexuality 'fully' and without incoherence (Butler 1990: 122), that there is no coherent heterosexuality:

> heterosexuality offers normative sexual positions that are intrinsically impossible to embody, and the persistent failure to identify fully and without incoherence with these positions reveals heterosexuality itself not only as a compulsory law, but as an inevitable an intrinsic comedy . . . a constant parody of itself.
>
> (Butler 1990: 122)

The very fact that Butler is saying that heterosexuality is a constant parody of itself *and* that it is a compulsory law illustrates the sticking point. One may want to name as the 'instability' of gender this constant parody of itself. But if one is also saying, with Butler, that heterosexuality is a compulsory law, and that one cannot wish oneself to a 'post-gender' position, then one is saying that heterosexuality as a compulsory law is *sustained* by the fact that it is a constant parody of itself. One may want to call this subversive, but the question will be what this achieves in terms of political strategy. This is a reasonable question, given Butler's own criticisms of Kristeva in terms of political strategy. But to put aside the debate about subversion, Butler's emphasis on the way in which instability, ambiguity, 'trouble' work to *sustain* gender norms is particularly useful.

31

Butler did not argue that she was 'subverting' gender or that gender was definitively subverted because it is unstable. Nevertheless, she rhetorically linked the ideas of gender instability and subversion. If gender was an entirely natural, binding, coherent, unparadoxical system, perhaps there would be no room for its subversion? Showing gender as unstable, paradoxical, dehiscent did show greater possibilities for its subversion than in a self-enclosed, stable system.

Because of the linking of the theme of constitutive instability with subversion, attention was deflected away from the fact that Butler's analysis could amount to an idea with a very different rhetorical edge. One could just as easily say, on the strength of her analysis, that because gender was constituted through its own 'trouble', its internal trouble should in no way be associated, even thematically, with the connotations of subversion. One could say that Butler's book was about constitution, not subversion. It was about how gender can be thought of as *constituted* through its own trouble. The focus in terms of which the book was taken up was the idea of gender as 'troubled'. But the focus should equally be on Butler's argument that gender is *constituted* so that the constitutive, rather than only the potentially deconstitutive, role of 'gender trouble' could receive more attention.

Accordingly, terms like 'instability' and 'subversion' figure less in Butler's subsequent work, *Bodies That Matter* (1993).[4] This language seems to have been de-emphasised, with the continuing emphasis that her work engages with concepts of performative speech acts and iterability, rather than performance or parody. Butler clarifies, 'I'm still thinking about subversive repetition, which is a category in *Gender Trouble*, but in the place of something like parody I would now emphasise the complex ways in which resignification works in political discourse' (Butler 1994: 33). Rather than an emphasis on sites of subversion, there is a balanced language of simultaneity. There is a focused emphasis on the way in which the repetition of norms is simultaneously 'hegemonic and subversive': we hear of sites which are caught in irresolvable tensions, sites which *simultaneously* legitimate and delegitimate (Butler 1993: 131), appropriate and subvert (Butler 1993: 128).

Does the critique of gender categories allow one to pass outside them? While this possibility has sometimes been attributed to queer politics, two of the key theorists associated with queer theory, Judith Butler and Eve Sedgwick, reject it. What, then, does the critique of gender achieve? And what of a gender critique which exposes the instability of gender categories? Does showing the instability of gender at least dislodge gender categories? To locate the presence of instability seems an encouraging move, but this feeling is lost when instability seems to support the status quo. The most important analysis may be the one which allows us to identify instability as simultaneous subversion and stabilisation, subversion and recuperation. But such an analysis must sacrifice the optimistic associations between instability and subversion.

In chapter 2, I shall consider debates surrounding the work of Jacques Derrida. Here again critics differ over the role that instability is understood to play. As essays in deconstruction, Derrida's projects have repeatedly been interpreted by critics in terms of 'nihilism, skepticism or relativism' (Derrida 1995a: 402). To locate deconstructibility has been taken to be a nihilist project, precisely because deconstructibility is taken by critics to undermine a given text or context. Yet Derrida has equally emphasised deconstructibility as rendering textual effects possible. Indeed, many critics, intent on recuperating interpretations of Derrida from nihilism, have made a point of defending his credentials as a philosopher. Derrida is then interpreted as analysing the conditions of possibility of textual effects. In a polemical moment, it might be declared that Derrida is not destabilising anything. But those who emphasise Derrida as identifying, analysing or reconstructing constitutive instability rather than destabilising discourse have tipped the scales too far. Constitutive instability simultaneously stabilises and destabilises.

It is fascinating to compare debate surrounding the work of Butler and Derrida. In the case of Butler, critics equate the analysis of instability with destabilisation, and positively interpret Butler's project as 'destabilising gender'. In the case of Derrida, critics equate the analysis of instability with destabilisation, and *negatively* interpret Derrida's project as 'destabilising philosophy'. In the case of Butler, I have argued that constitutive instability must be interpreted as simultaneously subverting and stabilising. I shall argue for the same interpretation of deconstruction.

2

DECONSTRUCTION IN
A RETROSPECTIVE TIME

This translativity of deconstruction destines it to erring and voyage.

(Jacques Derrida)

One sometimes hears comments these days about deconstruction being passé – but usually from those who were never much interested anyway, those who are pleased at the confirmation that there was never much there to worry about, and that it would eventually all go away. David Wills has described a form of conservatism where surprise is professed about 'the attention *still* given to Derrida's work in the United States' (Wills 1995: 255). Or, in Derrida's words:

> For more than twenty-five years, in fact, we have been told deconstruction is dying or that it is 'on the wane'.

(Derrida 1995b: 30)

An insidious phenomenon occurs when a complacency about theory dovetails with the fast turnover of that theory in the academic market-place. The most foreshortened versions of theorists proliferate, quickly drawn stereotypes being hard to unravel when interest just as quickly wanes. Theorists become institutionalised, lodged in books, arguments and conversation in their most reduced versions. In some ways, though, one might say that this has not been Jacques Derrida's fate. Thought of from this perspective, deconstruction seems to me exceptional in the sheer number of diverse classifications of his work which have proliferated since 1968. Sketchy stereotypes many of these may have been, but their mass has made it harder for any particular stereotype to gain overriding currency.

THE ERRINGS OF DECONSTRUCTION

In a scene from *Cyrano de Bergerac*, the hero outsmarts the provocateur who has insulted him with the unimaginative epithet 'bignose'. Cyrano replies with an exorbitant catalogue of possibilities for the mockery of his own outsize nose. Categorising twenty genres of possible witticism, Cyrano itemises: 'frank aggressive', 'pure descriptive', 'gracious', 'truculent', 'dramatic', 'insolent', 'naive', 'impressed', 'practical' . . . up to twenty. Teaching a course on the early work of Derrida, one day I found myself regaling the students with a list even more fabulous. There was I, itemising those ways in which deconstruction had been coded by various critics over the years: 'Dionysiac!',[1] 'anarchist!',[2] 'nihilist!',[3] 'apolitical!',[4] 'relativist!',[5] 'negative theological!',[6] 'self-contradictory!',[7] 'trivialist!',[8] 'pluralist!',[9] 'Barthesian!',[10] 'reversalist!',[11] 'strawman-ist!',[12] 'sensationalising!',[13] 'pragmatist!',[14] 'transcendentalist!'[15] . . . and my list continued.

Perhaps I was reminded of Cyrano because of the comic value in such an implausibly diverse list. In their context, most of the various codings of deconstruction have credibility.[16] Compiling the list, though, the mind curls with the curious effect of juxtaposing Derrida as anti-philosopher and philosopher, deconstitutive and reconstitutive. And then there is the dizzying phenomenon which, again that day in my course, I joked was the 'Brundle-fly effect'.

In David Cronenberg's science fiction film *The Fly*, the hero – scientist Seth Brundle – is accidentally synthesised with a household fly in a machine of his own invention. The result is a slowly transforming beast which becomes – as it names itself at one point – 'Brundle-fly'. Then there was also that phenomenon popularly, if briefly, known as the 'butterfly effect'. Through a chain of unpredictable and chaotically proliferating events, weather permutations – thunderstorms in Arizona, perhaps – could hypothetically eventuate from the flapping of the wings of a butterfly somewhere else on the globe. A butterfly effect occurred in the chain of unpredictable proliferations through various intellectual and popular domains caused by Jacques Derrida's flapping of wings. Thinking of the things 'Derrida' came to signify in these contexts, we might want to say that the 'butterfly effect' was really a 'Brundle-fly' effect. Consider the proliferating effects which something named 'Derrida' had in the context of debates around relativism, pluralism and pragmatism, for example.

This is the Brundle-fly effect: in *The Tain of the Mirror*, Rodolphe Gasché argued that Derrida is a 'transcendentalist' philosopher. He meant that Derrida was too often being interpreted as a smash-and-grab philosopher, disrupting texts and truths. Derrida, could, he pointed out, also be seen as someone who was talking about the 'conditions of possibility' of texts and truths. This is an interpretation we'll return to. In several essays, Richard Rorty directly responded to Gasché-like interpretations with sustained argument to the effect that Derrida is not, in this sense, a transcendentalist philosopher.[17] But by the time of Jürgen Habermas' first essay on Derrida in *The Philosophical Discourse of Modernity*, Derrida was being confidently referred to by Habermas as if he were simply a transcendentalist philosopher, with no supporting argument from Habermas for what is a highly contentious interpretation.[18]

In section III of Habermas' first essay, Derrida is one kind of Brundle-fly, what I would call a 'Gasché-Derrida'. Vertiginously, however, by Habermas' second essay on Derrida in *Philosophical Discourse*, I think Derrida has transmogrified into a different kind of Brundle-fly: a 'Richard Rorty-Derrida'. Habermas refers to the deconstructionist who 'deal[s] with the works of philosophy as works of literature' (Habermas 1987: 188).[19] Habermas then shifts smoothly (with what Derrida has described as a 'stupefying tranquillity', Derrida 1988: 157) from his 'Rorty-Derrida' to a kind of 'Paul de Man-Derrida' within the space of a page, as if there has been no transition: 'in his business of deconstruction, Derrida does not proceed analytically ... Instead, Derrida proceeds by a critique of style' (Habermas 1987: 189). Derrida has been the Rorty-Derrida-fly, for whom the standards of logic give way to those of literary effect, but he now evolves into a de Man-Derrida-fly. Remembering that *Blindness and Insight* is the title of Paul de Man's best-known book, consider Habermas' description of how, for Derrida:

> the text itself denies its manifest content, in the rhetorical surplus of meaning inherent in the literary strata of texts that present themselves as nonliterary ... Thanks to their rhetorical content, texts combed against the grain contradict what they state ... 'Blindness and insight' are rhetorically interwoven with one another
>
> (Habermas 1987: 189)

While Habermas does reference Rorty and de Man in this essay, he does not reference his interpretation of 'Derrida' as a 'Rorty-Derrida' nor yet as a 'de Man-Derrida'. It is not possible for any but a reader already conversant with the various interpretations of Derrida to distinguish 'Derrida' from the thing he became in de Man or Rorty's work. These 'Derrida-flies' become, in Habermas' essays, 'Derrida'. The criticism of deconstruction which then takes place in section IV of Habermas' essay is really criticism of de Man and Rorty, unreferenced as such, and ostensibly directed at Derrida.

It is a temptation to want to protect or protest the integrity of Derrida's philosophy against this kind of thing, to try, in Jonathan Culler's words, to demarcate 'orthodox deconstructive criticism from its distortions or illicit imitations and derivations' (Culler 1982: 227). Culler adds that a 'concern for purity is understandable among defenders of deconstruction, who are dismayed at the reception accorded ideas they admire'. Nevertheless he cautions that the concern for purity may lead one 'precisely to forget what deconstruction has taught one about the relation between meaning and iteration and the internal role of misfires and infelicities. Deconstruction is created by repetitions, deviations, disfigurations'

36

(Culler 1982: 228). In other words, isn't it inevitable that theory is open to a range of interpretations and passages, 'erring and voyage'? Isn't that possibility contained within the Derridean text we might think of as 'original'? Isn't it a mistake to think of these interpretations as 'perversions', since the 'origin' isn't original without containing the possibility of those very perversions? Wasn't Jacques Derrida always already the possibility of, didn't he always already envelop an invaginated version of . . . Jürgen Habermas' version of Derrida?

Deconstruction is not interpretative relativism, and one is not abandoned to an 'anything goes' position whereby all interpretations of deconstruction would be as good as each other. Always one can say of certain interpretations of deconstruction, as Derrida does say to Habermas' attribution to him of the view that rhetoric is primary: 'That is false. I say *false*, as opposed to *true*', and I defy Habermas to prove the presence in my work of that "primacy of rhetoric" which he attributes to me' (Derrida 1988: 157). To set up Derrida as the 'original word', to be plaintive about loss of purity, is problematic, if by this one imagines that a Derridean text could ever be pure, innocent and precede the possibility of its varied interpretation. However, this does not make all possible interpretations equally good ones, or indeed intellectually responsible and ethical ones. It is in these terms, also, that Derrida rejects Habermas' reading of him:

> here is the philosopher of consensus, of dialogue and of discussion . . . daring . . . to criticise without citing or giving a reference for twenty-five pages . . .
> Such procedures still surprise me, and I have difficulty believing my eyes, in my incorrigible naïveté, in the confidence that I still have, in spite of everything, in the ethics of discussion.
>
> (Derrida 1988: 157)

The problem of Brundle-flies, then, could be subjected at least to the values of an ethics of discussion. There has always been the critic ready to pounce: 'Derrida as "self-contradictory"'! 'Derrida deconstructs the "author's intention", but wants to retain control over the way in which his own work is interpreted!' For Derrida, however, this response is deliberately, wilfully trivial:

> And let me not be accused of denouncing errors of falsehood where I am supposed to have deprived myself of any right to such distinctions, as is so frivolously claimed.
>
> (Derrida 1995a: 401)

When a critic, A, interprets Derrida as, say, pragmatist, and another critic, B, attacks the merits of pragmatism through attacking what s/he names 'Derrida', then to redress critic B with faithful references back to

'Derrida's text' misses the mark. By now, the debate is about the merits of pragmatism, and the name of Derrida serves merely as an irrelevant stooge. Derrida has served as irrelevant stooge for a lot of debate in contemporary philosophy. But these debates *are* attributed, and with the most dismissive gestures, to Jacques Derrida. Certainly, all these debates take on their own momentum, so that conscientiously tracing them back to the real words of 'Jacques Derrida' would, at a certain point, be as appropriate to these debates as wondering what the butterfly 'really meant'. But, as I say, these debates *are* attributed to Jacques Derrida.

Casually, a colleague invokes Derrida's name in the context of a passing discussion of the merits of relativism, and I reach to slow down the discussion: 'Wait, but was he ever . . . ?' – but the moment's gone. Derrida gets lost in all the readings of cartoon readings of readings of cartoon readings of Derrida. For that colleague, Derrida is both passé, historicised, and filed as 'relativist'. The Brundle-fly effect has resulted from the work of so many difficult contemporary theorists. Despite all the strong, engaged work on Luce Irigaray (much of it refuting inter- pretations of Irigaray's work as 'essentialist') until a recent spate of new translations of her work reopened debate, Irigaray had very widely been demarcated as essentialist. It was difficult to continue to address this persistent interpretation when the work itself had also been shelved as 'old'. In the conjunction of fast classification of theory with fast turnover, the least complicated version of a theorist is seized upon, and the theorist is then discharged as uninteresting.

J. Hillis Miller has recently discussed a related phenomenon. It is clear that his concern is not with protecting the purity of an original Derrida, but with guarding against a drift towards neutralisation of the most complex and challenging aspects of particular theories. Miller discusses the way in which deconstruction has been 'falsely identified as nihilistic, as concerned only with an enclosed realm of language cut off from the real world, as destroying ethical responsibility by undoing faith in personal identity and agency, as ahistorical, quietistic, as fundamentally elitist and conservative' (Miller 1995: 82). Traditional ideas about identity, agency and responsibility have, Miller argues, in turn proliferated, or been reinstated. For example, on Tom Cohen's diagnosis, some scholars have supposed that deconstruction had to be denigrated (as nihilist) in the turn towards what is oppositionally designated as political engagement with the world (Cohen 1994: 2 cited in Miller 1995: 82). Hillis Miller's concern is less to rebut Gasché's reclamation of Derrida as philosopher than to express suspicions about what is really at work when 'everyone in literature, everyone doing cultural studies, feminist studies, studies of popular culture, "new historicism", or multicultural studies [breathes] a sigh of relief, and say[s], "Thank God. I don't have to take Derrida seriously any more' (Miller 1995: 83).

What did deconstruction represent when feminists first took it seriously? What does it represent when others think of deconstruction as cut off from the real world or as undermining concepts of identity, subjectivity or community valued in some feminisms? Rather than attempting to assert an orthodoxy of criticism, perhaps one does better to chart some of the vagaries of theory: the passages of Foucault, Derrida, French feminist theorists and others as they have been taken up. We might ask: which bits? By whom? In what contexts? What did they become? For whom? To what effect? What work did this do? What questions were asked? What questions elided? This would be to take the tack of meta-commentary: commentary about deconstructive commentary, analysis of how deconstruction has been analysed, working through how it was put to work, mapping where it travelled and what its effects were.

It is in line with the fast turnover of theorists that histories as well as commentary are now written about deconstruction. Adding to the enormous literature on and by Derrida, on deconstructive critics, by deconstructive critics, and literature on deconstruction *in* 'everything from architecture to 'the "Style" pages of the *New York Times* and the J-Crew catalog' (Wills 1995: 251) is a newer metadiscursive literature which constitutes a narrative out of the twenty-five years of those literatures. I am interested in following the work which certain Brundle-fly hybrids have been able to do for some contemporary critics. By 1997, we can ask 'what *was* that' – about a phenomenon which began in 1966, and now can just about be told as intellectual history. In *Deconstruction is/ in America* critics reflect on 'the present state of deconstruction in America' (Haverkamp 1995: vii). But the tone of many of the essays is retrospective. Gayatri Spivak opens her piece thus: 'I missed the first flush of Deconstruction in America (1966). I bought *De la grammatologie* off a catalogue . . . It was the mid-sixties. In those days . . . ' (Spivak 1995: 237).

DECONSTRUCTION IN AMERICA

In Derrida's words

Deconstruction, as we know it, will have been first of all a translation or a transference between French and American.

(Derrida 1995b: 27)

What was that? Histories which tell of deconstruction in America usually begin in 1966, when Derrida was invited to address a comparative literature conference held at Johns Hopkins University on Critical Languages and the Sciences of Man. A tale can then be told of four faces of deconstruction in America.

At first, deconstruction was taken up in American academia more in literary than philosophical contexts. One can turn for an account of the resulting genre of deconstructive criticism, associated with the Yale School of criticism, to Jonathan Culler's *On Deconstruction*. Here, Culler reviews a series of interpretations of literary texts representative of this period. Deconstructive criticism has been, for example, attentive to textual ambiguities. One might discuss the unresolved contradictions and the presence of hierarchies which are always breaking down. The deconstructive critic would avoid the urge to resolve contradictions located in texts (Culler 1982: 232–3). One might discuss competing interpretations of a particular text, each of which 'is based on premises that undermine the claim the interpretation supports', where 'the coherence of each interpretative schema is undone by the principle of signification to which it must appeal' (Culler 1982: 237–8). Or, the deconstructive critic might locate binary differences lurking in texts, and try to dismantle those differences or show them to be 'an illusion created by the workings of differences much harder to pin down' (Culler 1982: 241 citing Johnson 1980: x).

If Yale School criticism was one of the first faces of deconstruction in America, a second face was constituted by a series of books which appeared from 1986 onwards which claimed Derrida as properly philosophical, and whose prefaces made clear the desire to improve Derrida's legitimacy as a philosopher. Important instances here are Irene Harvey's *Derrida and the Philosophy of Différance* and Rodolphe Gasché's *Tain of the Mirror*. Irene Harvey went so far as to begin her book with an 'Open Letter to the Philosophic Community' which marked the transition of faces of deconstruction. Harvey declared:

> The contemporary philosophic community . . . has for the most part . . . outside of France, ignored or openly rejected *in toto* the work of Derrida
>
> (Harvey 1986: xi)

and also offered an 'Open Letter to Literary Critics' with the following statement of intent:

> the 'Derrida' and indeed the 'deconstruction' that you take to be all too familiar are not sufficient to provide a grasp of what it seems to me Derrida, the philosopher, is claiming, doing, and proposing. My aim, therefore, is to suggest a Derrida and a deconstruction . . . in a more rigorously *philosophic* way than hitherto.
>
> (Harvey 1986: x)

Hillis Miller has argued that a similar reclamation of Derrida as 'really a technical philosopher' involved the claim by Gasché that de Man, Hillis Miller and others had actually 'falsified' Derrida's work by using it in literary criticism. But Harvey, at least, was careful to qualify that hers was not an attempt to 'claim a privileged reading, nor to set up an orthodoxy

...but rather to illuminate aspects of Derrida's work which...have for the most part been neglected' (Harvey 1986: x). However, for Miller, by 1995 the problem has gone in the opposite direction. Derrida, he claims, is being bypassed in various academic domains because he is seen as too philosophical, and this is due in some part to the influence of interpretation such as that by Rodolphe Gasché.

One might say that a third face of deconstruction in America was constituted by a series of controversies, sometimes unusually violent, which took place around Derrida's work, from the 1980s onwards. These included concern about the influence of deconstruction on American graduate students (see Culler 1982: 227–8); concerns about the future of academic scholarship in the humanities; concern about the preservation of the 'canon' which deconstruction was supposed to undermine. It notoriously included unprecedented international protests from academics taking it upon themselves to defend the educational institutions and standards of other countries against Derrida. Derrida has recounted how his appointment as Director of the International College of Philosophy in France provoked a protest to the relevant French Ministry from a senior academic at Yale, claiming that the Ministry had been the victim of an intellectual fraud. Derrida's later nomination for an honorary chair at Cambridge provoked some twenty academics from around the globe to write similar letters of protest (see Derrida 1995a: 419–21):

> for the first time in history, to my knowledge, there has been the spectacle of academics at universities other than Cambridge, not even in England, claiming to protect the institution, that of Cambridge, and of the university in general.
>
> (Derrida 1995a: 403)

Controversy around deconstruction also included the depths of irresponsible public journalism when an academic 'scandal' was generated around the figure of deconstructive critic Paul de Man, whose wartime writing for a collaborationist newspaper re-emerged in the 1980s, leading, at worst, to associations of deconstruction with fascism, and prompting Derrida to protest at one point:

> Why has the press (most often inspired by professors, when they themselves did not write directly) multiplied denials, lies, defamations, insinuations against deconstruction...caricaturing ['deconstructive' texts] in a stupid and dishonest manner?...Why so much fear, hate, and denial of deconstruction? Why so much resentment?
>
> (Derrida 1988: 153)

Last, though not in chronological order, perhaps a fourth face of deconstruction in America could be said to be constituted by the heterogeneous bleed of deconstruction into a series of domains and disciplines: from architecture (Peter Eisenman) and psychology (discourse analysis) to everyday speech. It is here that questions about what deconstruction came variously to mean would be especially interesting: for example, in psychology, bringing to light contradictions in a subject's discourse, in architecture, separating the 'presence' from the 'meaning', the 'iconicity' from the 'instrumentality' of an architectural element (see Eisenman 1995: 136), in common speech, simply undoing or exposing a given. There is barely a domain within the humanities in which deconstruction has not come to signify somehow, barely a discipline in which there has not been speculation or negotiation of the possible work of deconstruction within that context.

Many essays in *Deconstruction is/in America* mark the deployment or indebtedness of a certain idea of deconstruction in the context of critical and cultural studies (Miller 1995: 82):

> One could argue that the shift [of critical interest] from the "purely" literary or philosophical to manifestations of, for example, popular culture, would not have been possible without, among other things, the conceptions of textuality and re- or decontextualisation that have been developed by Derrida.
>
> (Wills 1995: 255)

Deconstruction has been crucial to the formulation of feminisms of sexual difference, and to the rejection by some of essentialism and identity politics. It has been seen as a methodology for destabilising dichotomous oppositions, for decentring masculinity in relation to an 'othered' femininity, decentring heterosexuality in relation to an 'othered' homosexuality and decentring natural, normalised gender in relation to an 'othered' artificiality, as seen in the work of Judith Butler and Eve Sedgwick. Lastly, the earliest version of deconstruction in America took place with Gayatri Spivak's translation of Derrida's *De la grammatologie*. It is Spivak, and more recently theorists such as Homi Bhabha, who have negotiated deconstructive theories of postcoloniality. To unite all of these domains as a 'fourth face' of deconstruction may seem misleading, in that they are disparate faces of deconstruction. Yet collectively, they serve to indicate that a crucial aspect of deconstruction's passage is the extreme diversity, disparity and various far flung locales of its errings.

So the tale of deconstruction in American would span everything from Yale School literary criticism, violent reactionary criticism, accusation and inflammatory exposé, reclamation of Derrida as 'philosopher', denunciation of Derrida as anti-philosopher and anti-canon, deconstruction as feminism, postcolonialist theory, queer theory, cultural studies, architecture, a passage from intonations that deconstruction was 'not a method' to a templated deconstructive methodology of locating, reversing and displacing binarisms, to deconstruction as a term of general coinage.

NOT THE WORK OF A WRECKING CREW

I read a whole history of deconstruction in America in just one comment from Gayatri Spivak in an interview in *The Post-colonial Critic*. Here, then, is a deceptively simple statement:

> Derrida ... is not decentering anything. He's just descriptive when he talks about the possibility of [*sic*].
>
> (Spivak 1990: 147)

This represents one of the most important shifts in interpretation of deconstruction over the last twenty-five years. I have mentioned perceptions of deconstruction as 'anarchist!', 'nihilist!', which we see in a range of critics from Habermas (1987: 181) to Walter Jackson Bate and René Wellek (see Hillis Miller's discussion, 1987: 9). In the words of David Wills, 'Derrida's work is so often characterized in terms of a threat, the threat of damage, the work of a wrecking crew; deconstruction is so often reduced to destruction' (Wills 1995: 253). Derrida is notorious for his 'deconstruction of subjectivity', for, in Jean-Luc Nancy's words, a 'critique or deconstruction of interiority, of self-presence, of consciousness, of mastery, of the individual or collective property of an essence' (Cadava et al. 1991: 4). But when Nancy introduces the motif thus, he hastens to add:

> such a critique or deconstruction has not simply obliterated its object (as those who groan or applaud before a supposed 'liquidation' of the subject would like to believe).
>
> (Cadava et al. 1991: 4)

Nancy is reacting here to the fact that Derrida was widely understood to have pretended to have somehow obliterated or 'liquidated' the subject or to have claimed that the subject did not really exist. An example of this can be seen in the question Guy Scarpetta addresses in an interview with Derrida: 'you mark that "the subject of writing" does not exist, if one understands by this expression a master-subject' (Derrida 1981b: 87). From the first, Derrida tried to stave off such an interpretation. In the same interview, Derrida immediately declares to Scarpetta:

> I have never said that *there is not* a 'subject of writing' ... I was led to recall this to Goldmann, who also was quite worried about the subject, and about where it had gone.
>
> (Derrida 1981b: 88)

We can understand Spivak's statement that Derrida is 'just descriptive' when he talks about the 'possibility of the subject' as according with attempts by Derrida and his commentators to rebut connotations of nihilism which had proliferated around his work. Because an expression like 'decentring' the subject reinforced the loaded connotations of 'liquidation', and because such an interpretation had been so dominant in various circles, Spivak went so far as to protest: *'he is not decentring anything'*. What, then, was Derrida doing? Spivak exchanged the notorious concept of decentring – certainly one which Derrida had been known to use – for the concept of understanding how a subject is centred. Derrida was not 'decentring the subject', but was merely describing what constitutes the effect of the subject as authoritative, fully present and conscious to itself, masterful, interior:

> all that he looks at is the way in which the subject centers itself. He is not decentering the subject. The subject is – the subject must identify itself with its self-perceived intentions . . . to read Derrida as if he is decentering the subject is in fact, it is a very possible misreading.
>
> (Spivak 1990: 146)

Crucial to the critic's rejection of the nihilistic connotations of deconstruction was the concept of deconstruction as analysing 'conditions of possibility'. Remember Spivak's formulation, for example: he's just descriptive; he analyses *the possibility of* certain effects. Also, crucial to Derrida saying 'I never said there is not a subject' is his claim that the 'subject' should be thought of as an effect. For instance, consider how Derrida continues his rebuttal of Goldmann. Rather than saying that there is no subject:

> It is solely necessary to reconsider the problem of the effect of subjectivity such as it is produced by the structure of the text.
>
> (Derrida 1981b: 88)

Transforming the problematic of deconstruction to one of how 'effects of subjectivity' are generated is Derrida's means of insisting that he did not deny the 'existence' of subjects who identify with their self-perceived intentions. It is in this sense that we must understand Spivak's statement that he is 'just describing'. In line with this position, Derrida had often made statements about deconstruction not being 'a negative operation'. 'Rather than destroying', he explained at one point, what was necessary was to *'understand how an "ensemble" was constituted* and to *reconstruct* it to this end' (Derrida 1991: 272, my italic). Such comments have led to some critics claiming that Derrida is really a 'reconstructionist', not a deconstructionist. This is an ambiguous line, because such a claim is not intended to suggest that Derrida's aim is really to put back together or regenerate the most metaphysical ideals of philosophy. The claim simply continues the trend towards seeing Derrida as more 'analytic' – in Spivak's words, more 'descriptive', and less concerned with an agenda

44

of 'undoing' than is usually supposed. Derrida's deconstruction should be seen as a project of 'reconstruction' only in the sense of analytic reconstruction: in other words, in the sense of reconstructing the scene of the crime.

Derrida has certainly made sufficient statements to sustain the twist on deconstruction given by Spivak and McCarthy in the contexts discussed here. In particular, Derrida's description of deconstruction as 'understanding' how an ensemble is constituted and 'reconstructing' it to that end obviously lend themselves especially well. Still, I would suggest that it is important to understand those statements, and the insistence of Spivak, as related to a specific context constituted by the tenacity of interpretations of deconstruction as nihilistic; as motivated by strategic concerns to correct those interpretations; and perhaps, as motivated by the frustration at their tenacity. I suggest that all statements of the genre 'deconstruction is merely description' could be read as icons of the specific story of how deconstruction was *received*. This is why I have suggested that a whole history of deconstruction in America could be read in Spivak's surprising claim: 'Derrida is not decentering anything.'

Such a claim represents a significant shift in interpretation of deconstruction. The shift is often – though, I'll argue, erroneously – understood as a shift from literary to philosophically centred reception of deconstruction. It is also a shift which is not without its risks. The risks relate not to the proliferation of deviations and derivations of Derrida, but, to repeat Hillis Miller's phrase, to the neutralisation of theory. Miller thinks that theory is neutralised when it is not engaged with. Repeated claims that Derrida should be seen as a technical philosopher have meant, Miller argues, that he has come to be broadly perceived as an arcane theorist with whom one does not have to engage. However, I shall suggest that a different kind of neutralisation is risked by the position I have outlined here. Deconstruction, when interpreted as 'describing', 'analysing', or 'reconstructing' (the conditions of possibility of certain effects), runs the risk of being interpreted in terms almost indistinguishable from the movement to which Derrida addressed a very substantial body of critique: structuralism. I shall argue that the interpretation of Gasché is, in this sense, particularly misleading. For to echo Harvey: 'Deconstruction is not . . . structuralism' (Harvey 1986: 23). 'Neutralisation' is a good term to describe the problem. I am not lamenting the loss of an orthodox deconstruction, but the loss of what makes deconstruction importantly different from structuralism. A homogenisation of theory occurs when deconstruction, despite all its critical work on structuralism, ends up sounding like structuralism after all. The critical intervention which one body of theory makes into another is thereby muted.

THE 'BECOMING-STRUCTURALIST' OF
DECONSTRUCTION-AS-PHILOSOPHY

In his prefatory comments to *Tain of the Mirror*, Rodolphe Gasché accuses certain critics of deconstruction of having 'chosen simply to ignore the profoundly philosophical thrust of Derridean thought', (Gasché 1986: 3). Gasché reassured those who might have had concerns on this point that Derrida's intention is certainly not to try to 'do away' with philosophy in some way. Gasché wanted to defend Derrida's city-rights as a philosopher. He asserted that the notorious 'displacement' by deconstruction of traditional philosophical issues really amounted to an 'account' (in other words, a *description*) of the 'inevitable inconsistencies' grounding some traditions of philosophical thought.

Inconsistencies are inevitable where philosophical systems attempt to erect certain concepts which express what Jean-Luc Nancy has called 'a passion of the origin' (Nancy 1992: 37). Such a passion might be manifest, for example, in a philosopher's conception of a mythical state of nature preceding, and so pure of, the degradations of civilisation; or a concept of human soul intrinsically autonomous of the confusions of the body; or a concept of rational, civilised man sharply opposed to a primitive other, or a conception of truth as universal and eternal, independent of human knowledge. Such conceptions could be said to express a passion for origins because they are all conceived as in some way originally 'pure' of the other : either temporally, as in the state of nature which is imagined as originally prior to its corruption by civilisation; or in terms of essence, as in the idea of spirit being only inessentially attached to the body; or in terms of a kind of logical primacy, as when the primitive is thought of as a paucity of rationality, whereby Western is 'primary' or original, and the primitive the privation of Western values and so conceptually derivative. When Plato devalues writing in relation to speech, for example, in the *Phaedrus*, he does so on the basis that writing is tributary to, secondary to, since merely a 'copy' of, speech. Here, speech is original in relation to its other, writing, which is supposed merely to reproduce it.

The interpretations of Derrida offered by Gasché and Harvey emphasised the inevitable instability of texts which attempted to sustain such ideal conceptions of origin or purity as were implied in philosophical discussions of the state of nature, or the primacy of speech, or the rationality of man. Gasché described Derrida's analyses as aiming to establish how and why what is supposedly pure, ideal, original or transcendent is unavoidably contaminated by its opposite. For example, he explains, speech in its purity cannot be thought except by reference to writing. In relation to a philosophical opposition between speech and writing, a deconstructive reading might 'includ[e] an account of the factual return of debased writing in the form of metaphors (for instance) in the very attempt to describe the purity and self-presence of the logos' (Gasché 1986: 273). Gasché is referring to the fact that in explaining the primacy of speech over writing, Plato ends up describing speech as a form of writing, a phonic inscription of thought.

Interestingly, however, Harvey and Gasché both take the position that in offering a location of such instabilities in philosophical systems, Derrida should actually be thought of as specifically committed to the philosophical enterprise, indeed, in Harvey's words, in some ways *safeguarding* it:

> Such is the deconstructive allegiance to philosophy as such, we might add. Thus he safeguards that which he deconstructs, in a certain sense, but at the same time seems to threaten it
>
> (Harvey 1986: 80)

Why should the location of instability in a philosophical text be seen as a safeguarding enterprise? Harvey reveals Derrida's argument to be that instability is necessary to philosophy. An easy way to put this is: if philosophy is going to sustain *impossibly* pure ideals, a necessary correlate, indeed a condition, of its attempt to do so must be that those ideals be unstably, incoherently formulated. Any attempt to sustain an impossible ideal will undermine itself. Or, one can reverse this and say that self-undermining is the 'condition' of sustaining the ideal. A brief way of saying this is that the condition of possibility is the condition of impossibility, and this is exactly what Gasché does say:

> Derrida's inquiry into the limits of philosophy is an investigation into the conditions of possibility and impossibility of a type of discourse and questioning that he recognizes as absolutely indispensable.
>
> (Gasché 1986: 2)

Still, why should Harvey say that in some way such an analysis *safeguards* what it deconstructs? It is here that the context of deconstructive commentary is crucial. We are seeing again the rebuttal of the nihilistic connotations of deconstruction. For Harvey is explaining here:

> The search for the conditions of possibility of 'X' should not destroy 'X', Derrida seems to insist, but rather show how this became *necessary*.
>
> (Harvey 1986: 80)

Harvey reassures us that in some ways Derrida could be thought of as 'safeguarding' the text he is deconstructing, specifically in opposition to the possible reading that he was somehow 'destroying' it. She thinks that he is also doing something else, showing how it is safeguarded, showing *how* it is generated. Her reassurance is that Derrida does think that philosophy is safeguarded – it is *effected, generated, made possible* . . . just in case the reader might have thought that Derrida somehow did not believe in the possibility of philosophy. Not so, says Harvey. He is 'showing' its *'conditions of possibility'*. We have also seen Gasché's reassurance that Derrida's inquiry into philosophy is an investigation of a type of discourse that he recognizes as *'absolutely indispensable'* (Gasché 1986: 2, my italic). Now, Derrida does make statements suggesting that there is no question of doing away with philosophy, in early interviews in *Positions*, for example. But he is explaining the limits of deconstruction: one can't think that one will simply be free or pure of metaphysics just because one is invested in a deconstructive enterprise. One can't just 'get outside' of metaphysics, even with the best of deconstructive intentions. But notice that when Gasché conveys this tenor in Derrida's work the 'indispensability' of philosophy is somehow relayed as more of a soothing sentiment of the genre: 'oh, no, no, I assure you, philosophy is absolutely *indispensable'*.

And lastly, all this can be seen as safeguarding the philosophical enterprise if one appeals to the idea that analysing conditions of possibility is an eminently philosophical thing to do. This is another sense of Harvey's 'such is the deconstructive allegiance to philosophy', one that we also see in Gasché, and in others, for example, Christopher Norris:

> [W]riting is the very *condition* of knowledge . . . it can be shown to precede and articulate all our working notions of science, history, tradition etc. . . . What Derrida is using here is the form of 'transcendental' reasoning which Kant first brought to bear upon the central problems of philosophy. In fact I shall go on to argue that deconstruction is a Kantian enterprise in ways that few of its commentators have so far been inclined to acknowledge . . . A 'transcendental' question takes the form: what exactly are the *presuppositions* of our reasoning on this or that topic if the upshot is to make any kind of intelligible sense?
>
> (Norris 1987: 94; see also 183)[20]

What is striking about these influential interpretations of deconstruction which emphasise Derrida as analysing conditions of possibility of 'working notions' such as subjectivity is their propensity to collapse into a somewhat different kind of language. For example, we see Rodolphe Gasché claiming that Derrida offers an analysis of philosophy's 'laws of possibility', a location of philosophy's so-called 'infrastructures'. Inevitable textual instability becomes, in Gasché's language, an internal structure whose model we could reconstruct:

> To deconstruct . . . is to construct the signifying structure or system of referral that accounts for both exclusion and contamination.
>
> (Gasché 1986: 273)

Not only does deconstruction now sound like a theory which claims that texts are organised by internal 'structures', or 'systems', or 'infrastructures', but Gasché goes so far as to suggest that for Derrida these are internal, organising 'laws':

> Derrida's analyses . . . [aim] to establish the law that governs the 'contradictions' of philosophical discourse, the law that explains why and how what is supposedly pure, ideal, transcendental, and so on is unavoidably contaminated by its opposite.
>
> (Gasché 1986: 273)

What was the promise of structuralism? If we look at work by Roland Barthes, for example, in his high structuralist period, we'll see that it is the account of the narrative having a structure 'which is open to analysis, no matter how much patience its formulation requires' , a structure with 'an implicit system of units and rules' (Barthes 1984: 80–1). And in the most classic statement of the promise of structuralism, Barthes explained the approach in terms which had a certain scientistic connotation:

> The goal of all structuralist activity . . . is to reconstruct an 'object' in such a way as to manifest thereby the rule of functioning . . . of this object. Structure is therefore actually a *simulacrum* of the object . . . [which] makes something appear which remained invisible or . . . unintelligible in the natural object. Structural man takes the real, decomposes it, then recomposes it . . . there occurs something new . . . the generally intelligible . . .
>
> A structuralist *activity* . . . [involves] a veritable fabrication of a world which resembles the primary one, not in order to copy it but to render it intelligible.
>
> (Barthes 1972: 214–15)

Are we not told by Gasché that to deconstruct is to locate infrastructures, to construct the signifying structure of texts? It is precisely because structuralism did conceive of the internal rules organising a text that something seems to be amiss when we are told that deconstruction reveals the internal rules governing the text, or constructs (entirely in the sense of 'analytically reconstructing') those rules.

Pierre Macherey criticised this structuralist ideal of reconstructing a model of the internal structure or internal 'rules' or 'laws' governing a text so as to understand that structure, or those rules. He suggested that to conceive of the internal 'structure' of a text in such terms 'goes back to the entirely unscientific hypothesis that the work has an intrinsic meaning . . . So that . . . to extricate a structure is to decipher an enigma, to dig up a buried meaning' (Macherey 1978: 141).

Of course, structuralism rejected the approach to literature according to which the meaning of a text lay with the author's intentions, thought of as

49

preceding the text. A kind of *hors-texte*, a purported position outside the text, the author's intentions (his or her creative activity), was thought of as ruling over or governing the meaning of the created text. To interrogate the meaning of the text was, on such a model, to ask what the author meant to say, or do.

Critics of structuralism suggested that the concept of the text's 'structure' constituted a collapse back into appeals to the *hors-texte* of the text. Didn't structure come to occupy the place of the author's intentions? Rather than the real meaning of the text being the author's intention outside and governing the text, the structuralist would have instituted another 'real meaning': the structural rules which the structuralist imagines are governing the text. Just like the 'author's intention', the structure is thought of as governing the meaning of the text, overseeing, organising, and thus *hors-texte*. The governing rules of the structure would take up the old position of the governing intention of the author. The critic of structuralism responds by asking: does a text have some kind of a final meaning? If it isn't, *pace* the structuralist, the author's intention, then it shouldn't be the rules of the structure, either.

Perceiving just such problems, Barthes turned away from his earlier, optimistic accounts of the structuralist activity. In so doing he made reference to the criticisms that Jacques Derrida offered of structuralist criticism. For example, in *The Semiotic Challenge*, in a form of retrospective auto-critique, Barthes challenges the idea that in attempting to recon-stitute the structure constituting the rules which govern textual elements, the critic would be revealing the final signified of the text (Barthes 1988: 241). *Does* a text, he asks, possess a final signified? Even that of its own structure? Appealing to Derrida on this point, he continues:

> Jacques Derrida's philosophical investigation has taken up in a revolutionary fashion this problem of the final signified, postulating that there is never ultimately, in the world, anything but the writing of a writing: a writing always finally refers to another writing, and the prospect of the signs is in a sense infinite. Consequently to describe systems of meaning by postulating a final signified is to side against the very nature of meaning.

> (Barthes 1988: 241–2)

For the critic of structuralism, something has gone wrong when we think of a text's set of rules or its governing structure. When we do so, we imagine that it is a closed, whole unit. Such metaphors led to the structuralist fantasy of being able to reconstruct a model of that structure.

Consider the conceptual problems faced by the critic with structuralist analytical hopes. How must the critic be conceiving of 'the structure' of a text to have such hopes? Where and what is 'the structure'? Is the structure the laws which govern the rules of a particular genre such as a realist novel (that there must be resolution of the romantic narrative, a continuous linear sequence and so on)? Is the modernist novel subject to the different rules of a different structure? Or are both novels subject to the structural possibilities of the same structure, within which there is a rule-governed 'choice' of either a discontinuous or a continuous sequence of events? What are the limits of 'the structure': the sum total of the rules of combinatory possibility of which every narrative that ever existed was a version? Or is 'the structure' which governs a text narrower in scope than that? If it is so broad, how could we hope to reconstruct the model of it? And if it is smaller, how would we draw the limits delimiting it as a self-contained, mappable unit governing a particular narrative?

Then there are those who see the structure simply as the sum total of the intersection of the units within a particular text: all the relational elements of that text. But what is the relationship of the structure to the text? The structuralist might think that s/he has brought out, rendered visible, something invisible which resided in the text, through a textual analysis. But 'where' did it reside? *How* is it implicit? Obviously, part of the problem is thinking of the text as having a structure reconstructible as a unit, since one thereby conceptualises the structure as a whole 'thing' somehow different from and governing the text. In abstracting 'structure', what is overlooked is the possibility that 'it' might not be such a whole 'thing' that could be so reconstructed. Thus, says Derrida,

> structure . . . has always been neutralized or reduced, and this by a process of giving it a center or of referring it to a point of presence, a fixed origin. The function of this center was . . . above all to make sure that the organizing principle of the structure would limit what we might call the *play* of the structure. By orienting and organizing the coherence of the system, the center of a structure permits the play of its elements inside the total form.
>
> (Derrida 1978: 278–9)

In general, Derrida speaks against any conceptual horizon for the analysis of texts which is overly totalising, or which pretends to 'permit the reassemblage of the totality of a text' (Derrida 1981b: 45).

It is true that, as we have seen, Derrida has made statements which lend themselves to the interpretation that I am suggesting is risky. We have seen him stating that deconstruction involves understanding how an ensemble is constituted. We could add to this statements that he is trying to show how 'writing "structurally" carries within itself . . . the process of its own erasure and annulation' (Derrida 1981b: 68) or about following the 'strange "logic"' of différance (Derrida 1981b: 40). But quite often, these comments are ironic, playing on the pretensions of structuralism and analysis. Terms are often placed in scare quotes: 'logic' and 'structurally'. Derrida makes clear that he does not think that texts are governed by stable structures of which one could reconstruct models. For example, in the very passage where he speaks of the strange 'logic' of différance, and where he does invoke the concept of 'structural conditions', what he is emphasising is the structural *impossibility* of limiting or containing or closing the network of concepts and textual configurations through which différance is 'pulled' (Derrida 1981b: 40).

It is ironic that the interpretations of Gasché and Harvey are associated with the reclamation of deconstruction from the domains of literary criticism. Some accounts of deconstruction in the context of literary criticism take for granted to some extent the orientation which Gasché and Harvey vigorously defended. For example, when Jonathan Culler describes deconstructive literary criticism, he similarly claims that deconstruction treats any textual 'position, theme, origin, or end as a construction', or an effect, produced by discursive forces which can be analysed:

> Deconstruction treats any position, theme, origin, or end as a construction and analyzes the discursive forces that produce it.
>
> (Culler 1982: 259)

But because Culler is not demonstrating that Derrida is a 'philosopher', he does not insist so much on this point. There is some history to philosophers reconstructing conditions of possibility in quite a formal sense. In the understandable desire to suggest 'a Derrida and a deconstruction ... in a more rigorously *philosophic* way than hitherto (Harvey 1986: x) such critics end up showing that one could think of Derrida's discussion of 'conditions of possibility' as not unlike traditional philosophical enterprises. But this propels a reading of Derrida in which he would be constructing structures and establishing the internal laws of texts.

Perhaps it will seem that Culler's language is not entirely devoid of this emphasis. He does claim that deconstruction treats positions, themes, origins, or ends as constructions produced by discursive forces which can be analysed (Culler 1982: 259). He does refer to the logic of the text:

> The achievements of deconstructive criticism ... lie in the delineation of the logic of texts.
>
> (Culler 1982: 260)

And again, Culler states that deconstructive criticism is not the application of philosophical lessons to literary studies, but 'an exploration of textual logic in texts called literary' (Culler 1982: 227).

It is important, however, that with such comments Culler is not referring to the internal logic of 'the' text, which would presuppose that 'the text' was a stable entity with an internal 'logic' which could be reconstructed. Like Derrida, Culler refers to the notion that différance has a curious logic, which we could think of as 'textual logic'. This is entirely different from references to *a* text's 'logic'. Textual logic, as conceived by Derrida, precisely is thought of as an unstable, endlessly deferred, and hence *un*reconstructible *non*-'unit'. To speak of the textual logic of différance is to say, precisely, that neither 'the text', nor some kind of 'structure' of the text, is 'a whole'.

I am arguing that it is in part the keenness to demonstrate the philosophical credentials of Derrida that led to an over-insistence on the way in which Derrida could be thought of as analysing the logic, laws, structures, or infrastructures of texts. Yet Derrida has manifested the greatest wariness about pretensions to posit, or reconstruct a text in terms of, the text's supposed 'infrastructures'.

DECONSTRUCTION AS INTERVENTION

Let's say that we define logocentrism as the imposition of the values of 'propriety, of a proper meaning, of proximity to the self, of etymology, etc. [which] impos[e] themselves in relation to the body, consciousness, language, writing, etc.' (Derrida 1981b: 54–5). I have suggested that sustaining those values involves textual instability: for example, the displacement on to 'the other' (the body, writing, etc.) of devalued attributes which will also be found to pertain to the privileged terms associated with 'proximity to self' etc. We could say, therefore, that the logocentrism of a text renders it unstable, with a particular kind of instability that Derrida has called 'différance'. And we can say that the instability or différance of logocentrism is the condition of possibility of the text. In one kind of context, then, we might want to emphasise the idea that différance ensures the impossibility or dysfunction of a text: its internal incoherence. But we have seen another context – the context in which deconstruction was constantly associated with an anarchic enterprise – in which one would instead emphasise what, on the Derridean account, one can also say: that instability, différance, logocentrism *enable* or *render* effects of presence generated by the text. Instability and différance constitute the conditions of possibility of the text. Thus, in her discussions of deconstruction, Gayatri Spivak has stated of logocentrism (and phallocentrism, gynocentrism), 'all of these things *enable*' (Spivak 1990: 146, my italic).

Obviously, logocentrism, différance, instability, constitute *both* the conditions of possibility and the conditions of impossibility of the text. However, there are historical reasons for emphasising one or the other of these aspects of the deconstructive analysis. The moment that the latter (conditions of impossibility) are emphasised, Derrida becomes the anarchist who does not believe in the 'existence' of subjects, consciousness, truths, etc. But, I have argued, the moment that the former (conditions of possibility) are emphasised, the risk is run of Derrida's indistinguishability from structuralist reconstructionism of textual laws and infrastructures.

It is a risk that Gayatri Spivak indicates in the same passage:

> As Derrida says . . . 'Logocentrism is not a pathology,' it is the thing that enables us – except, if because it enables us, we say that it is correct, it would be a mistake.

(Spivak 1990: 146)

Here, Spivak indicates one of three dangers which I am suggesting are run by interpretations of deconstruction which present it as analysing or reconstructing 'conditions of possibility'. First, I have been suggesting the risk that it is neutralised, collapsing back into structuralism. Second, Spivak points out that to speak of deconstruction analysing conditions of possibility, or describing that which 'enables' certain textual effects, may give the connotations of an analysis which somehow 'approves' (or at least is neutral in relation to) that which it analyses. For example, one can say of the work of différance or logocentrism that it 'renders' operative certain textual effects of presence. From one perspective this is correct – Derrida does claim that certain textual effects are enabled – rendered – by the work of différance. Yet, if one uses the term 'operative' or focuses too much on a term such as 'enabled', one seems to affirm the work of différance. Something crucial is lost here: Derrida's critical work of intervention. The deconstructive project is to 'destabilise', unveil or in some way perform a certain critical work on that which is deconstructed. If we simply see it as analysing, then the critical aspect of the deconstructive project is entirely lost. Similarly, if we only see texts as 'effected', or 'enabled' by their own instability (in a way that is merely 'described' by deconstruction), then the critical aspect of the deconstructive project is, again, entirely lost. One needs to emphasise that deconstruction analyses the conditions of possibility *and* impossibility of the text. One needs to emphasise that the conditions of possibility are simultaneously the conditions of impossibility of the text. The third danger, then, is that presentations of deconstruction as 'descriptive' do not do justice to Derridean affirmations such as: 'Deconstruction, I have insisted, is not *neutral*. It *intervenes*' (Derrida 1981b: 93). Deconstruction 'describes' différance as the condition of possibility of a logocentric effect of presence. But the description is not neutral. It does destabilise an account of origin, or reason or of truth, to suggest that such values are sustained in a text by the work of différance. A deconstructive analysis would have it that such a text cannot 'avow' that its values are sustained or effected by the work of différance. This is precisely why the work of différance constitutes the conditions both of possibility and of impossibility of the text. Any presentation of deconstruction must commit itself to a simultaneous emphasis of deconstruction as describing the conditions

54

[handwritten annotation at top: question of subversiveness contingent on "destabilizing within" — but both B + S don't assume there's a "without"]

of possibility and impossibility, so as to retain what is in fact the promise of a deconstructive reading: not to be neutral, but to intervene.

BUTLER AND DERRIDA

In chapter 1, I reviewed critical debate surrounding the work of Judith Butler, and in this chapter, critical debate surrounding the work of Jacques Derrida. The two contexts rehearse a similar controversy concerning the project of locating internal instability in a given context. The controversy turns around what kind of intervention locating internal instability amounts to: Analysis? Destabilisation? Troubling? Reconstruction? Deconstruction?

A pattern of controversy repeats itself around the two bodies of work. In the case of Judith Butler, debate turns around whether a given site of instability – such as the need for repeatability of gender norms, or the way in which gender parody illustrates the parodic nature of gender – 'destabilises' gender norms, or 'really just uphold[s] the status quo'. In the case of Derrida, debate turns around the critic's understanding of deconstruction as nihilist, or as inconsequential, versus the critic's attempt to see deconstruction as the analysis of how an ensemble is constituted. If instability is understood as reinforcing the status quo, then analysing that instability will not easily be seen as a 'troubling' critical activity. Readings of homophobia by Halley, Butler and Sedgwick[21] suggest that instability of definition does conserve the status quo. But, if instability of definition is understood as 'destabilising from within', then the critic's work of exposing instability is more likely to be seen as similarly destabilising.

Where Butler's work has been celebrated for the extent to which it seemed to 'destabilise' gender, Derrida's work has been *stigmatised* by some critics for the extent to which it seemed to 'destabilise' philosophy. This interpretation came from all of those critics who saw Derrida as trying to bring down the best ideals and texts of philosophy. In the case of interpretations of Butler, those which embraced Butler were probably those which saw her as 'troubling' gender. Interpretations of Derrida which embraced him least were probably those which saw him as 'troubling' philosophy. And since interpretations of Derrida as anarchist and nihilist were influential, and led to considerable confusion, the reaction of other critics was to emphasise the Derrida who simply looked at how an ensemble was constituted, or who 'was not decentering anything', or who 'safeguarded' what he deconstructed', or 'analysed the discursive forces which produce any position, theme, origin, or end, thought of as a construction'.

In the case of interpretations of Butler, the temptation is to counterbalance her analysis by emphasising the extent to which instability can and does contribute to the status quo. In this light I presented the work on homophobic law by Halley. This is an important counterbalance in the context of a debate which presupposes a connection between instability and weakening the grip of gender norms. In the case of interpretations of Derrida, the temptation has clearly been to emphasise the extent to which instability, according to a deconstructive reading, rather than 'destroying x', constitutes the conditions of possibility of 'x'. What has been emphasised – the 'contributing to the possibility of x' interpretation of instability, or the 'destabilising' role of instability – has clearly depended considerably on the vagaries of critical interpretation of Butler and Derrida .

This comparison illustrates the pitfalls of abstracting and emphasising either the destabilising aspect of the project in question or its analytic or descriptive aspect. The critic who only sees Butler's project as 'troubling' certainly runs the risk of omitting the analysis of instability as reinforcing the status quo – something Butler also wants to emphasise. The critic who only emphasises Derrida's project as reconstructive, analytic, descriptive, omits the point of the deconstructive reading: that it is not neutral, that it does intervene.

To conclude this chapter by returning to Judith Butler's position, how is it not neutral, but an intervention, to describe gender as always already internally troubled? Here, we need only return to some of the first premises of *Gender Trouble*: that gender becomes naturalised and normalised, that what Butler names as the 'foundational categories of identity – the binary of sex, gender, and the body– can be shown as productions that create the effect of the natural, the original and the inevitable' (Butler 1990: viii). Butler's reconstruction of the conditions of possibility of the naturalisation of gender is not a neutral reconstruction. It does contribute to a politics of rendering visible, and so denaturalising, those processes of naturalisation.

Butler argues that 'Gender is a kind of persistent impersonation that passes as the real' (Butler 1990: viii). Such an analysis locates paradox at the heart of gender categories: for example, that natural gender is both opposed to gender impersonation, but is itself a kind of impersonation. An extended concept of 'gender trouble' might refer generally to the idea of paradox lurking at the heart of gender categories. I am going to extend the concept of 'gender trouble' beyond Butler's analysis of the self-deconstructive operation at work in gender as performative, or iterative. I am going to shift ground to a different genre of feminist theory and move to the body of feminist re-readings of the history of philosophy, a context which has repeatedly located the contradictions and inconsistencies in historical accounts of women, femininity, sexual equality or sexual difference. I consider the way in which those feminist re-readings of the history of philosophy which so like to stretch from book V of the *Republic* through book V of *Emile*, culminating with the holes and slime imagery of

Sartre and Beauvoir, have analysed inconsistencies in the discussion of women and femininity in this history, and used the inconsistencies to expose the philosopher in question.

This book thereby stages an intersection between three recent theoretical tendencies. The first is the theorisation of sex and gender as identity effects riddled with internal instability or gender 'trouble' in post-structuralist feminism, the main steps of which are followed in chapter 1. In this chapter, I have isolated the second tendency: characterisations of deconstruction as the analysis of the 'conditions of possibility' of textual effects of identity and presence. Derrida is interpreted as reconstructing paradoxical textual structures through which identity effects are generated by the internal 'différance' which also destabilises them. In the chapters which follow, I introduce these two pivots of feminist theory and deconstructive criticism into a third context: feminist re-readings of the history of philosophy over the past decade.

This is a context in which deconstructive feminism has typically been associated with controversial feminisms of difference. Deconstruction has, however, shown its ability to be many different things to different disciplines. It promises to feminist interpretation of the history of philosophy the deconstructive interpretation of textual instability as constitutive in phallocentric arguments about the nature and role of women. How are such arguments enabled by their own self-contradiction and paradox? Recent theorists such as Judith Butler and Eve Sedgwick have moved towards interpreting gender effects as operating through, or as generated by, internal instability. The debates presented in this chapter represent a reminder to theorise instability as simultaneously constitutive and deconstituting. This is a reminder which I shall deploy in feminist interpretations of the history of philosophy.

In turning to French feminist theory, I turn to a domain which is often discussed in terms of feminism of difference versus feminism of equality. In presenting the work of three French feminist philosophers, Michèle Le Dœuff, Sarah Kofman and Luce Irigaray, I hope to shift the ground of such characterisations. The following chapter adds to the resources of the theorist of constitutive instability. I have emphasised this orientation in the work of Butler and Sedgwick, and in some interpretations of deconstruction. I shall locate this orientation in the work of Le Dœuff, Kofman and Irigaray. In chapters 1 and 2, cautionary tales were also derived for the theorist of constitutive instability. The first chapter serves as a reminder that instability constitutes, rather than simply destabilising. The second chapter serves as a reminder that instability deconstitutes, while simultaneously constituting. Chapter 3 will produce cautionary tales of a different kind. Le Dœuff, Kofman and Irigaray serve as instances of theorists who, to different degrees, combine theories of constitutive instability with an occasional tendency to see textual contradiction either

as deployed by extra-textual subjects or as an expression of the contradictory aims of extra-textual subjects. The theorist may look behind the
contradiction to its possible causes. I favour an approach which focuses on
the rhetorical work performed by contradictions, rather than speculating
on why they might be deployed, or what they might express of the
author's aims or anxieties. I shall assess Le Dœuff, Kofman and Irigaray's
different approaches to constitutive instability from this perspective.
I shall also suggest that Irigaray's work is strong in terms of the issues
considered in chapter 2. Irigaray offers a strong theory of phallocentric
accounts of femininity as simultaneously constituting and deconstituting,
hegemonic and subversive, destabilising and stabilising.

3

LE DŒUFF, KOFMAN AND IRIGARAY AS THEORISTS OF CONSTITUTIVE INSTABILITY

> Under the influence of deconstruction, both Irigaray and Cixous . . .
> re-instat[e] the female body and the feminine.
>
> (Moira Gatens)

Deconstructive feminism has often been associated with feminism of difference. For Genevieve Lloyd, deconstruction represents a genre of feminism committed to opening the space for new symbolic representations of women (Lloyd 1993a: ix). This might entail an Irigarayan project of reconceptualising sexual difference or other strategies for 'reconceptualizing the feminine in non-dualistic terms' (Lloyd 1993b: 74 citing Hekman). Similarly, in *Feminism and Philosophy* Moira Gatens states that 'some feminists are engaged in the deconstruction of these traditional ideals and the construction of other meanings and other significances of female experience' (Gatens 1991: 99). Gatens makes reference to deconstructive feminism as an alternative to a feminist politics which essentialises and reifies women's experience. Lloyd argues that deconstructive feminism has not managed sufficiently to break from the reification of a mythic feminine specificity. What is common to the two theorists is that the nexus between deconstruction and feminism is the terrain of feminism of difference. The question not posed is what the coupling of deconstruction and feminism has to offer the discipline of these theorists: feminist interpretation of the history of philosophy.

In their works, Gatens and Lloyd offer different methodologies for reading the history of philosophy, for identifying the historical sex bias of reason, or for locating infrastructural or implicit sex bias in apparently sex-neutral theories. French feminism, and feminists of difference, are referred to by Gatens and Lloyd for their contributions to concepts of a mythic feminine specificity, but not for their contributions towards rereadings of the history of philosophy. While Lloyd and Gatens take different positions about Irigaray, they concur in only factoring Irigaray in terms of her reconceptualisation of the 'female body and the feminine'.

We don't hear about Irigaray as a reader of Descartes, Spinoza, Kant, etc. I wish to shift the emphasis away from debates about feminism of equality versus feminism of difference, or debates about essentialism versus social constructionism and instead work to cluster a group of contemporary French feminist philosophers insofar as they offer diverse methodologies for feminist interpretation of the history of philosophy.

In grouping Michèle Le Dœuff, Sarah Kofman and Luce Irigaray, I do not suggest that they constitute a school or a genre. Their projects are dissonant. Le Dœuff resists being seen as any kind of -ist (Foucauldian, Derridean, etc.) and is wary of feminism of difference, which, at her most caustic, she styles thus: 'One may like jam and knitting . . . but it is a big step from there to accepting . . . that every woman should conform to this model' (Le Dœuff 1991: 227). Sarah Kofman relentlessly identifies with Nietzsche, Freud and Derrida, but like Le Dœuff is wary of *écriture féminine*. As she explained in an interview, 'Je n'admets pas qu'il y ait une écriture propre aux femmes. Je suis partisane de la clarté, j'aime les discours rationnels et bien construits' (Kofman with Jaccard 1986: 7).[1] Irigaray is the French feminist of difference par excellence. While she has not always rejected feminism of equality, she has always argued that women's rights, and demands for equality, need to be reformulated in a language of difference.

The work of these theorists can be distinguished in terms of these generalised positions. However, I have grouped them to provide an alternative narrative of 'French feminism' thought of in terms of analytic methodologies, to feed into a domain of feminist philosophy that has styled French feminism in terms of issues of difference. Le Dœuff, Kofman and Irigaray analyse the way in which women and femininity have been rendered 'other' in the history of philosophy. All three are particularly attentive to moments of breakdown or unease in a text. They analyse the relationship between representations of femininity and moments of self-contradiction or unstable logic in philosophical texts. While they can be distinguished in terms of their positions concerning feminism of equality and feminism of difference, I wish to distinguish them in terms of the methodologies they deploy in the interpretation of the history of philosophy. In particular, I shall distinguish their approach to the interpretation of textual instability relating to tropes of women and femininity in the history of philosophy.

MICHÈLE LE DŒUFF

The philosophical imaginary

Michèle Le Dœuff is best known as an analyst of imagery in philosophy. As she explains, 'My work is about the stock of images you can find in philosophical works, whatever they refer to: insects, clocks, women, or islands. I try to show what part they play in the philosophical enterprise' (Mortley 1991: 86). She criticises the grandiose pretensions of philosophy, whereby philosophical thought is regarded as entirely understanding itself, and philosophers are taken to 'know absolutely what they are saying' (Le Dœuff 1991: 166):

> Whether one looks for a characterization of philosophical discourse to Plato, to Hegel or to Bréhier, one always meets with a reference to the rational, the concept, the argued, the logical, the abstract.
>
> (Le Dœuff 1989: 1)

In accordance with these pretensions, philosophy has distanced itself from literature: 'Philosophy is not a story, not a pictorial description, not a work of pure literature' (Le Dœuff 1989: 1). If philosophy is purportedly concerned only with the pure idea, the rational sequence of thoughts, it pretends to have no need of the ornamental image, the evocative allegory. For example, Kant refers to examples and illustration as merely 'bright coloring', 'an aid to clearness'. Le Dœuff points out that certain key images and metaphors are deployed in *The Critique of Pure Reason*. However, Kant asserts their absence from this work, an absence he justifies partly with the argument that examples and illustration are 'necessary only from a *popular* point of view ... Such assistance is not required by genuine students of science' (Kant 1929: 13).

Despite such repudiations of ornament, Le Dœuff notes the constancy with which philosophy has always indulged in, in Colin Gordon's words, a surreptitious trafficking in the world of images' (Le Dœuff 1989: vii). There are island metaphors which represent understanding in Kant, garden and building metaphors for knowledge in Descartes, theatre images for utopia in Bacon and so on. The excuse for the use of imagery in philosophy has often been that it translates difficult ideas for those who might not have the stamina for the dry austerity of pure argument, for those who might need anecdote, illustration and metaphor to aid comprehension. The serious philosophical reader should not be overly sidetracked by the ornaments and anecdotes s/he may find in a text. They have been put there for the benefit of the common reader. As Le Dœuff writes:

> The images that appear in theoretical texts are normally viewed as extrinsic to the theoretical work, so that to interest oneself in them seems like a merely anecdotal approach to philosophy.
>
> (Le Dœuff 1989: 2)

Thus, it would be inappropriate, trivialising, to interrogate too closely Kant's appeal to Bacon's island metaphors in *The Critique of Pure Reason*, for that textual element is merely the ornament, not the kernel of his argument. However, Le Dœuff effectively asks the following question: what is the effect, in a piece of philosophical writing, of the presence of textual elements which are not interrogated closely because of their purportedly marginal role? Among the textual work which imagery can thereby do is to 'conceal', or substitute for, problems in a philosopher's argument. Le Dœuff suggests that often a philosopher resorts to a piece of imagery at points where the argument has become unstable. Le Dœuff states the narrow version of her hypothesis:

> the interpretation of imagery in philosophical texts goes together with a search for points of tension in a work. In other words, such imagery is inseparable from the difficulties, the sensitive points of an intellectual venture.
>
> (Le Dœuff 1989: 3)

Le Dœuff considers the imagery in question to be textually operative, and not merely ornamental. She considers that the ornamental status in particular is operative because it serves to distract the reader from the rhetorical work which imagery performs, such as covering over difficulties in argument. Le Dœuff can be thought of as a theorist who analyses the textual effects of an inconsistent position or a contradictory refrain. She asks what is enabled in an argument when a philosophical text both devalues the role of imagery and draws fundamentally on imagery:

> The perspective I am adopting here . . . involves reflecting on strands of the imaginary operating in places where in principle, they are supposed not to belong and yet where, without them, nothing would have been accomplished.
>
> (Le Dœuff 1989: 2)

Le Dœuff argues that the contradictory status of imagery serves to enable or sustain philosophical arguments. It is precisely because the imagery has a double status as 'present' and yet not seriously 'present' (only a trivial embellishment) that it is able to perform important rhetorical work in an argument, unnoticed.

The contradictory status of women

Le Dœuff also focuses on the constancy with which women have been figured as 'other' in the history of philosophy. 'Stupid utterances . . . about women' are made by the very philosophers 'who, in principle, have no right to stupidity' (Le Dœuff 1991: 13). What is called 'woman' or the 'feminine' in philosophical works is a fantasy, an imaginary being (Mortley 1991: 85–6). Thus, in accordance with her general claims about imagery, she proposes that phallocentric imagery about women and femininity 'usually betray[s] a theoretical weakness, a difficulty that the philosopher has been unable to overcome' (Le Dœuff 1991: 13). Indeed, Le Dœuff has said that she first came to formulate her theories about the philosophical imaginary through her work on phallocratic images of women found in philosophical texts.

In 'Long Hair, Short Ideas', Le Dœuff discusses the contradictory status of women in philosophy. On the one hand, philosophy is 'permissive' towards women: women are 'admitted' to the domain of philosophy (Le Dœuff 1989: 101): from Hipparchia, Descartes' correspondent Elizabeth, Héloïse, Themista (one of Epicurus' disciples), Madame de Staël, Sophie Volland (one of Diderot's correspondents), the women who attended Henri Bergson's seminars, and Simone de Beauvoir to all the women who sit philosophy examinations in France today, and august commentators on history of philosophy such as Marie Delcourt, Geneviève Rodis-Lewis and Cornelia de Vogel. On the other hand, philosophy constrains the ways in which women participate in philosophy: 'women are ... admitted to philosophy ... in ways which reiterate an archaic permissiveness (and restriction)' (Le Dœuff 1989: 101). The admission of women into philosophy is really an exclusion of women within philosophy. The admission of women into philosophy seems to undermine a philosophical masculine/feminine division. But the division is subtly reinstated within philosophy. 'Permissiveness', she claims, 'is a sly form of prohibition' (Le Dœuff 1989: 103). Women are valued in marginalising ways: as disciples, commentators, admiring correspondents, intelligent readers, good pupils, daughters, lovers of male philosophers. This, then, is the contradictory status that women occupy within philosophy. Like imagery in philosophy, women are present, but not really present. Le Dœuff argues that this contradictory status which women occupy within philosophy performs important rhetorical work. Since women are 'present', philosophy appears not to marginalise women, and need not avow such marginalisation. What need not be avowed, then, is the important role that women as other play within philosophy (as less capable of philosophy, as lovers, daughters, correspondents and disciples). Le Dœuff argues that (marginalised) imagery is necessary, not incidental to philosophy. Similarly, she argues that 'these women' (the lovers, daughters and disciples) 'were necessary', not incidental, 'to their masters':

> The theoretical devotion of a woman is very comforting for someone experiencing his own lack ... How can it not be gratifying to be seen as a plenitude when one is oneself caught in incompleteness and disappointment?
>
> (Le Dœuff 1989: 107)

Woman, when considered as 'less capable' of philosophy, is invoked 'in a strictly fantasy-oriented sense, as a purely negative otherness, as an atrophy which, by contrast, guarantees a philosophical completeness . . . To say that women are incapable of philosophical knowledge, or to be a Diderot and benefit from Sophie Volland's listening in admiration, is one and the same thing' (Le Dœuff 1989: 112).

A distinctive feature of Le Dœuff's philosophy has been the way in which an analytic approach which she developed in her study of philosophical imagery has been redeployed in continuing studies of the sexism inherent in everyday behaviour and social practices. The essays in *The Philosophical Imaginary and Hipparchia's Choice* and elsewhere integrate Le Dœuff's analyses of the history of philosophy with her feminist analysis of education policy, abortion laws, public policy, the admission of women into public institutions, representations of women in advertising, the media and elsewhere, and legal reform. Le Dœuff analyses the contradictory logic governing the role of women in such contexts, in a way which integrates with her analyses of contradictory logic in the history of philosophy.

Consider one example, the essay 'Pierre Roussel's Chiasmas' in *The Philosophical Imaginary*. In her interpretation of the eighteenth-century philosopher Pierre Roussel, Le Dœuff notes a curious feature about his comments on women. At one point, Roussel overtly denounces unscientific, medieval prejudices about women and menstruation. He speaks in the name of the necessary limits of scientific knowledge, and speaks against supporting unjustified assumptions. However, in the same work Roussel propagates a series of wildly unwarranted prejudices about women, in areas beyond the scope of his competence. Looking for a name which might represent the phenomenon, Le Dœuff proposes 'the chiasma'. The chiasma occurs when one proclaims that one shouldn't be dogmatic before proceeding to rampant dogmatism about everything under the sun. The chiasma is what Le Dœuff describes as the 'negation which counter-weighs the general movement of the text' (Le Dœuff 1989: 147). More specifically, Le Dœuff is interested in the phenomenon of protesting against dogmatism in one's own area of expertise before proceeding to be dogmatic in areas not of one's own expertise.

Having located and named the chiasma through the device of the reading of Roussel, Le Dœuff goes on within the same essay to address a contemporary book of popular science – Evelyn Sullerot's controversial 1978 book *Le Fait féminin*, offering the unexpected explanation that 'elements in Roussel's discourse remain present today in quite widespread collective representations and practices' (Le Dœuff 1989: 158).

What interests Le Dœuff in Sullerot's work is the reappearance of the chiasma. It is precisely when Sullerot denounces confusing ideology and science that she does that very thing. Similarly, in a work which claims that femininity threatens to dominate masculinity, Le Dœuff points out that it is exactly where the author denounces sociobiology that various appeals to the sociobiological are made (Le Dœuff 1993a: 178). Le Dœuff offers the following formulation of the chiasma:

> The theoretical position of *any* savant who purports to draw global consequences from his partial knowledge came to strike me as a paradoxical one which falls under the sign of the chiasma: if the shoemaker wants to dogmatise *ad lib* over and above the matter of the shoe, he first has to neutralise the force of his local knowledge.
>
> (Le Dœuff 1989: 169)

Le Dœuff has synthesised her approach in analysing philosophical imagery with her approach in analysing 'everyday widespread collective representations and practices'. This can be seen in the close analyses she offers of contradictory logic in the latter. She may argue that the very gestures of overtly disavowing prejudice (such as speaking in the name of human rights or valorising women's writing) dovetail and act in conjunction with, *and blind one to*, concurrent gestures which marginalise women. For example, Le Dœuff analyses chiasmas in contemporary culture and public policy. She analyses the rhetorical work performed by their contradictory logic. The reader/recipient is distracted by the overt statement made or message sent in a certain context: 'I am well disposed towards women', 'You will find nothing but our best efforts to combat prejudice', etc., from the prejudices reinforced within that context.

Le Dœuff thinks that we can use an alertness to the logic of the chiasma as a warning signal, just as she thinks that the appeal to imagery can serve as a warning signal in a philosophical context where its use is also devalued. Le Dœuff offers a particular reading strategy whereby overt protestations of good intentions make one particularly alert to the presence of prohibitions, just as she argues that the 'permissiveness' with which the institution of philosophy has allowed women access as faithful readers, disciples, historians, or in otherwise marginal roles is really a sly form of prohibition.

One example is Le Dœuff's analysis of contradictory logic in legal judgements relating to women's status. She discusses the 1936 ruling which first laid the foundation for legislation concerning sexual equality in France. It states that women are as fit as men for the public service – however, the nature of some positions will necessitate the exclusion of women (Le Dœuff 1991: 231). The very laws which protect women's equality, and which could be seen as protesting the legislature's best intentions, blind one to the reconsolidation of inequality. And indeed, reviewing French law over the twentieth century, Le Dœuff argues that laws which seem to protect women on closer analysis frequently *retract* that same protection:

All the texts of the laws proclaiming equality – the Bobard ruling, the Law of 19 October 1946, the Law of 10 July 1975 – are in fact constructed on the same linguistic model. First comes the principle, which is proclaimed or reproclaimed whenever necessary, pleasant or useful to a government's image. Then ... at once the vessel is scuppered: 'However, when the nature of the functions or the conditions of their exercise justify it ... ', 'nevertheless, the particular régime in force in the ... ', 'subject to provision for the discretionary right of government to waive ... ', and so on. Each time that the principle is proclaimed, what is in fact being reproclaimed is the imprescriptible and inalienable right of the government to ignore it.

(Le Dœuff 1991: 232)

Similarly, the 1974 Veil law is generally considered a progressive measure because it amounts to the legalisation of abortion in France. But Le Dœuff again argues that the law is grounded in contradictory logic. It is both progressive and regressive towards women. The Veil law, she argues, is not a legalisation of abortion but instead a provision for *dispensation* from a 1920 law in which abortion, information on abortion and information about contraceptives were illegal. The apparently progressive measure blinds one to the fact that through the contradictory logic it adheres to, the Veil law is actually a *reproclamation* of the 1920 law: 'the legalisation of an exception amounts to letting go of one element in order to uphold the fundamental point' (Le Dœuff 1991: 247).

Le Dœuff's point is that the rhetoric and even certain isolated gains of equality politics can co-exist comfortably, indeed, thrive with a reconsolidation of the exclusion and silencing of women. An isolated gain for women may simultaneously undermine women's goals, as when an 'exemption' from the illegality of abortion simultaneously reconfirms the illegality of abortion. In analysing imagery in philosophy, she argues that its contradictory status (playing a functional role in covering tension points while provided with the pretext of being 'merely ornamental') enables the effect of the stable philosophical text. The lowly status which many philosophers attribute to imagery deflects our attention from the crucial work it performs. In analysing the contradictory logic of public institutions, Le Dœuff argues that the contradiction between the rhetoric of good intentions towards women and the fact of actually undermining women is again operative. Our attention is deflected from the way in which public policy and the implementation of laws are regressive by the pretext that the intentions of the state (media, education board, etc.) are nothing but good.

The 'deployment' of contradictions

One distinctive feature of Le Dœuff's work is her integration of techniques deployed in her analysis of the history of philosophy with her analysis of public policy, producing an interpretation of operative contradiction in both contexts. However, because Le Dœuff analyses the work performed by contradictions, there is sometimes a tendency towards the suggestion that contradictions have been deployed by agents so as to perform the rhetorical work in question. Language which ascribes intentions is manifest in her shoemaker metaphor: 'si on veut dogmatiser'. If one wants to be dogmatic, suggests Le Dœuff, one first has to express modesty about the force of one's local knowledge. Dogmatism can then take place under the cover of one's alibi of modesty. In her initial discussions of imagery in philosophy, there is a similar tendency:

> If the images of philosophical texts are so functional, so organic in their very dysfunctionality, might we not guess that they are made to measure?
>
> (Le Dœuff 1989: 4)

Similarly, in the discussion of the exclusion of women from philosophy, Le Dœuff's use of the language of the 'sly' reinforces the motivational analysis of contradiction. The permissiveness of philosophy towards women is really a sly form of prohibition: such language leans somewhat towards the suggestion that a devious stratagem has been deployed in order to manipulate women into the role of philosophy's other which is convenient to the male philosopher. In the strongest expression of this tenor in Le Dœuff's work, she claims that 'a closer look at any sexist fantasy – say in Sartre's *Being and Nothingness* – will show . . . a special blend of sexism *devised in order to* sustain Sartre's system and hide its blunders (Mortley 1991: 89, my italic).

Certainly, Le Dœuff's analyses are not always framed in such language. In one essay, she discusses how French intellectuals such as Pierre Bourdieu, Jean-Luc Nancy and others protest against racism and prejudice using rhetorical formulations which marginalise women. For example, they may speak of the 'droits de l'homme' which are defended by 'hommes de lettres' (Le Dœuff 1993b: 129). Le Dœuff directs her attention to an analysis of the rhetorical work performed by the chiasma. The message of combating prejudice serves to distract one from the effective silencing of women which does occur when concerned contemporary intellectuals are described as men of letters. She is only able to make this point because she brackets questions about the relevant psychological motives. Her claim is not about what the sender of the message is 'trying' to do. Le Dœuff hardly thinks that the anti-racism of Jean-Luc Nancy is an elaborate stratagem to consolidate sexism without being noticed. In this case, Le Dœuff's ability to analyse the rhetorical effects of his chiasma is premised on the analysis not engaging in questions of motives or intentions, but simply of effects.

Furthermore, at times Le Dœuff explicitly resists intentional or motivational language. For example, in 'Red Ink in the Margin', where Le Dœuff discusses inconsistent pronouncements by the nineteenth-century philosopher Boutroux, she comments, 'It matters little how such a duplicity is possible psychologically' (Le Dœuff 1989: 87). The important thing is less to speculate on why the contradictory status of imagery occurs, more to examine how it operates rhetorically in various contexts. Often, in the examples in *The Philosophical Imaginary* we have seen Le Dœuff suggest that imagery covers over weak points in argumentation. However, in her work this is very rarely a claim that the author is attempting to deceive the reader with an appeal to distracting imagery at the moment of weakness in the argument. It is a claim about the rhetorical work performed by a textual element whose official status is 'present' but 'not really present'.

I have represented Le Dœuff's work in terms of its analysis of the rhetorical work performed by unstable or contradictory refrains: for example, a piece of imagery which performs important work in the argument under the pretext that its role is merely ornamental, the feminine which is marginalised within philosophy under the pretext that philosophy is very glad to have women present, the marginalisation of women by the law, or by intellectuals, in the guise of the best intentions of equality and justice. I have suggested that there are two tendencies in Le Dœuff 's work. One performs such analyses by bracketing questions of what texts, philosophers or politicians are 'trying to do', issues of intention, strategy, ruse and motive. In other words, Le Dœuff avoids a causal-explanatory approach, in which the theorist speculates about the reasons, the intentions, the desired aims which might have caused the textual instability in question. A second tendency in her work is to be seen when Le Dœuff partakes more of this kind of language, as we have also seen in the above discussion.

Focusing on Le Dœuff's analysis on the rhetorical work performed by the contradictory refrain, I have suggested two tendencies in her approach. One leans towards a causal or motivational approach. The other is more 'effects based': it analyses the rhetorical work performed while avoiding issues of what the philosopher in question might have meant or be trying to do. Addressing the work of Sarah Kofman and Luce Irigaray, I shall build on to the framework of a distinction between these two tendencies. Kofman is an adversary of Luce Irigaray, and like Le Dœuff, she resists feminism of difference. I wish, however, to contrast their work not in terms of the equality versus difference debate, but in terms of the two tendencies I have located in Le Dœuff's methodology.

For my own purposes, what is distinctive in Kofman's work is her greater *causal* leaning towards the causal-motivational analysis of contradictory textual tendencies. By contrast, I shall suggest that one valuable aspect of Luce Irigaray's analysis is a greater emphasis on an 'effects-based' analysis. *effects*

SARAH KOFMAN

French philosopher Sarah Kofman's corpus of over twenty books includes extensive studies of how femininity functions as part of a phallocentric sexual economy manifest in the texts of figures such as Nietzsche, Freud, Comte, Kant and Rousseau. Kofman identifies her methodology as both deconstructive and psychoanalytic. These methodologies coincide insofar as she appeals frequently to a distinction between what texts declare and what they really do, or describe. This is a distinction which Kofman references to a deconstructive methodology, but also to a methodology of symptomatic reading inspired by Freudian psychoanalysis. The methodological distinction between what texts declare and describe, or do, can be seen in Kofman's interpretation of Freud's paper 'Femininity', for example. Kofman argues that Freud means to 'deconstruct' common popular prejudice about sexual difference. This, then, is the 'declared' level of Freud's text, in which many assurances are made by Freud about his good intentions concerning women. However, Kofman claims that his texts are heterogeneous, and also reconsolidate traditional phallocentric ideology (Kofman 1985: 107, 158). This is the level of what Freud's texts really do, or describe, as opposed to what they declare.

I shall focus on Kofman's interpretation of Rousseau in *Le Respect des femmes – Kant et Rousseau* (1982)[2] as exemplary of her methodology. Kofman argues that for Rousseau, femininity is multiple, split into opposed facets. She opens her study by citing his 'Vers sur la femme', which evokes the divided account of women:

> Objet séduisant et funeste, que j'adore et que je déteste . . . abîme de maux et de biens.
>
> (Kofman 1982a: 59)[3]

Women represent enigmatic, distanced figures, who fascinate but also inspire a 'respectful' caution. In this economy woman also serves as a figure for that which is enigmatic: thus 'nature' and 'truth' take on feminine connotations. As a divided figure, woman is both idealised and vilified. The Rousseauist figure of woman is represented by the exaggerated opposites of virtuous Sophie and the deceitful, worldly Parisienne. Woman is the Janus figure whose opposite faces are inseparable: the good and the bad mother, or the virgin and the prostitute.

Kofman focuses on Rousseau's use of the term 'respect' in his account of ideal relations between the sexes. This notion of respect for women is intended by Rousseau to have a positive rather than a pejorative connotation. Nevertheless, Kofman argues that it represents an ideal of deference towards and admiration for women *via* an ideal of holding women at a distance, the fear of contamination of men by women, a wariness of the effects of women's proximity to men, and an indirect account of the fragility of masculinity. Kofman interprets Rousseau's repetition of the word 'respect' as a symptom of a complex structure of ambivalence towards women.

Unlike many other feminist commentators on Rousseau,[4] Kofman has little interest in the vilification of Rousseau, either on the grounds of his self-contradiction or on the grounds of his misogyny. She is interested in mapping the contradictory pattern of his misogyny, but not with the aim of simple condemnation of the author. This movement of the 'both and' is for Kofman the starting point for analysis. The interpretation she offers is functional. She asks how the contradiction in question operates and what it conserves. Respect, she argues, is a kind of esteem for women which also expresses mastery over women. In the cleavage at the heart of the conception of woman, some women are brought down and rendered base, so that a conception of other women as pure and chaste may be conserved:

> Le clivage à l'intérieur du sexe féminin n'est pas l'effet de la distance sociale, mais d'une coupure opérée par le sexe masculin qui, pour les besoins de son économie sexuelle, rabaisse, méprise certaines femmes tandis qu'il élève les autres sur un piédestal, souille les unes et tente de conserver les autres pures, intactes, en les mettant à une distance qui les rende intouchables.[5]
>
> (Kofman 1982a: 14–15)

Certainly Kofman is not the only feminist commentator on the history of philosophy to note the contradictory, divided account of women in Rousseau's work. A good description of it is provided by Susan Moller Okin, for example.[6] The difference in Kofman's approach is its more 'functional' interpretation. Both Okin and Kofman note that woman is presented as 'la vierge *et* la putain', but Kofman inclines more towards pursuing the question of what the contradiction enables in Rousseau's account. She argues that some women in Rousseau's texts must play 'la putain' *so that* the generalised Rousseauist conception of woman may be accounted for as 'la vierge'. She claims that the moral notion of respect for women actually works to the profit of a masculine sexual economy by protecting man from confrontation with woman-as-castrated through elevating and distancing her.

There is a connection between Kofman's emphasis of the fact that two contradictory meanings are intertwined in the one French word *respect* and her emphasis of the fact that two contradictory connotations are intertwined in the Rousseauist sense of 'woman'. Kofman draws on the phenomenon of the two senses of 'respect' being intertwined to highlight the inseparability of the contradictory notions of women. Through the device of the repetition of the word 'respect', Kofman emphasises the functional aspects of contradiction in Rousseau's text. She argues that woman is represented as both pure and corrupt in Rousseau's texts because only by allotting some women a corrupt role can the threat of women as a 'generalised corruption' be prevented (Kofman 1988: 134). It is *in order to* 'protect' the identity of woman as pure, says Kofman, that Rousseau allocates the threat of woman as corrupt and dangerous to the 'vénale', reviled woman, symbolised by the women of Paris. Pointing out that 'respect' condenses a contradictory meaning, Kofman manipulates this double entendre as an echo of Rousseau's double account of woman, which like 'respect' has a double entendre: 'pure and impure'. Just as the two meanings of the term 'respect' are an inseparable part of the same word, the two senses of 'woman' are similarly inseparable parts of the same economy. Rather than contradicting it, the account of woman as corrupt and emasculating safeguards the account of woman as pure (Kofman 1982a: 16–17). For this reason, Kofman describes the Rousseauist account of woman as 'putain' as having an *economic* function. In other words, the account is functional or operative – it serves to protect the investment in woman as modest. Kofman's analytic starting point is to ask how the two contradictory accounts operate together and what they enable in Rousseau's texts. Her conclusion is that the Rousseauist contradiction salvages the account of woman-as-chaste.

Kofman's interpretation of 'respect' as having an economic function also involves an unmasking or demystification of the philosophers she re-reads. Both Rousseau and Kant present their ideal of distance from women in elevated moral terms, as part of their moral philosophy. Kofman, 'exposing' Kant and Rousseau, claims 'Cette fonction économique . . . du respect – plus ou moins dissimulée derrière le masque de la morale – relève d'une loi générale' (Kofman 1982a: 17).[7] Where Kofman interrogates the functional aspect of textual contradiction, she asserts that it enables a dissimulation whereby respect for women is disguised as a moral sentiment. The contradiction whereby 'respect' for women involves both protection from women and an economy of admiration for women is operative insofar as it conceals the masculine desire to keep a distance from women.

Insofar as Kofman inclines more towards an explanatory approach to the operation of contradictory logic in Rousseau's texts, she offers several suggestions concerning how that logic is sustained. Kofman reminds us that Rousseau curiously conceives the reversal of men's supremacy over women to be a part of the order of nature. Woman's modesty gains her the ascendancy over man, for man is thereby always at the mercy of women's concession of feminine charms and sexual favours, always straining towards her and never entirely satisfied. The 'double effect' of women's modesty is therefore the simultaneous protection of and the disruption to men's supremacy. Respect for women is seen by Kofman as the resolution of the problem posed by the double logic of modesty. One contradictory account of women (that of respect) is invoked as a result of and to resolve another contradictory logic – that of modesty which both protects and jeopardises masculine supremacy. Women's modesty is understood as both undermining and ensuring the stability of relations between the sexes, and so the contradictory account of 'respect' for women is invoked in order to protect the ascendancy of men jeopardised by women's modesty (Kofman 1982a: 70–3). The contradictory notion of 'respect' compensates for the contradictory function of women's modesty.

We also see Kofman employ a functional analysis of Rousseau's contradictions where she considers his use of what has been termed by Derrida and Freud a 'kettle logic' (Kofman 1982a: 89).[8] In a kettle logic, three incompatible explanations are sustained at once. Rousseau, points out Kofman, employs a 'kettle logic' in relation to the question of why nature might have endowed women with modesty. Although the given explanation is that modesty protects men and women from the certain doom that would follow if there were no natural restraint on their sexual desires (Rousseau 1991: 358–9), Rousseau also states that animals have no need for modesty because their sexual urge is governed by the demands of reproduction. So, Rousseau must explain why nature would not have allowed men and women to be similarly governed. In answer, he argues both that man is not like an animal and that animals are in fact more governed by modesty than we know. Even, he says, if he 'does agree' that in fact modesty is not natural but conventional, modesty is still 'necessary' (Rousseau 1960: 86–7).

Kofman notes that where Rousseau uses this 'kettle logic', he suddenly darts from the question of women's modesty to that of the need to confine women to the private and domestic sphere. Therefore, she concludes that Rousseau has used this 'kettle' or contradictory logic to phallocratic ends, in order to justify the confinement of women, where there is some threat posed of woman's mastery over men. Although woman's mastery is still allowed for, her ascendancy is restricted to her dominance in domestic matters (Rousseau 1991: 408), and thus the threat to man's more general ascendancy is limited.

Kofman's reading attempts a degree of functional explanation of some of the contradictions and paradoxes in Rousseau's account of women. However, what becomes apparent is that Kofman offers far more analysis of what enables the contradictory logic to function than of what the contradictory logic facilitates or produces in Rousseau's work. We have seen that, on Kofman's interpretation, women's modesty both undermines and ensures the stability of relations between the sexes, and so the contradictory account of 'respect' for women is invoked in order to protect the ascendancy of men jeopardised by women's modesty (Kofman 1982a: 70–3), as is the use of a contradictory 'kettle logic'. Thus, although Kofman emphasises the economic, operative function of contradiction (she argues that 'kettle logics' and the contradictory notion of 'respect' compensate for the contradictory function of women's modesty), her account is strongly oriented towards a causal explanation of Rousseauist contradiction. Although she does ask what the contradictions enable, her analysis is directed far more to how their occurrence can be explained and to what motivates them.

As we have seen in the work of Michèle Le Dœuff, this leads to a degree of assertion about the stratagem lying behind the deployment of contradictions. For example, Kofman's discussion of Freud's textual ruses is reminiscent of Le Dœuff's discussion of the logic of the chiasma. Freud modestly emphasises the limitations of psychoanalysis in addressing the issue of sexual difference. However, Kofman points out that his text effectively undermines the contributions of literature and other sciences, thereby reinstating the authority of psychoanalysis, and thus his own authority. Kofman suggests 'his modesty is feigned and tactical . . . Freud only pretends to be giving way to the specialists . . . whose "truths" he exhibits the better to criticise or deconstruct them' (Kofman 1985: 104).

But unlike Le Dœuff, Kofman frequently refers to the author's unconscious intent, from the perspective of a psychoanalytic interpretation. She proposes, in her introductory comments, that man's ambivalent, split representation of women represents his difficulty in coming to terms with the contradictory experience of the maternal figure as both phallic and castrated. The moral notion of respect for women, through elevating and distancing them, expresses Rousseau's unconscious fear of a confrontation with woman-as-castrated. Furthermore, where Rousseau describes women as threatening to suffocate, render passive and emasculate men, he is expressing his guilt at having 'suffocated' and 'rendered passive' (killed) his mother in childbirth (Kofman 1982a: 125).

Kofman's working tool is the presumption of the mechanism of a contradictory, unconscious Rousseauist logic, where the one account may at the same time amount to its opposite.[9] At one point Kofman argues that contradictory elements occur because, where Rousseau expresses abhorrence of certain women, he is at the same time expressing his desire for those same women (Kofman 1982a: 122).[10] Horror and disgust, says Kofman, are always the sign of the opposite in Rousseau (Kofman 1982a: 131). Since Rousseau cannot tolerate the notion of woman/the mother as castrated (passive, dead), and cannot tolerate the ambivalence between whether women are phallic or castrated, he therefore splits women into two radical images, the 'good and bad object' (Kofman 1982a: 125), and by displacing *all* of the 'bad' version on to the image of woman as impure, he manages to maintain the extreme version of the remaining woman as pure.

We should note that Kofman herself states a desire to avoid a 'reductive' reading in which Rousseau's account of women would be seen as the expression of a singular case of pathology – 'le cas Rousseau'. It is for this reason that she argues that aspects of Rousseau's account of women are common to all men, or to a certain kind of man (Kofman 1982a: 19).[11] So, while Kofman reads Rousseauist contradiction in terms of a form of psychoanalytic explanation of the text, it seems also to be with a view to more broadly accounting for the function of contradiction in a general-ised, masculine 'phallocratic' deployment of the theme of respect for women. According to the terms of her introduction, men are always trying to 'mend' or make compensation to (*réparer*) the image of woman that throughout history they have sullied and debased; to 'repair', in other words, the maternal body by trying to ingratiate themselves with women or the maternal ('se raccommoder avec elles'). So the 'feminism' of men – their tendency to laud, elevate and respect women – is the opposite side of the coin of which the first side is their misogyny. The conclusion of the text is also in accordance with the interpretation of a more general 'masculine pathology' about women. Men, says Kofman, always want to rummage in their mother's entrails (explore the secrets of the earth), to 'penetrate' her, rather than live side by side in proximity to her. Therefore, their own (self-inflicted) punishment is 'castration' – the notion of 'respecting' the secrets of the earth, the wariness of the drive for total knowledge. Kofman distances herself from an account which interprets the Rousseauist double logic in terms of a unique pathological case history and claims instead that the double account is a systematic masculine vision of women.

Despite this attempt to generalise a masculine pathological ambiva-lence in relation to women, Kofman concludes her text with a very particular reading of Rousseau: that his own constant urinary inhibition could be connected to his guilt that his mother, in 'excreting' him, had perished. The text then finally concludes with a reversion to Kofman's disclaimer, her rejection of psychoanalytic readings of Rousseau's texts which make inferences about his pathological case-history.[12]

Kofman serves as an example of an analysis of contradictory elements of the text which projects Rousseauist authorial, or unconscious, 'intention'. For her, the divided role of women allows Rousseau to salvage his ideal vision of women as pure. Kofman claims that the account specifically operates to serve 'men's' interests, and that it is a means for Rousseau to make reparation to the maternal figure, by the idealisation of the figure of woman. The contradictory notion of 'respect' is interpreted as resolving the contradictions inherent in feminine 'modesty'. The various contradictions are understood as serving 'phallocratic' ends. Rather than sustaining an explanatory account of what is produced by contradiction, Kofman's interpretation constructs a *causal* account of 'le cas Rousseau' and the author's unconscious demands and desires which are made manifest in his text.

Kofman does ask what is facilitated by contradiction. In this case, she claims that both Rousseau and Kant attempt to conceal the stakes of their dual account of women behind the mask of a 'moral' account of women. But here the claim about 'ends' is still a claim related to Kofman's account of dual, contradictory, *psychic motivation* (the desire to make reparation to the mother, the desire to conceal the dual impulses towards the feminine under a blind of morals and ethics, the desire to salvage the account of women as ideal and pure).

Kofman relies on the presumption of Rousseau's unconscious aims where she claims that Rousseau 'attempts' to make reparation to the maternal in idealising women through dividing the account of the feminine. Rousseau desires by his contradictory version of the feminine to make reparation to the maternal, to salvage the account of women as pure, and to *dissimulate* these intentions under the blind of a 'moral' account of sexual relations. In Kofman's account, these Rousseauist 'intentions' are unconscious, and the analysis of contradiction as functional is tied to the interpretation of what Rousseau (unconsciously) desires. In arguing that this is the way in which Rousseau desires the contradiction to function, Kofman infers a series of unconscious Rousseauist intentions. In locating contradiction, she often affirms a tension between Rousseau's conscious and unconscious avowals. Kofman's account of what textual effects (as opposed to unconscious satisfactions) are achieved by the Rousseauist contradictions is, in this sense, limited.[13] The interpretation is directed more at what motivates and facilitates the contradictory logic in Rousseau work than at what it enables. Kofman offers only a very limited analysis of what the contradiction itself enables.

LUCE IRIGARAY

In reading Irigaray, I am shifting the emphasis away from the thematic of sexual difference which she introduces into texts to the methodology she uses to do so. I shall suggest that Irigaray analyses the textual exclusion of sexual difference as contradictory. Taking one Irigarayan thematic – her concept of the divine – I shall examine the interconnection between her representation of women and femininity in terms of sexual difference and her methodological work on textual instability.

In her major work, *Speculum of the Other Woman*, Irigaray analyses a series of philosophers, from Plato and Plotinus through Descartes, Kant and Hegel to Freud, all of whose references to women, materiality or femininity suggest that the feminine has been appropriated or colonised so as to represent the 'other' of masculinity. 'The "feminine"', she claims, 'is always described in terms of deficiency or atrophy, as the other side of the sex that alone holds a monopoly on value: the male sex' (Irigaray 1985b: 69). For example, in reading Freud, she notes that females are only represented as (if girls) 'little men' (thus as the equivalent of little boys) or (if women) 'desiring babies' (thus as complements to the male) and 'desiring the penis for which the baby is a substitute' (thus as aspiring to be like men). There is room only for the feminine to be represented in terms relational to the masculine: as the same as, the other of, or the complement of the masculine: 'Freud does not see *two sexes* whose differences are articulated in the act of intercourse' (Irigaray 1985b: 69).

In focusing on representations of femininity in the works of philosophers, Irigaray analyses what she takes to be indications of theoretical weaknesses in those works, in the very reliance on the representation of woman as other to sustain a certain ideal identity of the masculine subject. Masculine identity, contrasted with femininity as a negative other, is all the more associated with positive qualities. Where women represent idle chatter, men represent rationality; where women represent the minus, men represent the plus (Irigaray 1985a: 22). To Irigaray, what suggests the fragility of associations of the male with reason, strength, civic responsibility, etc. is the 'othering' of woman to represent the emotional and irrational, the weak and the irresponsible. These strategies of othering suggest weakness and difficulty in the philosophical texts in which they occur. Irigaray suggests that representations of femininity serve as such an indication. She locates moments of self-contradiction or unstable logic in Freud's description of women, as when Freud both rejects and reinstates an opposition between activity/passivity to represent the opposition masculine/feminine.

Like Le Dœuff and Kofman, Irigaray focuses on the constancy with which women have been figured as 'other' in the history of philosophy. Like them, she locates points of tension, unease or contradiction surrounding this othering of women in the history of philosophy. But, on the basis of her assessment that woman has always been defined as the necessary complement to, or the negative image of, masculinity, Irigaray then attempts to go further by articulating the unsaid in philosophy. Instead of analysing how femininity or women are represented, she attempts to describe how they are *not* represented. Certainly, one can say that women have not been represented in terms which are not relational to a masculine reference point. Rather than making a claim about what women are really like, Irigaray analyses how a given text (in this case, Freud's) does *not* represent women. Once this 'not' is generalised by Irigaray to a series of thinkers throughout history, she has generated a claim about how women 'can not' be represented, or a claim about what sorts of representations of women have been 'excluded' throughout history. And, having made this claim, Irigaray then proceeds with an argument about the paradoxical, or self-contradictory, nature of exclusion itself. Irigaray uses the following kind of language to describe what has happened to representations of women and femininity: the philosophical logos has had the power to *'reduce all others to the economy of the Same'*. Its project, she maintains, had been to *'eradicate the difference between the sexes'* (Irigaray 1985b: 74).

How can one 'exclude' a representation of women without, at the same time, gesturing towards the possibility (even as one excludes it) of representing women in the excluded terms? How can one 'reduce' others to the economy of the Same without recognising that they exceed the economy of the Same? How could philosophy have 'eradicated the difference between the sexes' without implicitly indicating that which it eradicated? Irigaray plays with logic here: there must be 'something' to eradicate, even if that 'something' is an excluded possibility, the femininity which has never become culturally coherent or possible, what Irigaray names 'sexual difference'.

In this way, Irigaray generates a concept on which she has continued to rely throughout her work. This is a concept of the feminine whose status is neither that of the buried or repressed truth of the feminine nor that of a utopian, new possibility of femininity. It is neither empirical nor some unknowable 'outside' of language and culture, 'neither on the near side, the empirical realm that is opaque to all language, nor on the far side, the self-sufficient infinite' (Irigaray 1985b: 77).

Instead, it is a conceptual possibility which is, as Irigaray formulates her idea, both within and without, or on the border of histories of representation of femininity. Not within, because it has been excluded. Not entirely without, because insofar as it has been 'excluded', it has been indicated or gestured towards as an excluded possibility. Thus the concept of femininity Irigaray has generated has a paradoxical inside/ outside, possible/impossible status. Irigaray's point is that 'the recognition of a "specific" female sexuality would challenge the monopoly on value held by the masculine sex alone' (Irigaray 1985b: 73). Thus, with this concept Irigaray proposes the project of disruption of traditional representations of masculinity and femininity and the reinvention of those representations:

> what is important is to disconcert the staging of representation according to *exclusively* 'masculine' parameters, that is, according to a phallocratic order ... disrupting and modifying it, starting from an 'outside' that is exempt, in part, from phallocratic law.
>
> (Irigaray 1985b: 68)

77

Here, Irigaray describes the conceptual status of the feminine she is reworking, not as outside, but, using scare quotes, as 'outside' (both inside and outside, or occupying the paradoxical border position that the excluded always holds). She does not say that it is exempt from the phallocratic order, but that it is exempt in part. When, in later work, Irigaray refers to 'women's identity', women's bodies, women's nature, women's Gods, etc., the status of femininity and women has the paradoxical status she has generated early in her work. Speaking in the name of a feminine identity whose status is this paradoxical 'inside/outside', Irigaray incurred being accused by critics of pretending to describe the truth of women. However, Irigaray began her career with clear statements deflecting the interpretation she was to incur. She specifically rejects the idea of asking 'What is woman?' (Irigaray 1985b: 78). She proposes an alternative to that kind of question, one of 'repeating/interpreting the way in which, within discourse, the feminine finds itself defined as lack, deficiency, or as imitation and negative image of the subject, [and one] should signify that with respect to this logic a *disruptive excess* is possible on the feminine side' (Irigaray 1985b: 78).

Irigaray can be understood as diverging from Le Dœuff and Kofman from the point at which Irigaray attempts to argue that any concept of femininity exceeding the terms of 'man's other' must 'have been' excluded. Above all, they part company at the point at which, as a disruptive strategy, Irigaray uses the device of attempting to insert into the philosophical texts she reads, and into language and culture generally, a concept of femininity which she takes to be excluded, a concept of femininity in terms of difference, rather than relativity to the masculine.

Relentlessly, then, Irigaray emphasises in her work the need for a feminism of sexual difference, and this translates into a wariness about feminist aspirations which are limited to 'equality with men':

> women merely 'equal' to men would be 'like them', therefore not women. Once more, the difference between the sexes would be in that way cancelled out, ignored, papered over.
>
> (Irigaray 1985b: 166)

And, in a more recent statement:

> To demand equality as women is, it seems to me, a mistaken expression of a real objective. The demand to be equal presupposes a point of comparison. To whom or to what do women want to be equalized? To men? . . . To what standard? Why not to themselves?
>
> (Irigaray 1993b: 12)

It is because of such statements that debate about Irigaray tends to be overshadowed by this equality versus difference controversy within

Deutscher equates "internal destabilization"
& with a sort of internal externalization
of ? for the sake of appearing stable

LE DŒUFF, KOFMAN AND IRIGARAY

feminism. Certainly, Le Dœuff, Kofman and Irigaray can be distinguished in terms of their positions on feminism of difference, since Le Dœuff and Kofman are extremely wary of this theoretical position. However, I have concentrated on the arguments of all three that phallocentric accounts of women are sustained by unstable and contradictory textual elements, and I want to continue by examining Irigaray's position in this regard. Irigaray argues that a paradoxical structure generates masculine and feminine identity. Masculine and feminine identity are, therefore, always already destabilised, but these identities function *on the strength of* this internal destabilisation: they are the effect of structural instability.

Sum
?

Irigaray focuses on what she takes to be the conditions of possibility of identifications of masculinity with presence or positivity and femininity with absence or negativity. Thus, Irigaray interprets the generation of man's 'identity' as presence and positivity in terms of its dependency on the identification of woman as his 'other' and as a kind of negative alter ego to the masculine. As we've seen, she claims that the association of man with rational and positive qualities depends on the production of woman as man's 'negative mirror':

> phallic currency . . . can immediately be assumed to need its other, a sort of inverted or negative alter ego . . . Inverse, contrary, contradictory even, necessary.
>
> (Irigaray 1985a: 22)

We have seen that Irigaray's claim relates, in part, to what she asserts is the peculiar fragility of the masculine identity because of this dependence on the identification of the feminine as 'not' being those qualities in terms of which the masculine is represented. What I now point out is that for Irigaray, a structural paradox constitutes the 'conditions of possibility' of masculine identity. On the one hand, the feminine as absence and negativity (as 'Not-A') is conceptually dependent on the notion of masculinity as presence and positivity. That is to say, the feminine as 'irrationality', for example, would seem to be conceptually tributary to the notion of the masculine as 'rational'. However, Irigaray argues that the notion of the masculine is generated through its opposition to its (feminine) 'negative mirror'. Thus, the masculine both is and is not conceptually 'dependent' on the notion of the feminine. The very same 'A/Not-A' dichotomous structure which produces the identity of masculinity as presence, positivity, and autonomy from the feminine also renders the masculine tributary to the feminine in the sense that the effect of masculine identity is dependent on its opposition to the feminine. For Irigaray, it is the negative 'interpretative modality' of the feminine which actually 'sustains' masculine 'moves', the masculine 'pursuit of a certain game', and acts as the 'hinge' for exchanges between men (Irigaray 1985a: 22).

This is one contradiction which Irigaray considers to be necessary and operative in the production of masculine identity as presence and positivity. Irigaray also perceives a certain paradoxical 'necessity' whereby woman is constructed both as nothing but 'man's negative mirror' and yet also as 'in excess' of her role as negative mirror to the masculine. Here, Irigaray proposes that because of the dependence of the representation of masculinity in terms of presence and positivity on its opposition to the feminine-as-absence, any intimation of a feminine other than, or in excess of, its role as alter ego to the masculine destabilises masculine identity. Irigaray has indicated the following paradox: the 'action' of producing the feminine as 'negative other' is itself a gesticulation towards a feminine more and other than its role as man's 'negative other'.[14] The same gesture which excludes the feminine as other than 'man's other' simultaneously indicates that feminine 'remainder' and thus simultaneously destabilises itself. In other words, Irigaray's proposal is that the very same gesture which excludes woman-as-excess also, paradoxically, indicates that excess. Consequently, only by remaining in excess to her role as negative other can woman be produced as man's negative other. Thus, the feminine simultaneously supports and destabilises masculine identity.

Irigaray sometimes uses the metaphor of 'materiality' in her discussion of this conceptual problem. Woman has historically been associated with materiality, ground, earth, matter.[15] Irigaray adopts or 'mimics'[16] this association by redeploying the metaphor of materiality to describe the feminine as the matter out of which man fashions his alter ego. If man, she argues, has fashioned his alter ego out of matter, then woman, as the matter out of which man fashions his alter ego, must be in excess of that fashioning. Woman-as-matter is 'in excess' of any particular 'fashioning' of that feminine 'matter'. Woman is thus conceptually in excess (as 'matter') of her role as 'negative' mirror. It should be noted that the sense of woman's 'excess' is particular. I use the term 'conceptual' in an attempt to situate this notion, because it has a peculiar epistemological status. Irigaray does not (in her early work) argue that sexual difference is a real fact, and that women are simply misrepresented in terms of atrophy. Where she accounts for women as exceeding representations of the feminine in terms of atrophy, she does not invoke a distinction between feminine reality and the representation of the feminine.[17] Rather, she argues that the representation itself is paradoxical. It is the representation which limits the feminine to atrophy. However, such representations necessarily destabilise themselves. Because of this, we are able to articulate the concept of an 'excessive feminine' as a hypothetical possibility, currently excluded from language and culture.[18] In this way, then, Irigaray emphasises another 'condition of possibility' generating man/woman dichotomies in the history of philosophy. This is the exclusion of an 'autonomously conceptualised' notion of woman. Irigaray proposes

[handwritten margin notes at top: "are 'moments' we — in order / that which on — the instability / hone in on 'expose' that is automatic / to 'expose' that there."]

that one can trace in the texts of the history of philosophy not just the representation of woman as lack and atrophy but also the simultaneous, necessary auto-destabilisation of that representation. Moments of auto-destabilisation will be said to have occurred where a text, in the midst of a production of woman as man's negative other, gesticulates to a conception of femininity as in excess of that role.[19] Irigaray effectively suggests that constitutive instability is necessary to the production of man's identity in terms of presence and positivity.

Man, the divine and the feminine

Irigaray also affirms that man/woman oppositions should be interpreted in terms of an interwoven cluster of concepts, and in particular, concepts relating to the projection of transcendental ideals. Accounts of 'man' and 'woman' are seen as interconnected with the projection of man's ideal identity: God. As with the positioning of a particular feminine, Irigaray also argues that the positioning of a particular 'God' sustains masculine identity. In considering the relationship between representations of man and representations of God, many of Irigaray's texts assert that the Western masculine-paternal God serves as a masculine 'ideal-ego'. In *Speculum*, Irigaray asserts that there is a relationship between man and God in which 'some (male) One has taken on omnipotence as one of his attributes ... [and] ... the child can "fantasise" himself identical to Him – to an ideal ego' (Irigaray 1985a: 356). God is positioned as a mythical, ideal point of pure, self-contained knowledge, of radical autonomy of the other, of the ultimate transcendence of materiality and mortality. The projection of a masculine-paternal God is a projection of a masculine ideal:

> this figure of love [Christ/God] must continue to be unique, remaining eternally captive to the lure of a (male) Same ... Is it not the pattern for the mask that completes, to the point of inappearance, man's identity with himself? The dream of becoming the self without contradictions, of reabsorbing into the self all things opposed and different, of subsuming under the self the transcendent of oneself. Of one day finally being divinely the self.
>
> (Irigaray 1991: 186–7)

The claim is that the masculine-paternal God has been conceptualised in terms of the needs of a masculine genre, just as the feminine has been conceptualised in terms of the needs of the masculine genre.

A masculine/paternal, Occidental God acts both as 'guarantor' (*caution*) of man's identity and also as the absolute, external guarantor of the knowledge attained by man in his identity as the 'man of reason'. In exercising reason, man transcends his own materiality, which is associated with (or displaced on to) the identity of the feminine. Thus, Irigaray comments :

81

[handwritten margin note at bottom: "?? consider this in rel to law/rights"]

Man has been the subject of discourse: whether in theory, morality or politics. And the gender of God, the guardian of every subject and every discourse, is always *masculine and paternal*, in the West.

(Irigaray 1993a: 6–7)

Thus, in the chapter on Descartes in *Speculum*, God is positioned as that which confers the truth of the objective reality of our ideas, and as the guardian of 'immutable truths' (Irigaray 1985a: 197). The positioning of a God, or a divine realm regarded as original and as coinciding with a point of ultimate truth, allows the 'man of reason' in his pursuit of knowledge the conviction that he approaches a stable realm of truth. It is also in this sense that the projection of the Platonic divine realm of Forms serves as a kind of guarantee that man, in his cultivation of the philosophical life approaches more closely to a higher realm. It is in this sense that God is said to play the role of 'conferring the truth', or the objective reality, on the ideas generated by a philosophical life associated with masculinity, as Irigaray phrases it.

Irigaray accordingly argues that masculine identity is produced through two different kinds of 'prop'. On the one hand, man is opposed to woman as his alter ego. On the other hand, man identifies with God as his ideal-ego and as the 'guarantor' of masculine identity. Yet, just as we have seen Irigaray argue that the production of feminine identity must destabilise masculine identity at the same time as it supports it, Irigaray makes the same claim about the relationship between God and man. There are several senses in which Irigaray argues that while God acts as 'guarantor' to masculine identity, at the same time God is the blind spot to masculine identity:

Thus, 'the father's image' will be rediscovered in the soul of the son ... how much that image owes and denies to specular projection and inversion. [Otherwise] he would already have recognised that the 'father' is that which is reproduced in him in order (not) to be mirrored in his absence (of self). The cover over a *blind spot* in consciousness which he fails to recognise.

(Irigaray 1985a: 314)

The above passage suggests that the masculine owes a considerable debt to the divine image of the 'father' but that this debt must also be denied. Here, Irigaray suggests that the role of the divine as masculine-paternal ideal ego is similar in structure to the paradoxical relationship between masculine identity and its other, the feminine. In each case, because Irigaray asserts a relationship of dependence of masculine identity on its (divine and feminine) props, she suggests that the ideal relationship with these props is simultaneously compromised.

Where the masculine is aligned with a divine ideal-ego of immateriality, autonomy and self-identity, Irigaray suggests that the masculine is dependent on the identification with the divine, 'in order (not) to be mirrored in his *absence (of self)*' (Irigaray 1985a: 314, my italic). The divine is an ideal of self-coincidence and self-sufficiency that the masculine *necessarily* falls short of. In this cited phrase, it is unclear whether the masculine identifies with an ideal (divine) specular image in order to be reflected as an atrophied version, or precisely in order not to be reflected as an absence of divine self. In other words, man is both opposed to and aligned with the divine.

Irigaray might well have selected as an example Saint Augustine's waverings between whether man is like or not-like God.[20] As man's ideal, God must be simultaneously the opposite of man and the ideal of man. God thus confirms man's 'absence of divine self' in the same movement as providing an ideal of self-coinciding, disembodied, all-knowing self. Furthermore, insofar as the divine 'props' up masculine identity, the masculine is dependent on that 'prop' and so is confirmed in that fragility by the same support that provides the ideal.

Irigaray locates a further series of internal tensions in this relationship between man and God where she considers the role of the divine as 'legislator', and as guarantor of man's pursuit of knowledge. How can God as 'radically other' be drawn on as a voice legitimating the laws of man? The ineffability of God, which gives those laws their legitimacy, also makes them unknowable to man once the divine has been declared as ineffable. As Irigaray writes in her reading of the Platonic metaphor of the cave in the *Republic*, a radical divide is projected between the realms of man and God, precisely in order to produce God as an ideal other:

> A *paraphragm* – a diagonal, a diameter, or even a *diaphragm* manu-
> factured for specula(riza)tions bars and – forbids the access (to) the
> excessiveness of an 'other' side. God-the-Father, no doubt, thereby
> gains a bonus of power.
>
> (Irigaray 1985a: 361)

The problem is how the laws of God can coherently be considered as translatable into the laws of human philosophy. How can there be a coherent account of the passage between their difference, and how can this passage occur given the limitations of mortal perception? Thus, in her reading of Hegel she raises a problem in relation to the radical division between the so-called 'laws of God' and the laws of philosophy, and between the laws of the female and the male. 'What', she asks accordingly, 'will be the passage of their *difference* in the subsequent movement of the mind? Or rather, how will that difference be resolved?' (Irigaray 1985a: 224).

Man both projects God as radically other and also refers to divine directives to legitimate the prescription of sexual difference. Where God's

83

laws are radically other, how can they be referred to reliably? This implies a knowledge of the divine order excluded by man himself insofar as he projects God as the radical other. How can man undertake to speak for God, and how can man undertake to relegate woman to a secondary position on the basis of a divine law which he *also* projects as being ineffable? This would seem to be the question Irigaray evokes when she continues.

> How does the mind acquire, in a variation of deferred action (après coup), the right to make laws and official statements about (the) matter, when a certain process of statement has already excluded difference in its desire to return to sameness?
>
> (Irigaray 1985a: 224)

Thus Irigaray insists, as does Derrida, on the fact that in Plato's *Dialogues* Being cannot appear.[21] The mind's grasp can only have 'an intuition of Being in the rarest and highest moments of the loving contemplation of the Good or the Beautiful' – and then only an intuition. She comments:

> Finally Being does not appear or even appear to appear. It slips away from the mind's grasp, even as it forms the foundation of mind. Is this the mystery – the hysteria – of Being? Hidden in its crypt where no-one, however skilled in philosophy, has glimpsed it? Only at the rarest and highest moments of loving contemplation of the Good – or of the Beautiful? – will the wisest man receive some 'intuition' that can barely be put into words. Here then, man does not yet have the plenitude of Being *within him*, but instead a whole range of theoretical tools . . . are being worked out to form a *matrix of appropriation* for man.
>
> (Irigaray 1985a: 150–1)

The aporia in the guarantee established by God of masculine identity is the (necessary) *evanescence* of God. Thus, as in the case of Derrida's analysis of Plato in *Dissemination*, man's identification with a divine point can be reinterpreted as an '*appropriation*' of the plenitude of divine Being. It is an appropriation (in other words, it is *inappropriate*) because man privileges masculinity (mind, reason, knowledge) in opposition to a devalued femininity (body, emotions, passions) on the strength of a ('masculine') alignment with a point of divine plenitude that the same system organises as incoherent as an ideal ultimate state of the 'masculine'.

So, God must also be seen as a fragile guarantee of masculine identity. It is the *schism* between man and God which renders God a meaningful, transcendent ideal, but the schism between man and God simultaneously leaves man severed from his own guarantor. Conceptually cast adrift as mortal limitation, suspended between an ideal of being 'like God' and a condition of being radically 'not God', man is promised an eventual communion with the divine, but only as a transcendence of his mortality, his physical embodied materiality. The promise of the eventual becoming-immortal of man does not alter the fact that man qua *man* (qua mortal), while he must cultivate a transcendence of the sensible, is radically severed from the divine. The terms according to which the masculine is opposed to the feminine and the feminine depreciated are in fact the terms of an ideal which the masculine necessarily also falls short of.

Irigaray frames her problematic specifically in terms of the production of the effects of masculine and feminine identity. She asks what the conditions of possibility of these two sexual identities are, what produces their effect, what they rely on and what they necessarily exclude. Irigaray analyses the paradoxical conditions of masculine and feminine ('A/Not-A') identity. Thus, we can interpret Irigaray as proposing that several contradictions are constitutive in this regard. These include the paradox whereby the dependence of the masculine on both the feminine as 'negative' and on the transcendent as 'ideal' render the masculine simultaneously supported and destabilised. Irigaray also claims that the very exclusion of any femininity exceeding the 'Not-A' also indicates the conceptual possibility of such an excess. Thus the role of the feminine as a 'negative mirror' to the masculine is also auto-destabilising. We have also seen Irigaray claim that masculine identity is dependent on its identification with a transcendent entity as ideal-ego, and as guarantor of the reason which man cultivates in opposition to the feminine. Here, Irigaray suggests that masculine identity is again destabilised by its own 'guarantor'. The projection of a transcendent realm legitimates the 'laws' of man and sustains the masculine/feminine opposition. Simultaneously, that legitimation is auto-destabilised precisely because it is projected as transcendent and thus ineffable and exterior to man.

Irigaray herself is most known for her argument that 'man/woman' ('A/Not-A') oppositions rely on the exclusion of any feminine in excess of that opposition. I have pointed out Irigaray's argument that such exclusion is auto-destabilising. Commentary has focused on Irigaray's attempt to develop new conceptual frameworks for masculinity and femininity, her attempt to articulate a hypothetical feminine in terms which would interrupt this 'A/Not-A' conceptual framework. I have considered how Irigaray argues that contradiction is constitutive in the production of sexed dichotomies and I suggest the importance of not obscuring the internal contradictions organising these oppositions. In other words, the history of philosophy should not be described as if man has simply been coherently and consistently aligned with positive qualities such as rationality, and women with nature, emotion and the body. Such an analysis is overly complicit with the textual *effect* of para-doxical conceptual structures and helps to cover over the extent to which such structures are self-contradictory and auto-destabilising. The contradictory structures I have suggested here are those whereby man must be both aligned with and opposed to his transcendent, legitimating ideal.

OUTSIDE THE TEXT?

Irigaray's strategy of inserting concepts of sexual difference into phallocentric texts relies to some extent on assertions about what those texts mean to say. For example, in her reading of Freud, Irigaray makes various assertions about Freud's desire. According to her, Freud desires to reduce women to phallocentric terms. Such assertions support Irigaray's argument that a concept of sexual difference is subversive of Freud's account of femininity. To some extent, an authorial Freud is constructed, with phallocentric desires and intentions. Indeed, this is the ground of Kofman's criticism of Irigaray. Irigaray is so sure, Kofman protests, that Freud wishes to speak exclusively among men about women; that Freud wishes to deprive women of the right to the logos and the phallus alike; that he wishes to present a phallocentric account of women; that he does wish to hold on to the old words 'masculine' and 'feminine' (Kofman 1985: 104, 115). How can Irigaray abstract this stable position with such confidence out of the complexity and heterogeneity of Freud's text?

However, the contrast with Kofman demonstrates how much stronger this very tendency is in the latter. We have seen in her interpretation of Rousseau the exaggerated nature of her reconstruction of Rousseau's unconscious desire, and her supposition that such desires are made manifest in the text. While Kofman criticises interpretations of Rousseau's texts which rely on the projection of an extra-textual authorial psyche, her own text does nevertheless conclude with an interpretation of Rousseau's text in terms of what Kofman projects as Rousseau's particular neurosis. Kofman often refers to Derrida in support of her own approach. The influence of deconstruction is manifest in the string of textual references to Derrida and *Of Grammatology*. Yet it is far from clear that Derrida would accept Kofman's projections of Rousseau's 'unconscious' in her interpretation of the instability of his texts.

For example, Derrida resists a psychoanalytic interpretation of Rousseau if, he says, 'by that we understand an interpretation that takes us outside of the writing toward a psychobiographical signified, or even toward a general psychological structure that could rightly be separated from the signifier' (Derrida 1976: 159). For such an approach obliges us to posit a mythic position exterior to the text, an *hors-texte*, such as the author's psyche, or the author's unconscious'. And Derrida suggests:

Reading ... cannot legitimately transgress the text toward something other than it, toward a referent (a reality that is metaphysical, historical, psychobiographical, etc.)

(Derrida 1976: 158)

Both Kofman and Irigaray focus on textual tensions and contradictions in the work of canonical figures such as Rousseau and Freud. However, like Le Dœuff and to varying degrees, they occasionally interpret those textual tensions in terms of authorial aim. For example, on occasion we hear of Sartre's sexism having been devised in order to hide the blunders of his system, of Rousseau's contradictory acount of women as an expression of his guilt over his mother's death, or of Freud's castration anxiety.

Kofman references her methodology to Derrida. However, in chapter 5, I shall interpret Derrida's reading of Rousseau in *Of Grammatology* as avoiding the transgression of the text to the kind of psychobiographical referent which sometimes seems to be manifest in Kofman's work. I shall suggest that this enables more emphasis on the constitutive role of Rousseau's unstable arguments. Derrida's interpretation concentrates more on the effects rendered by those instabilities, since it is not preoccupied with attempts to look behind Rousseau's texts to possible causes of such instability ranging from Rousseau's motivations to his authorial ruses or his psychobiography.

Both Le Dœuff and Kofman express wariness of the work of Luce Irigaray, and of feminism of sexual difference. Yet I have suggested alternative terms in which to assess Irigaray's readings of the history of philosophy. While Irigaray, like Kofman, does make reference to the author's desire or the author's ruses, I have suggested that her strongest focus is on textual instability as constitutive of phallocentrism. Her texts drift less towards reconstructions of the author's psyche, and bear more with the focus on textual instability. Her work is oriented less towards questions of what causes such instability. Contradictory tensions constitute phallocentrism, she argues, which must simultaneously exclude and acknowledge the conceptual possibility of sexual difference. Sexual difference is both interior and exterior to phallocentrism. In this sense, phallocentrism is constituted in its own instability. Irigaray does not argue that phallocentrism is destabilised by such instability. But she does argue that the possibility of destabilisation is opened up by the contradictory constitution of phallocentrism. While constitutive instability is not subversive, it does allow the possibility of subversion. The instability of the simultaneous exclusion and gesturing towards the possibility of sexual difference creates the conditions of possibility for Irigaray's intervention: the generation of disruptive, exorbitant concepts of sexual difference, which are then inserted back into such texts. In the light of the discussion in chapter 1, it is interesting that Irigaray's readings do not seem preoccupied with the issue of whether constitutive instability is 'really subversive' or really hegemonic. She argues, coherently, that constitutive instability both is hegemonic and opens up the possibility of her own subversive intervention.

4

JEAN-JACQUES ROUSSEAU
AND THE INCONSTANCY
OF WOMAN

> Rousseau's arguments for confining women to private life are a
> farrago of contradictions.
>
> (Margaret Canovan)

French feminism has been discussed by feminist philosophers in terms
of the debate between feminisms of equality and difference more than
as a source of methodologies for the interpretation of the history of philosophy. In the remainder of this work, I shall offer readings of canonical
figures in the history of philosophy who are significant from a feminist
perspective. My readings focus on constitutive instability in arguments
which constrain or devalue the role and nature of women. I address the
work of Jean-Jacques Rousseau, Saint Augustine and Simone de Beauvoir.
I rely on methodologies drawn from the work of Le Dœuff, Kofman and
Irigaray, and also draw from debate about the role of constitutive
instability which has been generated around the work of Judith Butler and
Jacques Derrida. The work of, and debate surrounding, these various
theorists provides cautionary tales and a resource pool for the analyst of
constitutive instability. Le Doeuff and Kofman lean sometimes towards
attempting to explain instability rather than analysing its effects. Debate
about Butler's work represents the risk of overly focusing on constitutive
trouble. Some interpretations of Derrida (those which see his work as
anarchist/nihilist) also represent this risk. Other interpretations of
deconstruction represent the risk of overly focusing on Derrida as an
analyst who reconstructs. I have argued for the need to interpret deconstruction as the analysis of how instability generates effects of stability,
and simultaneously disrupts those effects, with an even balance on both
arms. Irigaray represents a strong theorist of constitutive instability from
my perspective, analysing instability as both subversive and stabilising.
In the readings which follow, I shall not be taking an approach which
is specifically Derridean, nor specific to Butler, Le Dœuff, Kofman or
Irigaray. Instead, the approach taken in the following interpretations
of accounts of women in the history of philosophy results from reflection

on these theorists and, in particular, on debate surrounding their work. This will be evident in the specific orientation of the readings, according to which instability in the arguments of Rousseau, Augustine and Beauvoir is analysed as constitutive: as both subversive and stabilising.

FEMINIST APPROACHES TO THE HISTORY OF PHILOSOPHY

One can read the history of philosophy for its symbolic alignment of men (and masculinity) with reason, culture, strength, the investigating subject, the public sphere; and the alignment of women (and femininity) with nature, the body, the emotions, weakness, the investigated object, the private. In relation to the man of reason, woman has repeatedly been represented as a passionate, sensitive, irrational creature of the private sphere. Narratives about the consistency of phallocentrism in the history of philosophy are reinforced by anthologies and the work of Okin, Elshtain, Spelman, Pateman, Lloyd, Gatens, Green, Tuana and Nye, and many others.

I recall as a student being struck by the anomalies in the canonical texts in which reason was, directly or indirectly, associated with masculinity. If men represent mind, and women the bodily, how was it that men were also associated with bodily strength in opposition to the bodily weakness of women? Even the simplest symbolic binary association (mind/body: masculine/feminine) seemed a complex structure requiring further analysis. Rather than contenting ourselves with the narrative that mind has been attributed with the symbolic connotations of masculinity, and embodiment the symbolic connotations of femininity, we need to analyse the complex conceptual structure of a binarism which enables man *both* to be opposed to the bodily *and* to be associated with the bodily, even in the most simple and familiar of these dichotomous oppositions.

There is no shortage of texts which confirm the narrative that reason has been associated with masculinity, the body and the passions with femininity. But what if we read the history of philosophy differently? What if we do not look for confirmation that stable sexed binarisms (man = reason; woman = passions) have occurred in the history of philosophy? Instead, what if we read for the presence of internal disruption of those binarisms – the presence of exceptions, instability, contradictions, slippage? I do not contest the accuracy of the narrative about the man of reason. I contest the way in which this narrative has sometimes been told. Instability, contradiction, tension and paradox have always been integral to the symbolic association between reason and masculinity. In our concern with exposing the history of this phallocentric association, its consistent instabilities have sometimes been downplayed.

90

Such downplaying is related to the role attributed to textual instability. The argument that the masculinity of reason is unstable might seem an attempt to suggest that the story is not so bad after all. It might be thought that the instability of the masculine connotations of reason weakens or mitigates those connotations. The existence of contradictory refrains might be taken to mean that the overall misogyny of the text is somehow less. Such suppositions rely on a subtractive approach to inconsistency. One refrain is subtracted from the other, leaving a stabilised, definitive textual refrain. In this second half of this book, I shall challenge interpretations of canonical works in the history of philosophy which take just such an approach to textual instability. Such an approach causes critics and readers to neutralise, or look away from, or behind, the instability of the man of reason and gendered dichotomies. By contrast, I shall argue that feminist interpretation should be focusing right on such instability. In this and the next three chapters, I shall consider feminist interpretation of Jean-Jacques Rousseau, Saint Augustine and Simone de Beauvoir. In each case, I shall be arguing that feminist interpretation of the history of philosophy needs rich, complex methodologies for its analysis of the contradictions, inconsistencies and instability in that history.

To return to my question, what if we do not look for confirmation that stable sexed binarisms (man = reason, woman = passions) have occurred in the history of philosophy? What if we read *for* the instability of those binarisms? Perhaps we shall find that man is often associated with the bodily – for example, as the merely human in opposition to God. We shall find many apparently progressive arguments that reason is gender-neutral which also maintain associations between femininity and irrationality. We shall be faced with the crucial, often incoherent, conceptual dislocation of 'femininity' from 'woman', 'masculinity' from man. We shall find that the ability to describe women as masculine and men as feminine frequently *stabilises* the supposed identities of man as masculine and women as feminine, and enables many a phallocentric account of sexual difference. We shall encounter the elasticity with which the public sphere, as Carole Pateman has pointed out, can incorporate working women and still retain a coherent alignment between the man/woman and public/private oppositions (Pateman 1988: 227–9).

Now is a time in feminist theory generally when gender and sex binarisms are being interrogated as the site of instabilities and anomalies. In chapter 1, we saw two examples in the work of Judith Butler and Eve Sedgwick. Is it also time to shift our analytic focus away from the stability and consistency of the man of reason and the woman of passions towards the presence of contradictory, unstable elements in such binarisms, and in canonical philosophical accounts of equality and difference between the sexes? An important period in feminist interpretation of the history of philosophy has occurred with the discussion of how men and women have been differently represented in relation to ideals of reason. The question is how feminists should best interpret the presence of contradictory tensions in that history. Can we tell the tale of the man of reason in ways which do not suppress the ambiguities inherent in that tale? Given an analysis which does try to represent those ambiguities, how best to analyse them? What methodologies to draw upon?

True, it is no new undertaking in feminist theory to *indicate* the presence of contradictory tensions relating to man/woman dichotomies. Indeed, arguing that these dichotomies are riddled with contradictory tensions has become a familiar theme in feminist analyses of the history of philosophy. Second only to the simple argument that reason has been masculinised in the canon, exposing contradiction has been one of the most reliable feminist devices for offering critiques of classical accounts of women. Consider the example of many feminist re-readings of Rousseau's *Emile*. Establishing the presence of contradiction has provided the basis for every manner of feminist critique of that philosopher from the eighteenth to the twentieth centuries, from the work of Mary Wollstonecraft to that of Susan Moller Okin. Still, feminist methodologies have often been limited to simply exposing the incoherence of Rousseau. Such an approach does not analyse the operative role of instability in his phallocentrism. The instability is taken to undo the phallocentrism, forestalling an analysis of the sustaining role it also plays. As I argued in chapter 1, the problem with such an approach is its presumption that gender normativity's good operation relies on its coherence of definition. If one rejects this presumption, then stronger methodologies are needed than simple exposure of instability of terms and incoherence of definition. As we have seen, this argument arises in the context of debate around the work of Judith Butler. I am proposing that it be redeployed in the context of feminist readings of the history of philosophy.

I shall use the example of feminist interpretation of Jean-Jacques Rousseau in this chapter in a discussion of the methodologies which have tended to inform the genre of feminist readings of the history of philosophy. Rousseau is a philosopher notorious for his self-contradictory and unstable account of sexual difference. Taking a cross-section of feminist responses to Rousseau, I propose an analysis of methodologies deployed in the interpretation of the unstable and contradictory textual elements grounding phallocentric accounts of sexual difference.

THE INSTABILITY OF ROUSSEAUIST SEXUAL DIFFERENCE

Rousseau's most sustained account of a necessary 'sexual difference' is presented in the fifth book of *Emile*, where he describes Emile's ideal partner, Sophie. Rousseau argues that the society contemporary to him

violates nature's dictates. At different times, Rousseau identifies degradation in the mining and plundering of 'mother-earth' (Rousseau 1987b: 66;
Rousseau 1979: 113); in large, anonymous urban communities in which
there is a loss of immediacy between humans (Rousseau 1966: 72–4); in the
loss of empathy with the other (Rousseau 1987b: 54); in the enslavement of
men and in war (Rousseau 1987b: 68, 70, 74); and in man's excessive
cultivation of reason, manifest in the practices of science and philosophy
(Rousseau 1987a: 10).[1]

One of the worst symptoms of degradation from nature's dictates
can be seen in the confusion between the sexes. Sexual identity has
become confused where society 'confounds the two sexes in the same
employments and in the same labours' (Rousseau 1991: 363). The sexes are
confused literally in that they live too much in each other's proximity
and intermingle excessively in society (Rousseau 1960: 100). Even when
married, a man and woman should maintain a certain distance (Rousseau
1960: 100, 107; Rousseau 1991: 479). In modern cities such as Paris,
men seek out the society of women too often, as when they frequent
female salons. They thereby jeopardise their masculine identity, for man is
rendered feminine or effeminate by too much contact with women
(Rousseau 1960: 100–1).

There is a distinct sexual identity (a series of attributes and practices)
which pertains, or *should* pertain, distinctly to each sex (Rousseau 1991:
363). The masculine sex, he declares in *Emile*, ought to be active and
strong, and the feminine sex passive and weak (Rousseau 1991: 358). The
denaturalisation of the sexes is seen in the confusion of sexual identity –
the 'rendering feminine' of men, and the domination by women of men.
An unnatural redistribution of power relations between the sexes occurs,
where man, the natural master of women, loses his power of command[2]
and where woman adopts masculine practices (Rousseau 1991: 363,
408–9).

Thus, sexual relations have been denatured, first, when women and
men intermingle overly; second, when the power relationship between
them is perverted so that woman dominates man; and third, when men
and women take on each other's attributes or habits. In a denatured
feminisation, men take on a passive lifestyle, cultivate their personal
appearance and adopt an exaggeratedly mannered and powdered
gentility, as we typically see in the mores of larger cities (Rousseau 1960:
100–1). In a denatured masculinisation, women gather together to discuss
ideas, write literature, enter the public sphere, and lose their timidity and
modesty.[3]

Obviously, as Sarah Kofman and many others point out, the account of
sexual difference prescribed in *Emile* is oriented in terms of men and their
requirements, as opposed to those of women (Kofman 1988: 124). The
account of Sophie is structured in terms of the question of what kind of

woman is necessary to Emile. Rousseau does not ask what kind of man would be necessary to Sophie, and does not conceive of Emile's education accordingly (Rousseau 1991: 357). Instead, Sophie's education and character are presented in terms of the kind of companionship Emile will require. Woman is the natural complement to man and so should act accordingly: 'Woman is made specially to please man ... If woman is made to please and to be subjugated, she ought to make herself agreeable to man' (Rousseau 1991: 358).

Woman should be mistress of the domestic and maternal arts (Rousseau 1991: 368). She should acquire sufficient instruction from her parents to be an intelligent partner to her husband but not enough to be his equal (Rousseau 1991: 386, 409). She should receive no religious instruction since it is the man who educates a woman in these matters (Rousseau 1991: 377). She should be gentle, pure, dainty, fastidious, irreproachably faithful, dress simply, behave demurely and yet she should charm and delight. She should be wise, and prudent, and quietly oversee or manage her husband or guests in certain subtle ways (Rousseau 1991: 361, 370, 383). She should 'cultivate pleasing talents that will entertain her future husband with as much care as a young Albanian cultivates them for the harem of Ispahan ... a lovable and pure woman who possessed such talents and consecrated them to the entertainment of her husband would ... add to the happiness of his life' (Rousseau 1991: 374).

Rousseau rejects the suggestion that in recommending a 'sexual difference' ordered in this fashion, he is recommending a sexual 'inequality'. He rejects any suggestion that he is asserting the superiority of the masculine sex. The feminine sex becomes 'inferior' only when measured against the standard of the opposite sex. Because the sexes are different, they are not comparable. Thus, the sexes are considered to be 'equal' by Rousseau specifically insofar as they are understood in their own terms rather than the terms of the opposite sex. Each sex 'contributes equally to the common aim, but not in the same way' (Rousseau 1991: 358). Or as he reformulates this sentiment: 'Woman is worth more as woman and less as man. Wherever she makes use of her rights, she has the advantage. Wherever she wants to usurp ours, she remains beneath us' (Rousseau 1991: 363–4).

The entire project of *Emile* intertwines the prescriptive with the descriptive. Consider the formulation, 'man and woman *are* not and *ought* not to be constituted in the same way' (Rousseau 1991: 363, my italic). On the one hand, Rousseau's argument does not describe an actual sexual difference. Rather, it is a prescription for a state of affairs which should exist, but does not. We have seen many of Rousseau's justifications for this prescription. Sexual difference is in man's interests because it produces an ideal companion for him. Sexual difference saves him from being enchained to women. The cultivation of sexual difference is necessary because man is in danger of being rendered effeminate by women. Furthermore, we should cultivate sexual difference because it is 'natural', ordained by the 'law of nature'.

There is considerable slippage between the prescriptive and the descriptive levels intertwined in Rousseau's account. Arguing that men and women 'are' (naturally) sexually different, he slips from the account of ideal sexual difference to the account of actual sexual difference. The difference between the sexes is borne out by empirical evidence. For example, consider little girls – is it not true, he asks, that they are vain and coquettish from their earliest age (Rousseau 1991: 367, 369)? And furthermore:

> The children of both sexes . . . also have particular tastes which distinguish them. Boys seek movement and noise: drums, boots, little carriages. Girls prefer what presents itself to sight and is useful for ornamentation: mirrors, jewels, dresses, particularly dolls.
>
> (Rousseau 1991: 367)

As Starobinski points out, childhood has a special status for Rousseau. The state of childhood is parallel to the state of nature in the sense that both are states of innocence (Starobinski 1988: 11–12). Rousseau sometimes uses children as an exemplar of the uncontaminated natural.[4] Rousseau's reference to children to describe natural sexual difference is consistent with the account of childhood as a state of original, pre-social innocence. But the specifics of the reference are not. As Canovan argues, Rousseau vilifies woman's nature for faults which he also asserts are the product of social forces (Canovan 1987: 87–9). Rousseau both refers to the vanity of little girls in his argument that sexual difference is natural (boys and girls are different), and he also makes the reference to devalue adult women as vain. Yet Rousseau vilifies a modern, vain, civilised woman against a lauded natural woman. Rousseau uses references to the actual behaviour of children, women and men to explain his account of the natural difference between the sexes, but also to explain his account of actual masculinity and femininity as degraded.

One of the most crucial natural attributes of woman is her modesty. Since the sexes could be destroyed by the endless satisfaction of sexual desire, nature has endowed women with modesty in order to save man from their insatiability (Rousseau 1991: 358–9).[5] Women's modesty is a natural restraint to their unbounded passion. However, woman is represented as having to produce and generate masculine desire deliberately. Thus, in *Emile* Sophie must not always be available for Emile's sexual satisfaction. Sophie must measure out her favours, and be somewhat sexually resistant to Emile (Rousseau 1991: 477, 479). This agrees with a general analysis of desire outlined by Rousseau. Sophie does not display any immodest excess of decolletage or ankle, and dresses with simplicity and propriety. Precisely because Sophie is so modestly dressed she arouses the imagination and desire of the male: 'Her adornment is very modest in appearance and very coquettish in fact. She does not display her charms; she covers them, but, in covering them, she knows how to make them imagined . . . one would say that all this very simple attire was put on only to be taken off piece by piece by the imagination' (Rousseau 1991: 394). Similarly we are told in the 'Letter to d'Alembert' that the naked woman is less arousing than the peep of bare ankle from underneath a heavy long skirt (Rousseau 1960: 134). Here, as Kofman and Starobinski have argued at length, we see a dense Rousseauist economy of desire as generated by concealment, resistance and the veiled.[6] Women must deliberately generate and sustain masculine desire through resisting and provoking it.

Indeed, this necessity gives an impression of an otherwise lukewarm masculine attraction towards women. Masculinity is peculiarly fragile, anything but virile. Excessive contact with women is capable of jeopardising masculinity by rendering men effeminate. In *Emile*, an active virile man is supposed to govern a passive and obedient woman. Yet this account is destabilised by the description of man as easily overwhelmed and emasculated by woman, and by the description of virility as dependent on its incitement by women.

Note also the dual picture of women painted by Rousseau concerning artifice. On the one hand, artifice is dangerous. To act a part, to mimic what one is not, is anathema to Rousseau. Witness his devaluation of actors, of theatre (Rousseau 1960: 57, 80–1), and of women who only feign modesty. Nothing could be more threatening than the worldly Parisian woman acting out a modest femininity in order to manipulate man better (Rousseau 1991: 388–9). On the other hand, it is striking that the 'authentically' modest and demure Sophie is also required to manipulate man through feigning a resistance to his desire. Sophie resists Emile not 'authentically' – not out of a desire to resist his desire – but because through resistance she sustains Emile's desire (Rousseau 1991: 479).[7] Similar attributes are assigned both to the 'natural' woman and, pejoratively, to the 'degraded' woman of modern society. Similar characteristics are used both to elevate and depreciate women.[8]

The division in the Rousseauist account of woman between elevated and devalued women corresponds roughly to a division between 'ideal' and 'actual' women, and to the distinction which Kofman has drawn between Rousseau's divided account of woman as whore and virgin. Actual women pose to men the dangers of emasculation, engulfment, sexual destruction, artifice and deceit. However, the natural state and role of woman is represented quite differently. In her natural capacity, woman reinforces and sustains masculine virility, identity and mastery. She acts as the complement rather than a threat to man. This division between Rousseau's two versions of women should correspond to a division between real women (threatening, destabilising) and ideal, essential or virtual women (harmonious, supportive complement). Yet there is blurring between the two accounts. For example, while natural woman is opposed to artful woman, the natural woman must also be artful. The worldly, degraded woman is vain, but the young, natural Sophie also has tendencies towards vanity .

The slippage between Rousseau's descriptions of the natural and degraded states of femininity corresponds to a slippage between a description and a prescription of sexual difference. The difficulty arises from his argument that sexual difference is natural. Because contemporary society is in a state of degradation, relations between actual men and women are excluded as a reference point for the natural. Accordingly, Rousseau turns to a utopian account of the fictional Emile and Sophie: 'Emile is a man and Sophie is a woman; therein consists all their glory. In the confounding of the sexes that reigns among us, someone is almost a prodigy for belonging to his own sex' (Rousseau 1991: 393). Precisely because it cannot be empirically described, Rousseau prescribes sexual difference through turning to 'descriptions' of a fiction. He turns to 'descriptions' of hypothetical men and women as they would be under a utopian regime of radically modified educational and social practices. As Rousseau is recommending a hypothetical sexual difference, his 'description' of this hypothesis should be limited only by his imagination. But in describing sexual difference, he takes himself to be describing neither the fantastic, the fictional, nor his preferred state of affairs, but rather what is *natural*. For this reason, a conceptual difficulty hampers his ability to describe the natural state of sexual relations. As Sarah Kofman suggests, his references to this natural state are overlaid with 'kettle logic'. For example, Rousseau insists that modesty is natural, and yet also comments in an aside that *even if it is not*, it is still socially desirable and should be cultivated (Rousseau 1960: 87). Here is the ambiguity between the descriptive and the prescriptive in Rousseau's work.

The problem which arises from Rousseau's attempt to describe natural sexual difference is how one describes a hypothetical referent. As Paul de Man comments, 'What kind of epistemology can hope to "know well" a radical state of fiction?' (de Man 1979: 137). If the actual is not natural, where do we locate supposedly natural relations? And if we are ourselves corrupted, are we capable of identifying the natural? This is a problem not limited to the question of sexual difference. It arises with all of Rousseau's descriptions, hypotheses and inferences about nature as essential, original and legislative (for nature lays down laws which we must obey). As Derrida reminds us, the Rousseauist 'nature' is a *juridical* fiction (Derrida

1976: 274). The question is how accurately we may know its laws. As Rousseau himself says of other philosophers:

> Knowing nature so little and agreeing so poorly on the meaning of the word 'law', it would be quite difficult to come to some common understanding regarding a good definition of natural law . . . Writers begin by seeking the rules on which, for the common utility, it would be appropriate for men to agree among themselves; and then they give the name *natural law* to the collection of these rules, with no other proof than the good which presumably would result from their universal observance. Surely this is a very convenient way to compose definitions and to explain the nature of things by virtually arbitrary views of what is seemly.
>
> But as long as we are ignorant of natural man, it is futile for us to attempt to determine the law he has received or which is best suited to his constitution.
>
> (Rousseau 1987b: 35)

How does Rousseau isolate an account of the natural state of relations between the sexes? In *Emile*, he simply asserts that sexual difference is one of nature's 'laws' (Rousseau 1991: 358, 363), ignoring the epistemological problem of how we might know such laws. In fact, the most sustained accounts of women's nature occur in fictional and semi-fictional texts: *Emile* and *La Nouvelle Héloïse*. This facilitates an overriding of the epistemological problems. The literary genre, within which the lauding of the fictional personages of Sophie and Julie occurs, distracts from the problem of how Rousseau's understanding of the 'natural' is to be justified.

Other devices deployed by Rousseau include his location of the natural in the state of children (Rousseau 1991: 365); in pastoral or provincial communities (Rousseau 1991: 389); in Geneva (which Rousseau describes in the 'Letter to d'Alembert' as less denatured than a city such as Paris); in classical times (ancient Greece and Rome, Rousseau 1991: 360, 362, 366, 390–1); and in savage, barbaric or pastoral eras (Rousseau 1987b: 48, 62–3; Rousseau 1960: 33, 44–5). At different times, Rousseau describes the differences between the sexes which pertain to these various states as 'natural', even though these descriptions are not consistent. A methodological difficulty is faced (although not discussed) by Rousseau of how to locate, isolate and describe a virtual sexual difference. This difficulty is evident in his persistent slides between different uses of the term 'nature'.

When Rousseau refers to actual men and women as sexually different by nature, the term is used in the sense of what humans are 'like'. Here, our nature is how we can be described, how we actually are. But when Rousseau uses contemporary relations between the sexes as a counter-example against which to assert an ideal state of sexual difference, then the term nature refers to our essence. Here, our nature is that which lies underneath the distorted character of contemporary men and women.[9] At other times, nature is a kind of juridical entity akin to God's law. Rousseau asserts that sexual difference is a 'law of nature,' that which nature has ordained for relations between men and women. And at other times, 'nature' is used in the sense of the fictional 'state of nature': that sexual difference which would hypothetically have pertained to a primordial human state either before social organisation, or in early stages of social organisation.

In sum, a striking aspect of Rousseau's description of sexual difference as natural is the proliferation of different devices used to legitimate the account. Rousseau argues that sexual difference is natural, and also argues that it is socially desirable even if it is not natural. In referring to relations between the sexes in ancient epochs, he describes various barbaric cultures, relations in Sparta and relations in Rome, although these accounts conflict. We see a proliferation of ideal 'epochs' to which contemporary relations can be opposed. In book 5 of *Emile*, we are told that sexual difference has been prescribed by the voice of nature (Rousseau 1991: 358), *and* that it has been prescribed by the voice of God (Rousseau 1991: 359), *and* that it is prescribed by the voice of reason (Rousseau 1991: 382). In Rousseau's description of sexual difference there is a multiplication of the senses of the term 'nature', and there is a multiplication of different legitimating terms (laws of nature, of God, and of reason).

Rousseau makes a constant appearance in feminist work on the history of philosophy, particularly political philosophy. Reflection on interpretation of Rousseau within this genre, allows us to take a cross-section of different methodologies deployed in the analysis of phallocentric accounts of women's nature and role in the history of philosophy. Such methodologies range from the critical to the reconstructive to critique of reconstructive projects. Rousseau's contradictions are a constant focus of feminist discussion. This will allow some reflection on methodologies deployed specifically in the feminist analysis of such textual instability within the history of philosophy.

FEMINIST INTERPRETATIONS OF ROUSSEAU

What methodologies have been employed within anglophone feminist philosophy in its interpretation of Rousseau? A response seen from commentators as early as Wollstonecraft through to some contemporary critics has been the simple denunciation of Rousseau for his support for the subjugation of women, particularly in the context of his overall egalitarian philosophy (see Wollstonecraft 1975; Lange 1979: 51). 'In any feminist Chamber of Horrors', says Margaret Canovan, 'Jean-Jacques

Rousseau would occupy a prominent place' (Canovan 1987: 78). However, Canovan also asks what redress for women within the architecture of Rousseau's 'horror chamber' might entail. She thereby adopts an identifiably different kind of methodology, continuing a tradition also begun by Wollstonecraft, one which aims at rectification of sex bias. How might one salvage the positive aspects of Rousseau's theory and modify women's role within it? For Wollstonecraft, the project was plausible and involved extending the Rousseauist programme for a masculine rational education to women. Though Canovan perceives difficulties, still the issue for her is how Rousseau's conception of citizenship can be extended to women, although against his own intentions, through discarding Rousseau's beliefs about the different natures of men and women.

This second approach has been criticised by many feminist critics. Many have focused on the difficulties involved in extending Rousseau's account of the male citizen to include women. In what I designate as a third approach, Susan Moller Okin and Moira Gatens both argue that Rousseau's conception of the public sphere is structured in terms of the exclusion of women. The feminine private sphere, argues Moller Okin, is crucial as a support of men in Rousseau's public sphere. This is why the existing conception of the public sphere cannot sustain the inclusion of women.[10] Reworking the Rousseauist model would require such substantial intervention that the model would be entirely disrupted. The coherence of Rousseau's own account is lost in the list of all that would need to be changed if women were to be included within his conception of the public sphere. This kind of feminist response argues that the subjugation of women plays a crucial, structural role in the overall philosophy. This argument renders questionable feminist attempts to distinguish positive aspects of Rousseau's theory from his account of women's role, as if the latter were merely an unfortunate addendum to the overall philosophy.

For Carole Pateman, Rousseau's exclusion of women from the public sphere is just one of many examples of philosophers (including Hobbes and Locke) for whom the social contract between men is at the same time an unstated sexual contract involving the appropriation and deployment of women's labour:

> Juridical equality and social inequality – public/private, civil/natural, men/women – form a coherent social structure.
>
> (Pateman 1988: 229)

Indeed, for Pateman, this structure has ramifications for women's eventual entry into the public sphere after the eighteenth century. Often, women continue to occupy their traditional status. As Pateman diagnoses, public and institutional equality co-exist perfectly well with informal or private inequality (Pateman 1988: 229).

This point concerns the limitations of 'feminism by extension' (or by 'inclusion'). Extending to women the role of citizen traditionally restricted to men is a straightforward political reform. Analysts such as Gatens and Pateman, however, use an analysis of the history of political philosophy to argue that the role of an individual in the public sphere always presupposes an 'other' in the private sphere sustaining that role. Pateman continues the analysis thus: even when women gain a role in the public sphere, this might not automatically undermine the supposition that women will perform a certain role in the private sphere, or that some women will do so, or that some subordinate 'other' will do so. Interestingly, Pateman indirectly challenges theorists such as Canovan and Okin for whom Rousseau's account of sexual inequality undermines his account of social equality. One notices in Pateman a greater interest in suggesting how this apparent inequality actually constitutes a 'coherent whole', or as she suggests above, a coherent, phallocentric social structure. If we designate as a fourth approach the argument that Rousseau's account of women undermines his overall philosophy, then Pateman might represent a fifth possible approach. Like Gatens, Pateman suggests that the role of women, while contradictory, sustains the overall philosophy.

For Pateman, as for Okin and Gatens, dichotomous relations operate at a complicated infrastructural level. Okin's text focuses on the fact that Rousseau's social contract is structurally reliant on the exclusion of women from that contract. Gatens' text focuses on the implications for feminist analyses which, presuming that the sex bias is merely superficial, attempt to amend it through extending citizenship to women. Pateman's text again analyses traditional contract theory and makes the similar structural point that the social contract presupposes a largely unacknowledged sexual contract. Pateman also focuses on the implications for social change. Both approaches touch on the complexity of the dichotomous structure at work in the Rousseauist text. Dichotomous relations exist in a more complex interrelation than a simple series of opposites: man/woman, masculine/feminine, public/private, reason/emotion. We must grasp the interconnected nature of those dichotomies. The public sphere is dependent on the exclusion of the feminine. A dichotomous structure can accommodate a surprising degree of change without significant disruption.

Genevieve Lloyd also offers an analysis of dichotomous relations as woven with complexity. Examining the relations 'man/woman', 'reason/emotion' at work in Rousseau's texts, Lloyd points out that femininity is both 'construed as an immature stage of consciousness, left behind by advancing Reason, but also as an object of adulation, as the exemplar for Reason's aspirations to a future return to Nature' (Lloyd 1984: 58). Nancy Tuana agrees that the gender connotations of Rousseauist reason

101

are complex. Woman is affiliated with emotion, man with reason. But rationality, as she says, involves 'a complex interdependence between reason and emotion' (Tuana 1992: 47). Although Rousseau poses men and women as an extreme dichotomy, and although reason and nature are respectively aligned with men and women, nevertheless, reason and nature are not posed as a radical dichotomy. Instead, Lloyd points out, reason is 'a dynamic development from nature', rather than an external instrument controlling nature: 'Reason emerges from Nature and closeness to Nature is the mark of its authenticity. In this version of the progress of Reason . . . Nature lies both in the past, as an object of Reason's backward-looking nostalgia, and in the future, as the goal of Reason's fulfilment' (Lloyd 1984: 58).

Of all the commentators we have so far considered, Lloyd touches most closely on the density of this web in Rousseau's text: the disruption of radical dichotomies between reason and nature, the positioning of nature as both transcended, lost 'past' and 'future' ideal goal, the alignment of the feminine with nature, and yet the sustenance of a radical dichotomy between man and woman. Lloyd states that femininity 'slots into' the complexity of the reason–nature dialectic, representing both the threat of disorder and the inspiration of natural harmony. Yet she halts at the point of suggesting that where nature has a 'dual location', this 'creates new possibilities for woman as symbol' (Lloyd 1984: 64). The 'new possibility' is that woman represents dual contradictories such as order and disorder, while representing nature as both mythical lost past and future aspiration. Following the pattern of this kind of complexity could be designated as a sixth possible approach for a feminist reading.

So, we might pause at this point and try to characterise some key common features of the analyses considered so far. Each touches frequently on the problem of dichotomous opposition in the texts of Rousseau, and some particularly emphasise the complexity of the dichotomous structure. Some emphasise the indebtedness of the conception of the privileged, public rational masculine sphere to the positioning of the private feminine natural sphere. For some, this demonstrates the instability of Rousseau's philosophy. For others, the subjugated role of woman plays a key role in a coherent whole which is Rousseau's political philosophy. While most emphasise the interwoven complexity of Rousseau's oppositions, there is a tendency *either* to argue that the complexity stabilises *or* to argue that it destabilises the 'overall' political philosophy.

FEMINIST ANALYSIS OF ROUSSEAUIST CONTRADICTION

I want now to turn more specifically to the way in which feminist theorists have analysed the contradictory tendencies in Rousseau's work. Sometimes, there has been a tendency to analyse and reconstruct for the reader contradictory tendencies while ceasing the discussion with that analysis. For example, both Margaret Canovan and Susan Moller Okin accuse Rousseau of contradictions in his views of women. Asks Canovan, why does Rousseau vilify woman's 'nature' in terms of faults which he also asserts to be the product of social forces? Furthermore, she asks, doesn't Rousseau's own position that nature must be supplemented by a citizenship which is nevertheless 'unnatural', even for men, undermine his opposition to women's citizenship as 'unnatural' (Canovan 1987: 89)? Susan Moller Okin also accuses Rousseau of contradiction insofar as the principles which Rousseau holds to be of crucial importance for men – the principle of equality, the rejection of the right of the strongest, legitimation of government by general will – are violated by Rousseau where women are concerned (Okin 1979: 143). Among other tensions in the Rousseauist account, Okin argues that the role and education which Rousseau allots to women would actually lead to women subverting Rousseau's ideal institutions: the patriarchal family and the democratic republic. Are not women to be socialised so as to privilege the individual rather than the state, a love relation rather than the priorities of the outside world, the family's interests rather than those of the republic (Okin 1979: 176–7)? Carole Pateman agrees. And because women are, as Carol Pateman also notes, 'guardians of order and morality', Moira Gatens concludes that:

> women should play the additional role of guide or guardian to men; that is, they should, like Ariadne, spin the yarn that guarantees that Theseus will neither come to harm nor lose his way in the maze of culture. Rather, man will retain his relation to nature via his relation to the private sphere . . . a kind of 'time-warp' where the 'primitive' and natural patriarchal family is 'frozen'.
>
> (Gatens 1991: 11)

But since, as we have seen in Okin, women lie outside as the affective, domestic, nurturing support to the public sphere, their first interest is to the family and private interest and not to the public interest, and so Pateman comments that women are also the 'permanently subversive force within the political order' (Pateman 1980: 20).

How, then, might we characterise the ways in which critics have tended to approach the presence of textual contradictions relating to Rousseau's account of women? Sometimes the presence of contradiction is merely indicated as if this were criticism enough (Canovan 1987: 90). Sometimes, pinpointing contradiction serves a suggestion that Rousseau's argument is in some way auto-destabilising: that it invalidates itself, as in the approach of Susan Moller Okin. Sometimes the presence of contradiction is interrogated from the standpoint of how it may be explained. For example, both Sarah Kofman and, more recently, Linda Zerilli (1994) have attempted psychoanalytically informed explanations of Rousseau's contradictory images of women. Nancy Tuana takes the explanatory approach when she suggests that the tensions in Rousseau's doctrine of natural equality which occur when the doctrine is not extended to women are caused (can be explained by) his views about women: 'Rousseau's views on woman blinded him to this tension within his own theory' (Tuana 1993: 162). In a kind of salvage operation, the theorist might try to amend the contradictory elements. For Wollstonecraft, Rousseau's deprivation of women of their equal rights contradicted his commitment to equal rights. She tried to correct that element in his philosophy, extending his educational programme to women.

Another approach might argue that only one of the contradictory elements expresses Rousseau's 'real meaning', and that the other should in some way be disregarded. This tack is taken by Joel Schwartz. Of two opposing elements, one should be seen as 'merely rhetorical', thus:

> One can oppose equal opportunity for women either because it would make them men's superiors or because it would make them men's inferiors; one cannot oppose it for both reasons simultaneously.
>
> Of the two arguments given, the second one seems to me to be Rousseau's real one.
>
> (Schwartz 1984: 147)

Again, this is a kind of salvage operation. Rather than repairing the contradictory element, one resolves Rousseau's contradictions by demonstrating that they are only apparent, since one of two opposed arguments can simply be disregarded.

A similar kind of salvaging is seen with the suggestion that the contradictions are a mitigating factor in the assessment of the sexism in the Rousseauist corpus. That is to say, Schwartz also presents Rousseau as contradicting his own misogyny, and thus as *softening* the misogyny of his own account. Here the critic actually emphasises Rousseau's contradictions in an attempt to demonstrate that Rousseau is in fact more complex or more complicated than might have been appreciated by other feminist readings. This is a tack taken by Karen Green, for example, in *The Woman of Reason*:

> before completely condemning Rousseau . . . it is worthwhile considering his justification for these views . . . For although he believes that women should be different from men . . . he also ascribes a very

important place to [women] in society, and for each derogatory quotation a more flattering counterpart could be supplied . . . there is more to Rousseau's thoughts on women than a simple reliance on natural difference.

(Green 1995: 70)

At times, theorists such as Pateman, Gatens and Lloyd suggest that in some way Rousseau's contradictions could be understood as strangely coherent. For example, discussing what she describes as the contradictory view that for Rousseau women are both a threat to social stability and yet also the guardians of morality and order (Pateman 1980: 29), Pateman also argues that the two conceptions are nevertheless not opposed to each other. For Pateman, as for Lloyd, and also Gatens, this problem in Rousseau's argument relates to his curious account of the relationship between social organisation and nature. For Rousseau, culture is 'bad', a degradation from the natural state. Culture is also a necessary, remedying supplement both to our (mythical) 'fall' from the natural state and to the (mythical) natural state per se (as isolated, pre-linguistic individuals) from which we must inevitably 'depart'. Thus, returning to the point that women are positioned by Rousseau so that they are both the guardians of social order and the 'permanently subversive force within the political order' (Pateman 1980: 20), Pateman suggests that although this account of women's dual role is contradictory, nevertheless the two conceptions are 'not opposed'. Her point is rather like Gatens' suggestion that Rousseau's work 'reveals a thorough *and, for the most part, consistent line of argument* concerning what ought and what ought not to be the function and province of women' (Gatens 1991: 10, my italic). Lloyd, Pateman and Gatens have all wanted to suggest that there is a strange kind of 'coherence', albeit complex, to the contradictory elements.

Thus, where Lloyd and Gatens insist, not as a denunciation but rather as part of their exposition, on the fact that for Rousseau, culture is both degradation from and supplement to nature, we see them emphasise an idea of the 'strangely united' status of these opposites. Such an emphasis can be seen wherever these commentators underline some kind of 'both A and Not-A' logic operating in Rousseau's text. Another example is the point made by Pateman and Gatens that woman functions on Rousseau's account both as the support of and as the disruption to the social order, and that women are thus seen as both the guarantee of man's connection to the state of nature, and hence the ground and support of the social contract, and the threat to it. A similar logic is suggested by Lloyd in her emphasis on the fact that the feminine, as associated with nature in Rousseau's texts, is conceived of as both 'left behind' and 'aspired to', described by Lloyd as allowing 'a new resolution of the ambivalence of the feminine to enter Western thought' (Lloyd 1984: 58).

Such readings, emphasising unity in the contradictory accounts of the feminine, are certainly an advance on the analysis whereby Rousseau's account of women is assessed as 'far from impressive' since a 'farrago of contradictions'. Nevertheless, the question remains of how to interpret these contradictions and their textual effect. In this regard, it is Gatens who seems to come closest to an interrogation at that level. Because Gatens goes beyond the location of and the denunciation of contradiction in Rousseau's work, she is in a position to begin to chart the operation of that contradiction. Thus, she notes that the (contradictory) role of women functions to resolve the contradictory demand on men to be in proximity to nature and to culture at the same time. Gatens both is attentive to a 'strange unity' of the divided elements in Rousseau's texts and notes that woman's role is functional within Rousseau's account. Writing of the uneasy relations between nature and culture, the man and the citizen, the family and the state, Gatens proposes:

> By fulfilling her 'natural' role as wife/mother [woman] acts as a pivotal point around which the tensions in these dichotomies are resolved.

> (Gatens 1991: 95)

Of course, Gatens points out, the cost to women of fulfilling this role is considerable – woman, she says, is thereby neither citizen nor exactly 'woman' – rather wife and mother. Thus, somewhat like Moller Okin, Gatens notes that Rousseau's heroines are doomed to 'tragic ends'. And somewhat like Pateman, she notes the ironic situation in which women are both support of and threat to the social contract, whereby the social contract, as Carole Pateman points out, presumes the sexual contract, but, we can add, is at the same time disrupted by the sexual contract. This, says Gatens, is because, since women are not participants in the social contract, they are not bound by its rules and ideals although they are internal to it. Hence, she points out, it is common to see women conceptualised as 'uncivilised and hostile to reason and law'. For example, Gatens cites Rousseau's description of the 'disorder of women', Hume's comment that women are prone to violent and socially disruptive passions, and Hegel's account of women as the 'eternal irony of the community'.

However, Gatens' focus is less on the fact that the cost to women is considerable, or that his heroines are doomed, or that their role is dual and contradictory, and more on what is enabled by the dual and contradictory role of women. She argues that woman's role allows man to resolve the tensions in the series of contradictory dichotomies (both culture and nature) which he himself negotiates. For Gatens, the irony is that while woman's role functions to resolve the contradictory status of man's role, woman herself is left negotiating a contradictory status. However, while she describes this consequence as ironic, she certainly does not see it as accidental, for her analysis presents a Rousseauist logic whereby woman must be both without and within, support and threat to the social contract, in order to sustain man's status of proximity to nature and culture.

This is a strong alternative to seeing Rousseau's account of women as *limited* by its contradictions, an approach taken by many other commentators. Pateman, Gatens and Lloyd are all concerned to track the complexity of Rousseau's thinking. In analysing the reason/nature dichotomy, for example, Lloyd discusses the logic according to which reason should both govern nature and be governed by nature. Making this point is not 'exposing' Rousseau, for Lloyd, nor is it salvaging Rousseau. Her concern is to demonstrate what Pateman describes as the 'strange coherence' of Rousseau's thought, and she does so by pointing out that for Rousseau, 'Reason and Nature are not equal, independent terms, complete in themselves; and their interdependence is quite complex' (Lloyd 1984: 62). In a sense, then, Lloyd's approach is one of explaining Rousseau's contradictions. Where, for Kofman, the contradictions might be due to Rousseau's unconscious desire, for Tuana they are more simply due to his views about women, and for Lloyd they are due to the complex interdependence of the dichotomous terms. By contrast, when Gatens suggests that the contradictory role of women functions to resolve the contradictory demand that men be in proximity to both nature and culture at once, she exchanges the attempt to explain the presence of con-tradictory tensions for the suggestion that contradictory tensions might serve a rhetorical purpose. Gatens suggests that woman's contradictory role resolves the contradictory demands on man. In a brief moment, Gatens could be said to exchange the causal-explanatory account of Rousseauist contradictions (how shall we explain their presence?) for an effects-based approach. In other words, Gatens asks not how we can explain the contradiction, but instead: what is the textual effect of the contradictory tensions we have located?

If we pivot a feminist analysis of Rousseau more generally in this direction, we shall be confronted with a series of productive questions: What is facilitated in Rousseau's argument by the introduction of repre-sentations of women as dual and split? What is facilitated in Rousseau's argument by the split and contradictory definitions of nature? What is facilitated in Rousseau's argument by the fact that reason is both opposed to nature and aligned with nature? What is facilitated in Rousseau's argument by the role of culture as both degradation from and supplement to nature? Granted, Rousseau's arguments are destabilised by the incon-sistencies pinpointed in much feminist analysis. The overall coherence of his philosophy has rightly been called into question by many. But too much emphasis on the overall incoherence has tended to foreclose closer analysis of how Rousseau's phallocentrism is sustained and enabled by its contradictory elements. In other words, there has been concentration on the fact that Rousseau's argument is contradictory. There has been much less focus on how the contradictory elements sustain the phallo-centrism. I am arguing for a move in orientation from the 'that' to the 'how'.

There is a very well-known reading of Rousseau whose approach might be characterised specifically by its interest in analysing Rousseau's textual contradictions in terms of the textual effects they generate, of origin and of presence. The reading is disappointing for my purposes in its lack of analysis of Rousseau's account of sexual difference. Never-theless, my focus will be on the reorientation in feminist analysis of Rousseau which might be provoked by Jacques Derrida's material on Rousseau in *Of Grammatology*. In the second chapter, we considered different twists given by critics to deconstructive interpretation. For some, a deconstructive interpretation, exposing textual instability, poses a threat to a philosophical text. Against interpretations of deconstruction in terms of nihilism, anarchy or 'anti-philosophy', some critics argued that Derrida is not decentring anything, but reconstructing the conditions of possibility of effects of presence. Still, those 'conditions' amount to the work of textual instability. Textual instability renders stable effects of gender, presence, subjectivity, origin.

In this chapter, we have considered feminist approaches to the textual instability of Rousseau's phallocentrism. I have argued for the need to read canonical texts for such instability, so as not to reinforce the effect of a stabilised, consistent, untroubled history of sex bias. The sex bias of the history of philosophy has always been troubled. At the same time, this argument returns us to the question of whether feminist analysis which merely exposes such textual trouble is satisfactory. In this chapter, I have suggested that simply exposing sex bias does reinforce the effect of a stable sex bias, rather than highlighting its instability. But simply exposing the instability of sex bias is also not sufficient. Such an approach supposes that sex bias is undone by its instability. A valuable method-ology is one which is able to analyse sex bias as rendered, as 'done', rather than 'undone' by its instability. In returning to a deconstructive reading of Jean-Jacques Rousseau, I am suggesting that this is what such a reading is able to offer.

METHODOLOGIES FOR THE INTERPRETATION
OF ROUSSEAUIST CONTRADICTION

It would be possible to summarise and differentiate the approaches of many of the important twentieth-century European studies on Rousseau in terms of their approach to Rousseauist contradiction. An emphasis on his contradictions has sometimes been a means of discrediting him as a systematic or coherent philosopher. It has sometimes grounded psychologistic interpretations of his divided psyche.[11] Asserting the actual systematism or coherence of his contradictions has been a typical way in which he is 'salvaged' as a thinker. Alternatively, Rousseau is salvaged through an explanatory approach to the contradictions, for example, through the argument that they represent the evolution of his thinking (Philonenko 1984: 291). Some have argued that Rousseau's philosophy is only apparently contradictory or is contradictory without being incoherent (Groethuysen 1949: 392; Derathé 1979: 4; Beaulavon 1937: 334–5). His contradictions have been seen as deliberate, indeed a testimony to the complexity, not the confusion, of the author. Or it may be argued that the contradictions constitute a coherently dialectical organisation of theses and antitheses (Baczko 1974: 9, 232–3).

What we see in many of these approaches is a frequent attempt to recuperate Rousseau as a thinker through arguing that his contradictions are authorially under control. The contradictory elements of his work would be stabilised through the suggestion that they are intentional. We also see a supposition that his contradictions can be interpreted as playing an important role in his argument only if it can be argued that they are deliberately deployed by him. Thus commentators defend Rousseau in terms of his systematic complexity. Alternatively, if it seems implausible that Rousseau's contradictions are dialectical or otherwise 'under control', commentators suppose that the contradictions are incoherent (see Raymond 1962: 7–8).

Paul de Man has made the apt observation that much Rousseau commentary is 'accompanied by an overtone of intellectual and moral superiority, as if the commentators, in the most favourable of cases, had to apologize or to offer a cure for something that went astray in their author' (de Man 1971: 112). Although de Man affirms that 'one hears this tone of voice even in so sympathetic and penetrating a critic as Jean Starobinski' (de Man 1971: 112), Starobinski also alerts us to the same tendency in Rousseau commentary:

> Homme de la contradiction, Rousseau était traité avec condescendance: on pouvait beaucoup lui pardonner, parce qu'il avait été un magicien de la langue. Son cas personnel relevait du psychiatre.
>
> (Cassirer 1987: ii)[12]

An advantage of Derrida's approach is that it overrides the question of authorial intention in relation to Rousseauist contradiction.[13] Derrida's account of Rousseau's 'supplementary logic' emphasises what is produced by Rousseau's textual contradictions in a way not possible within a text overly governed by attempts at inferring Rousseau's extra-textual intentions, authorial control, or psychic state.

Derrida does attempt to distinguish between what Rousseau's texts 'describe' and what they actually 'declare'. This distinction may seem reminiscent of other attempts to discuss Rousseau's intentions. De Man argues that Derrida is too close to claims about what Rousseau's texts declare against his intentions. In actual fact, Derrida distinguishes what Rousseauist passages actually 'describe' against their own 'declarations'. Most tellingly, Derrida's distinction is not causally oriented. Where Derrida locates Rousseauist inconsistency or paradox, there is no suggestion that Rousseau-the-author has 'made a mistake', or has lost control of the text. There is no attempt to explain these textual elements in terms of the operations of the author. This is not because Derrida argues that 'Rousseau' was entirely in control of his argumentation. Derrida does not interpret in terms of an *hors-texte*, a point positioned outside the text from where the text would originate (Derrida 1976: 158). He therefore bypasses analysis of the causes of Rousseauist contradiction framed in these terms (i.e., whether they might have been caused by 'authorial' error). Rather, *Of Grammatology* is oriented towards asking how the text operates and what is effected by its paradoxes or contradictions. It is oriented towards analysing the effects of textual instability, rather than towards the attempt to explain textual instability with reference to an *hors-texte*.

Other important Rousseau commentators might seem to lean in this direction. For example, in his attempt to read Rousseau's methodological practice as dialectical, Baczko almost suggests that the 'antinomies' enable or produce synthesis and textual resolution. Yet such approaches are still causally oriented insofar as they rely on reference to and inference about Rousseau's methodological practice. Furthermore, they still might be considered to belong to those 'salvage operations' of Rousseau, insofar as they invoke dialectical interpretation as a means of arguing that Rousseau's contradictions are in fact resolved.

While Derrida does consider that Rousseau's textual contradictions could be described as coherent, this is not the same thing as arguing that the contradictions are resolved.[14] Specifically, I would suggest that according to *Of Grammatology*, Rousseauist contradictions remain unresolved.[15] They remain operative as contradictions. As such they can be seen as productive of effects of originality, interiority and presence, despite (or rather, necessarily simultaneously with) the destabilisation of those effects. This is a structure which is rendered by certain operations of Rousseau's 'supplementary logic'.

I have argued that the instabilities generating phallocentrism in the history of philosophy might have been suppressed in some feminist narratives about that history because of suppositions that to demonstrate the instability of phallocentrism is to demonstrate that its grip has been weaker, its history more inconsistent than a narrative about the consistency of phallocentrism might suggest. In this chapter, we have seen several critics who demonstrate the inconsistency of Rousseau's thought precisely in order to show that his most extreme moments are mitigated, or softened. In turning to Derrida, we find an approach to interpreting Rousseau capable of focusing on how instability generates, rather than subtracting from, phallocentrism. This is not an argument locatable in *Of Grammatology*, or locatable only in the book's footnotes and asides. Derrida focuses on instabilities surrounding the terms 'writing' and 'nature' (while acknowledging that nature connotes femininity in Rousseau's work). Nevertheless, I have posed the question of how we might reread the canon so as to emphasise the way in which phallocentrism is stabilised, rendered or effected only by the textual instability which also destabilises it. In the light of this question, Derrida's reading is extremely suggestive of new possibilities for feminist interpretations of Rousseau. I take up these possibilities in chapter 5.

5

CONSTITUTIVE INSTABILITY IN ROUSSEAU'S DEFENCE OF NATURAL SEXUAL DIFFERENCE

> If we accept that Rousseau's system has to include a contradiction in order to hold together, we should review and reinterpret it.
>
> (Michèle Le Dœuff)

Jacques Derrida identifies in the history of philosophy a series of imaginary ideals of original, self-identical self-presence, which would be unmediated by representation, by the sign, by the human. In the words of Jean-Luc Nancy, Jacques Derrida writes about the 'passion of the origin' (Nancy 1992: 37). Such ideals of original self-presence manifest themselves in contexts as diverse as theories of subjectivity, history, theology or metaphysics. As Kevin Hart comments, 'Upon Derrida's reckoning . . . [i]nstances abound: "*eidos*" (Plato), "*ousia*" (Aristotle), "*esse*" (Aquinas), "clear and distinct ideas" (Descartes), "sense impressions" (Hume), "Geist" (Hegel), "logical simples" (Russell), "pre-reflective intentionality" (Husserl)' (Hart 1989: 83). Derrida considers that Rousseau's conception of nature is another manifestation of this 'nostalgic desire for a stable origin' (Hart 1989: 148).

Derrida argues that such ideals of self-presence are sustained in the history of philosophy through a series of hierarchical oppositions such as: 'original/copy', 'primary/tributary', 'purity/degradation' and 'presence/ absence' (Derrida 1981b: 6–7, 9, 29, 41, etc.). The texts of Rousseau are organised by oppositions such as 'nature/culture', 'pastoral/city' and 'speech/writing', which intersect with the opposition 'purity/degradation'. Such oppositions can be seen as sustaining imaginary ideals of purity because they displace the spectre of degradation on to othered sites such as 'city-life', 'culture' and 'writing'.

In a well-known example, Derrida considers the opposition between speech and writing in Plato's *Phaedrus*, in which Socrates values speech for its greater 'presence' to truth, as opposed to writing, which is merely the copy, or material inscription, of speech (see Derrida 1976: 97–8).

112

In apparent contradiction, Socrates also describes speech as a form of writing. Living, animate discourse is, he says, 'written in the soul' (Derrida 1981a: 148–9).

Speech is identified with an ideal (truth) to which it is supposedly present and yet which it falls short of. Speech is present to truth but not at one with it. In fact, like writing, it is merely an 'inscription' of truth. What is of interest is Derrida's interpretation of this contradiction. First, he sees the contradiction as 'necessary'. By the very terms on which speech is considered to be superior to writing, and identified with ideal 'presence' (that it is 'closer' to truth), it must also be seen as absence from truth (it too is at a remove from truth). By the very terms on which speech is considered superior to writing, it must be seen as the equivalent of writing. Second, Derrida analyses the effects of the contradiction at work in Plato's argument. It is in order to be privileged over writing that speech must also be identified as akin to writing.

Analysing the textual effects produced, Derrida analyses the contradictory logic at work here as operative. The identity of speech is both presence to and distance from truth. Through its opposition to an other (writing) which represents absence, the effect of speech representing 'presence' is generated. But because of this simultaneous alignment with, and falling short of, a privileged term (speech) from an imaginary transcendent ideal (truth), Derrida argues that the hierarchical oppositions generating ideals of presence are internally unstable (Derrida 1981b: 59–60). Thus, he has notoriously commented, 'Texts deconstruct *themselves* by themselves' (Derrida 1986: 123).

Derrida uses the terms 'trace', 'différance' and 'supplement' to refer to the inability of a privileged term associated with presence to be entirely 'pure' of the devalued term it is opposed to. In the case of the speech/writing opposition, we can think of speech being 'mediated by the trace' insofar as the very terms by which it is valued and opposed to writing also align it with representation, distance from truth, inscription, 'writing'. In this sense, oppositions such as speech/writing can be understood as 'internally unstable' because the very terms which sustain the opposition also simultaneously undermine it. Derrida comments that différance (the deferral of a mythical, projected, original presence) 'produces what it forbids, makes possible the very thing that it makes impossible', stating, 'Without the possibility of différance, the desire of presence as such would not find its breathing-space' (Derrida 1976: 143). In the case of the speech/writing opposition, différance constitutes the extent to which speech is itself organised according to the model of inscription.

The identity of speech is limited to that of being (mere) copy or inscription in relation to the mythical point of self-coinciding self-presence: original truth. But the effect of this relationship between speech and truth is not the devaluation of speech as 'absence' from truth, but rather the alignment of speech with the 'presence' of transcendent truth. This is facilitated by the displacement of 'absence' on to speech's 'negative other': writing.

It is for this reason that we can see Derrida as a philosopher who understands contradiction as operative. But, as we have seen, this point is not always apparent when commentators overly insist on his conception of hierarchical oppositions, and concurrent ideals of self-presence, as 'internally unstable'. Certainly Derrida argues that philosophical texts which erect ideals of self-presence through hierarchical opposition necessarily and simultaneously undermine those conceptions because différance is the necessary condition to truth, the subject, and origin. However, he simultaneously argues that what *produces* 'effects' of the subject, 'effects' of truth, and in the case of Rousseau, 'effects' of an ideal, unmediated nature, *is* différance. Irene Harvey formulates of this problematic as follows: 'Writing, we should recall, is the condition of the possibility of language, but it is therefore also a certain condition of impossibility . . . A certain conflict is thus at work here, or a certain tension: two contradictory commands *that nevertheless produce the possibility of language*' (Harvey 1986: 150, my italic).

DECONSTRUCTIVE INTERPRETATION OF ROUSSEAU

Amidst his reading of Rousseauist oppositions such as speech/writing in *Of Grammatology*, Derrida explores Rousseau's nature/culture opposition (see Derrida 1976: 219) and his attempt to articulate a mythical genealogy of the passage of man from a hypothetical 'state of nature' to the social state of political organisation. The latter, for Rousseau, is a 'supplement'[1] to, even a degradation from, a mythical pure and immediate state of nature. But on the other hand, the advent of society is inevitable. This is because the ideal of a 'pure', pre-social state of nature is conceptually incoherent, containing an aporia or vanishing point.

Derrida comments, as does Paul de Man, on the 'dynamic' and indeterminate properties of the Rousseauist term 'nature'. He refers to the discrepancy between the state of nature as a 'primitive time' in the 'Discourse on the Origin of Inequality', in which the savage wanders in the forests 'without industry, without speech, without dwelling' (Rousseau 1987b: 57); and the account in the 'Essay on the Origin of Languages' in which, points out Derrida, 'the barbarian . . . has a family, a cabin and a language, even if he is reduced to "gesture and some inarticulate sounds"' (Derrida 1976: 252). Derrida analyses the variation in Rousseau's various accounts of primitive times. The details shift constantly (and are incompatible with each other) because the role of the

114

Rousseauist notion of the 'primitive' is that of a 'time before time' (Derrida 1976: 252). The one structural invariant about Rousseau's 'primitive times' is that there is 'nothing before them'. The difference between the two texts in terms of their account of the 'primitive' is related to the fact that there is a 'continuous sliding, that slow transition from nature to culture'. Derrida elaborates:

> For no continuity from inarticulate to articulate, from pure nature to culture, from plenitude to the play of supplementarity, is possible. The *Essay*, having to describe the *birth*, the being-born of the supplement, must reconcile the two times.
>
> (Derrida 1976: 255)

In Rousseau's texts, the point which is projected as the point of origin is unstable because it is constantly repositioned. The (mythico-genealogical) 'collapse' of nature into culture is inevitable. There is no conceptually coherent period of pure 'natural' plenitude before the social, there being no conceptually coherent account of a nature which does not collapse into the 'social'.

Derrida's argument is that Rousseau's conceptions of nature (even in those texts which address the question of a hypothetical passage from a state of nature to a state of social organisation) are *always already* social, even though they are by definition opposed to states of social organisation. They are 'always already social' because there must be an element within the state of nature which leads to the collapse into the social. Rousseau's conception of nature cannot be 'pure' of its opposite, because it must contain the element that leads to its degradation into or supplementation by culture.

The conceptual aporia at the heart of the nature/social opposition in Rousseau's work is particularly apparent in his attempts to explain the hypothetical passage from nature to the social in works such as the 'Essay' and the 'Discourse on the Origin of Inequality'. Here, two symptoms could be interpreted as indicating this aporia. The first, as I have suggested, is the constant repositioning of, and inconsistency in, the description of the natural state. The second symptom could be seen as the multiplication of accounts of the passage from nature to the social, the problem of how to explain that passage.

Rousseau describes this passage in various ways. It is located with the passage from a language of gesture to a language of speech (Rousseau 1966: 5), with the passage from the expression of need to the expression of desire and passion (Rousseau 1966: 11, 45), and with the passage from man's state of radical isolation, where he has no conception of the other qua other, to a state where he has a sensibility of the other (Rousseau 1966: 32). We are also told that the origin of man must be located with the point at which he is already 'linguistic' so that he can comprehend the 'language of God' (Rousseau 1987b: 38). We are told that the 'origin of man' need not be traced back to his origins in an animal state because that tracing is not relevant to the origin of man. However, we are also told that what restricts us from tracing man back to his animal origins is the lack of progress in comparative anatomy and natural science. Here, it seems that the restriction on seeing man as originating in the animal is not conceptual, but rather technical. Lastly, Rousseau also explains the passage from the natural state through the factors of both pity and speech. In the 'Discourse on the Origin of Inequality' we are told that pity is the first 'natural sentiment' (Rousseau 1987b: 55), and that which invokes a passage to the social, since it awakens a sensibility of the other. In the 'Essay' we are told that speech is 'the first social institution' and therefore owes 'its form to natural causes alone' (Rousseau 1966: 5).

It is clear from the juxtaposition of Rousseau's various notions of 'primitive times' that many of these placements of the 'origin' of man are incompatible. For Derrida, Rousseau's constant shiftings and repositionings of the passage from nature to the social are the manifestations of a 'supplementary logic'. That which is positioned as the 'supplement' (culture) is always already 'within' or conceptually 'prior to' that which is supposed to be original to it. Thus there constantly occurs a repositioning of the point understood as original. The repositioning distracts one's attention from the incoherence of Rousseau's concept of originality. For Derrida, it is a structural necessity that the notion of 'primitive times' has no content except that of being 'before'. It constantly shifts, being projected as that which is before whatever is positioned at a particular textual point as the 'social'. Thus, at one moment such a point may be a state of primitive family organisation. At another, the 'primitive' is that which precedes the state of primitive family organisation.

At one point, Derrida describes this as a structure which 'does not follow a linear genesis but indicates permanent possibilities which may at any moment reappear in the course of a cycle'. Thus we see contradictory accounts where 'the nearly-social state of barbarism may *in fact* exist before or after, indeed during and under the state of society' (Derrida 1976: 254). At another point, Derrida describes this as a circular structure:

In addition to the system of oppositions that controls the entire Essay (servitude/politico-linguistic liberty, North/South, articulation/ accent, consonant/vowel, capital/province// autarchic and democratic city), we may perceive here the strange workings of the historical progress according to Rousseau. It never varies: beginning with an origin or a center that divides itself and leaves itself, an historical circle is described, which is degenerative in direction

116

but progressive and compensatory in effect. On the circumference of that circle are new origins for new circles.

(Derrida 1976: 202)

The logic of 'supplementarity' is the organisation of certain terms as mere additions to (or degradations from) a privileged term which is nevertheless not autonomous of its 'supplement' but is rather, conceptually, *already* lacking or 'contaminated' by its 'other' in some way (see Derrida 1976: 144–5, 215, etc.). Thus according to the logic of the supplement, the 'outside' is 'inside' (Derrida 1976: 215). This is the case with all Rousseau's oppositions between various states of social organisation and the ideals of nature to which these states are opposed.

We have seen the mobility of Rousseau's descriptions of the state of nature and the passage from nature to culture. Any state understood as radically pre-social or original must still contain the factor which allows the passage to the social. This suggests that the flexibility in Rousseau's work in relation to where the barrier between 'natural' or 'social' is drawn, the flexibility about what is defined as 'natural'[2] and the flexibility of the factor understood as provoking the passage from the natural to the social is not accidental, but *necessary* to Rousseau's texts and their 'supplementary logic'.

We can now return to a feminist interrogation of the shifting and incompatible senses of 'nature'. As Margaret Canovan has asked: 'What connection can there be . . . between Rousseau's repeated references to the 'naturalness' of the patriarchal family and his account of the natural state of human beings in the *Discourse on the Origin of Inequality*?' (Canovan 1987: 87). The interpretation of Rousseau in *Of Grammatology* suggests that the two accounts are linked by a circular logic such that the relationship between 'origin' and 'supplement' (nature and the social) is of an extreme mobility and repeats incessantly. On the circumference of each nature/culture opposition is a new nature/culture opposition. Each organisation of the 'cultural' redivides again and repeats the opposition between nature and culture. For this reason, Rousseau's texts include multiple and incompatible accounts of the 'natural'. What is 'original', 'primitive' and 'natural' in the 'Essay' (the family organisation) is positioned as 'social' in the 'Discourse on the Origin of Inequality'. While the agrarian state is considered a 'fall' to the social in relation to the primitive family, it is also idealised as 'natural' in relation to the radically degraded, large city community of Paris.

From a linear point of view, the dichotomous oppositions (primitive/ agrarian, primitive/family, agrarian/city) which organise Rousseau's corpus are not structurally compatible. While the agrarian is at one point described as the social, at another point it is privileged as the 'natural' if another state is relegated to the status of the 'social' – for example, the

large city. However, from another (circular) point of view, these oppositions can be understood as structurally interconnected so that the same
state can be understood by Rousseau as both 'natural' and 'social',
through the supplementary logic which Derrida suggests is organising
Rousseau's concept of the natural.

We can also return to the suggestion by Carole Pateman about the
interconnection of dichotomous oppositions. Pateman proposes that
the dichotomous oppositions 'masculine/feminine' and 'public/private'
are curiously flexible. It is this flexibility which allows these oppositions
to accommodate the substantial upheaval which should disrupt them.
Thus, where women enter the 'public' sphere, the private/public opposition stretches and realigns so that within the 'public' sphere is repeated
the private/public opposition (and women take up secondary positions
within the public sphere). For Derrida, each concept of 'the social' repeats
the structure that divides the natural from the social. Another way of
saying this is that a supplementary logic allows the notion of nature to be
opposed to the social, and yet to accommodate further nature/culture
oppositions. Both Derrida and Pateman offer an account of the mobility of
privileged terms in dichotomous oppositions ('public sphere', or 'nature')
such that they are able to incorporate their 'other' (the feminine, society)
through their redivision within the public sphere, or of nature into the
internal oppositions 'masculine/feminine' or 'nature/culture'.

Carole Pateman's comments are oriented towards an explanation
of why the dichotomous oppositions 'public/private' and 'masculine/
feminine' are able to accommodate the social and conceptual change that
should, apparently, disrupt them. Derrida also could be said to offer an
account of how a nature/culture opposition can be sustained in tandem
with descriptions of nature as not autonomous of culture. But Derrida's
orientation can be framed differently. Derrida emphasises that which
is produced, or enabled, by the radical mobility and constant redivision of
dichotomous oppositions in a supplementary logic.

We have seen Derrida argue that in Rousseau's text the 'external' or the
'supplement' is *not* external to the 'interior' or 'original':

> it does not suffice to show, it is in fact not a question of showing, the
> interiority of what Rousseau would have believed exterior; rather to
> speculate upon the power of exteriority as *constitutive* of interiority:
> of speech, of signified meaning, of the present as such.
>
> (Derrida 1976: 313, my italic)

Rousseau would like to see advanced society as a degradation of man
in relation to a more natural state. But, responds Derrida, 'One can no
longer see disease in substitution when one sees that the substitute is
substituted for a substitute' (Derrida 1976: 314). Although Derrida
is arguing, in effect, that *there is no such thing as the interior* (that the interior

118

always contains that which is 'exterior' folded within it), he is *also* insisting on the fact that the structure of substitution and supplementarity 'are *constitutive* of the effect of interiority'.[3] One expression of Derrida's argument is the idea that there is 'no such thing' as interiority. Another is that the very structure which renders interiority a chimaera acts to produce the effect of interiority. The effect of interiority (of original nature) is rendered.[4] It is Derrida's insistence on the structure of supplementarity as (paradoxically) generating effects of origin and interiority which I have wanted to emphasise.

In the last chapter, I examined a cross-section of methodologies in feminist interpretation of one canonical philosopher: Jean-Jacques Rousseau. I focused on methodologies deployed to interpret Rousseau's contradictions. I noted attempts to explain those contradictions and several approaches which see the contradictions as invalidating Rouseau's misogyny. Certainly, Rousseau's contradictions do invalidate his misogyny, insofor as we expect from a philosopher coherence and consistency of terms. Still, the problem with the invalidation approach is its tendency to direct attention away from the way in which misogyny, like the homophobia considered in chapter 1, is sustained by incoherence and inconsistency of terms. The invalidation approach leads the critic to look away from the crucial rhetorical work performed by an incoherence of terms. The analysis stops short at the point of exposing the presence of incoherence, the invalidation of the philosopher's misogyny being a common aim of a feminist reading. As many feminist critics have noted, Rousseau's definitions of the natural are inconsistent. In this chapter, I shall ask how Rousseau's description of sexual difference is enabled by its incoherence of terms.

One cannot consider Rousseau's account of sexual difference in abstraction from the complexity of the Rousseauist conception of the 'natural'. What do we find, directing our attention right at the instabilities and contradictions surrounding this term? The authority grounding the 'law' of sexual difference is not singular, but plural. The prescription of sexual difference is legitimated by the 'voices' of nature, reason and God. The senses of nature multiply, as do the terms which legitimate the prescription of sexual difference. This multiplication is crucial to Rousseau's account of ideal relations between the sexes. The multiplication of legislative 'voices' is not in itself contradictory. There is no obvious contradiction in Rousseau's argument that sexual difference is prescribed by both God and nature. Nevertheless, contradictions arise about whether these prescriptions can be reliably known in civilised society. Can they be located within the continuum of social progress, or do they pertain to a state conceptually understood as preceding human society? Contradictory views on this point are necessary to Rousseau's prescription of sexual difference as natural. Contradictions relating to whether the law of sexual difference is located within or outside the continuum of social progress *assist* the operation of Rousseau's prescription of sexual difference. Rousseau's man/woman dichotomy should be interpreted in the context of the operative contradictions generated by the combination of the 'voices' of reason, nature and God in his apology for sexual difference. The Derridean reading of the unstable Rousseauist opposition nature/culture, in which culture is both interior and exterior to nature, rarely addresses the issue of sexual difference. Yet it provides key resources for a feminist interpretation of this issue, because the Rousseauist account of women is grounded in, and sustained by, the Rousseauist definition of the natural.

THE 'ELASTIC' FUNCTION OF PERFECTIBILITY AS 'NATURAL'

The relations between Emile and Sophie are described by Rousseau as natural. But the reader unfamiliar with Rousseau's work would be puzzled in turning to the account of sexual relations described as natural in texts such as the 'Discourse on the Origin of Inequality', or the 'Essay on the Origin of Languages'. There, what pertains to the hypothetical, primitive state of nature bears no resemblance to the domestic sexual relations recommended in *Emile* as natural. In *Emile*, natural relations between the sexes are organised in terms of a public/private division. Man takes his repose in the private haven created by women, which constitutes the 'happiness of his life ... when he [leaves] his office exhausted' (Rousseau 1991: 374). In the second 'Discourse',[5] natural relations between the sexes are primitive and anonymous. They are restricted to literal sexual relations which occur spontaneously. The family unit is not part of the 'state of nature': men do not know their children, and women only know them for as long as they suckle them and tend to their needs (Rousseau 1987b: 56–7 etc.). In the 'Essay', an isolated, primitive family unit is considered to pertain to the state of nature, but not the sentiment of love for a particular woman (Rousseau 1966: 44–5). What, then, can we make of the apparent incompatibility or self-contradiction of Rousseau's definitions of 'natural' relations between the sexes?

Many twentieth-century continental studies suggest that the inconsistent descriptions of the 'natural' do not constitute a simple incoherence on Rousseau's part. His understanding of humans as 'perfectible' must be taken into account. Perfectibility is the possibility of human self-modification through willed change and transcendence of the natural given. It is, for Rousseau, nature 'herself' who rendered humans perfectible. Perfectibility gives rise both to our enlightenment and to our errors, our vices and our virtues. Insofar as humans are naturally perfectible, it is 'natural' that they pass from a mythical state of nature to one of rudimentary society, 'natural' that they cultivate the reason which will lead to their own degradation from the natural:

> It would be sad for us to be forced to agree that this distinctive and almost unlimited faculty [perfectibility] is the source of all man's misfortunes; that this is what, by dint of time, draws him out of that original condition in which he would pass tranquil and innocent days; that this is what, through centuries of giving rise to his enlightenment and his errors, his vices and his virtues, eventually makes him a tyrant over himself and nature.
>
> (Rousseau 1987b: 45)

In imbuing humans with perfectibility, nature imbues them with the capacity for a natural passage from the state of nature to that of the social, and development through successive stages of civilisation. In this way, Rousseau is able to define coherently the state of nature, an 'early' pastoral state of social organisation, and the degradation into contemporary civilisation as all 'natural'. The definition of perfectibility as itself 'natural' imbues the term 'natural' with the capacity for an extreme elasticity in its meaning.

Human perfectibility also accounts for the representation of certain advanced aspects of culture (for example, a highly contrived education of the sort recommended in *Emile*) as the means of amending the state of cultural degradation in accordance with the prescriptions of nature. Because we have 'fallen' from the (mythical) state of nature, we must use contrived, 'unnatural', cultural means (such as education) to approximate the natural order. The notion of perfectibility accommodates both the idea that it is 'natural' that we 'fall'[6] from the pre-social to the social, from nature to culture, from the agrarian/pastoral community to highly civilised urban society, and also the idea that we may transcend a highly degraded civilised society through educational and other practices, for example, in accordance with the natural law. This is perfectibility, the constant transcendence by humans of their given state. Perfectibility allows the term 'nature' to stretch, with conceptual coherence, to accommodate both the mythical state of nature and the movement out of that 'original condition' as well as various succeeding states: primitive and barbaric societies, early Roman and Greek societies, and modern pastoral and provincial communities.

The concept of perfectibility provides two ways of considering as coherent the elaborate, artificial means of producing 'natural' men and women in *Emile*. First, Emile can transcend the contemporary state of degradation and sexual confusion through the human capacity for self-perfection. Second, the elasticity of the term 'nature' allows relations between the sexes in the 'golden age', small pastoral communities and the domestic relations between Sophie and Emile all to be understood as 'natural'. Perfectibility enables the 'natural' to refer to 'original' sexual relations, and to any stage of development out of nature, any degradation, and also any cultural amendment (such as education) which will generate a greater proximity to a social organisation supposedly 'ordained by nature'.

The contradictory employments of the term 'nature' are rendered coherent by the elasticity of the notion of perfectibility. This is how the contradictions surrounding that term can be explained. However, can this analysis be taken further? What do the contradictory meanings of 'nature' themselves enable? What is facilitated in relation to the prescription of natural sexual difference by the possibility of elastic and contradictory meanings of the natural?

Nature has at least three meanings. First, the sense of our 'essence', that which lies underneath the overlay of culture: 'Throughout the ages the natural relations do not change' (Rousseau 1991: 391). This sense of eternal 'natural relations' between the sexes is invoked in support of the ideal domestic arrangement between contemporary humans as embodied by eighteenth-century Emile and Sophie: 'the standards of what is or what is not suitable that result from [natural relations] remain the same' (Rousseau 1991: 391). The 'natural' is also a law for human relations which hangs over the degraded continuum of civilisation. In this sense, the 'natural' is again eternal and unchanging, but it is not internal to us. It is not our inner 'essence'; it is external to us. 'Nature' is a transcendent, legislative entity which ordains human relations. An invariable law of nature gives directions for the way in which men and women ought to act (Rousseau 1991: 358, 363). A third sense of the 'natural' refers to a hypothetical state which would have preceded man's social organisation. This refers to a primitive state of human relations. This is not a state understood as 'historical', but a hypothesis about what might pertain to a state preceding all that we ascribe to the 'social'.

The first sense of nature is 'interior' to humanity. The second and third senses of nature invoke exteriority, although in different senses. Nature as 'law' is transcendent to the human, but persists as a law which remains eternally valid throughout historical eras. Nature as 'original' is external to the human. It is that hypothetical primitive state which would pertain before minimal social relations. These senses of nature are not simultaneously compatible. In particular, describing a certain arrangement between the sexes as 'natural' can mean that it pertains to a hypothetical primitive state of pre-social, barbaric relations, or that it pertains to the true essence or 'nature' of modern men and women underneath the distortions of culture. Relations between the sexes could be natural in the first or second sense, but are often described by Rousseau as 'natural' as if this means the same thing.

The straddling of the term 'nature' across these different connotations is crucial to the description of sexual difference as natural. For Derrida, the constant organisation and reorganisation of the opposition 'nature/culture' leaves a Rousseauist 'nature' positioned as always exterior and interior to culture. Culture always 'precedes' nature and nature is never entirely 'pure' from the culture it is opposed to. Even the hypothetical 'state of nature' must still contain the factor provoking the 'fall' to the social. Derrida argues that there is an aporia at the heart of original nature. What, to reformulate this, is enabled by this aporia with regard to the legitimation of the Rousseauist prescription for sexual difference? What is enabled by nature's simultaneous connotations of exteriority and interiority in relation to the social continuum?

Nature's prescription of sexual difference needs to be positioned as exterior to culture for its legitimacy. Otherwise, the prescription could not be considered immune from the effects of cultural prejudice and degradation. Rousseau constantly insists on the pernicious, wide-embracing effects of such prejudice. To be legitimate, sexual difference must be located in a natural law which precedes culture. Nature is also positioned within culture as an immanent essence.[7] The concept of nature hovers between these different meanings. This straddling compensates for the distance between original nature and contemporary relations between the sexes.[8] Those relations between the sexes posited by Rousseau as original are incoherent as a blueprint for relations between Sophie and Emile. Rousseau protests that although he describes contemporary social relations as 'unnatural', his ideal is not the emulation of, or attempt to return to, an original 'primitive' state (Rousseau 1964a: 964). However, nature has a hovering, elastic meaning. Nature is positioned both prior to the social and also as the advent of the social, both exterior and interior to the social, both transcendent to and immanent in contemporary humans. Any state of sexual relations recommended as 'natural' is therefore legitimated by the connotation of that prescription as natural in the sense of 'radically original', 'exterior' to the social. Simultaneously, it retains the relevance and recognisability of a 'human nature' immanent within the social. For some critics, the slippage in definitions of nature can be explained. For others, the incoherence of nature is a destabilising factor. I am suggesting a sense in which the terminological slippage sustains Rousseau's argument.

The pastoral, domesticated family idyll pertaining to Emile and Sophie has been laid down as the law of nature. The notion of this 'law' straddles both transcendent and immanent connotations. It appears to be a problem for Rouseau's argument that relations between the sexes described in a text such as the second 'Discourse' are almost animal relations. Here, the sexes come together only temporarily for procreation, and the family unit is not original. The juxtaposition of these notions of 'nature' produces the double argument that Rousseau considers the family as both a natural institution and an unnatural institution. The account of the family as 'unnatural' seems to disqualify the recommendation of ideal relations between Emile and Sophie as 'natural'. But the slippage (between whether 'natural sexual relations' are those of the primitive state of nature or those of Emile and Sophie) is necessary to the description of Emile and Sophie as natural.

The concept of perfectibility renders coherent the alternate descriptions of these states as 'natural'. But the modern, domestic ideal of sexual difference is natural both in the sense of the 'internal natural' and in the sense of the 'external natural'. The straddling of the different (external and internal) senses of 'natural' gives the notion of contemporary sexual difference the legitimacy of the external sense of the 'natural' and the relevance to modernity of the internal sense of the 'natural'. Perfectibility does render coherent the alternate multiple meanings of 'nature', but not a concurrent sliding across those meanings.

Perfectibility also disqualifies Rousseau's devaluation of confused sexual identity. The state of nature, primitive and barbaric states, agrarian and modern provincial communities can all be understood as natural because this term refers both to a hypothetical original state and to various states of social organisation. The pastoral is valued as natural in opposition to city life, but is also a degradation from the natural. In relation to Paris, Genevan life is 'natural', but it remains degradation in relation to a simple pastoral life. Sexual relations in city life are described as unnatural. Men are rendered 'effeminate', women masculine. But in relation to some more catastrophic society, confused sexual relations in Paris should, according to the same logic, be comprehensible as 'natural' via that same elasticity of perfectibility. In short, degradation is natural because it inevitably follows from natural perfectibility, and this renders problematic the devaluation of particular states as degraded. Perfectibility specifically allows us to see mutability from projected 'original' relations between the sexes as 'natural'. Perfectibility disqualifies the prescriptive force of sexual difference as 'natural'. Nevertheless, the elasticity of perfectibility such that it encompasses both immanence and transcendence (the natural law as both internal and external to culture) is crucial to the prescription it also disqualifies. While bestowing the necessary connotations of transcendence and immanence on nature, perfectibility simultaneously renders incoherent the devaluation of contemporary social degradation as 'unnatural'.

The same term which makes possible the legitimation of sexual difference also makes it impossible, or destabilises it. This could be named an 'operative contradiction'. The prescription that 'sexual difference is natural' is enabled by the operative contradiction pertaining to the connotation of 'natural'. The prescription operates through the mobile effects of the concept of perfectibility, these effects being both the legitimation of the prescription of sexual difference and the disqualification of that prescription.

THE VOICES OF NATURE, REASON AND GOD

The transcendent location of nature's directives is essential to their legitimacy. But how trustworthy is knowledge of transcendent directives? In a state of degradation, our perception of the directives of nature and God is unreliable. Rousseau raises this problem in contexts such as the Vicar of Savoy's 'Profession de foi' in book 4 of *Emile*, the discussion of sexual difference in book 5, and *La Nouvelle Héloïse*.

Knowing the ineffable

In book 4 of *Emile*, the Vicar of Savoy considers what knowledge we may have of God and his directions. The Vicar sometimes asserts that God is radically unknowable and ineffable. Reason is limited in its ability to know the 'impenetrable mysteries [which] surround us on all sides' (Rousseau 1991: 268). The degradation of civilisation sometimes stifles the inner voice of our soul which helps us to decipher the voice of God (Rousseau 1991: 264). In the end, as Paul de Man points out (de Man 1979: 224–5), the profession of faith by the Vicar of Savoy is organised both by the argument that the voice of God speaks to man loudly and unmistakably and by the argument that the voice of God is faint and imperceptible because of the contemporary mediation of inner conscience by culture and prejudice (Rousseau 1991: 291). This is one formulation of the contradiction which I consider in this section. The 'Profession' tells us that we can rely upon the ability of our inner conscience to decipher God's law, but it also tells us that we cannot.

Again, this can be seen as a necessary contradiction. It is partly the fact that God's voice is rendered faint by the conventions of culture which legitimates the devaluation of those conventions. Yet, it remains the perception of God's voice which allows us to devalue the prejudices of culture as mere prejudice. If God's voice is rendered faint by culture, how can we be sufficiently sure of our perception of God's voice to devalue the prejudices of culture?

The same problem occurs in relation to Rousseau's legitimation of sexual difference by the voices of both nature and God. It is a 'miracle' that man should be masculine and that woman should be feminine in contemporary society. Society is accordingly unable to provide a referent for natural man and woman. Such an account must be virtual and/or fictional, as in the account of 'essential' sexual difference and the account of Emile and Sophie. The details of that fiction are legitimated by reference to the laws of nature and of God. Rousseau's ability to decipher those laws goes unquestioned in the discussion of sexual difference. But this ability is called into question in the 'Profession of Faith', which immediately precedes the account of sexual difference. Cultural prejudice affects the reliability with which our inner judgement or our inner sentiment perceives transcendent laws. In book 5 sexual difference is such a law: presented both as a law of nature and as a law of God.

The same problem is again raised in *La Nouvelle Héloïse*. Julie asserts that the form and love of the beautiful have been imprinted in her soul by nature. But she questions whether we can rely on the purity of this interior model. How can we know that this model is uncontaminated, for it is prone to an imperceptible corruption by public prejudice?

> Enfin, que le caractère et l'amour du beau soit empreint par la nature au fond de mon âme, j'aurai ma règle aussi longtemps qu'il ne sera défiguré. Mais comment m'assurer de conserver dans la pureté cette effigie intérieure qui n'a point, parmi les êtres sensibles, de modèle auquel on puisse la comparer. Ne sait-on pas que les affections désordonnées corrompent le jugement ainsi que la volonté, et que la conscience s'altère et se modifie insensiblement dans chaque peuple, dans chaque individu, selon l'inconstance et la variété des préjugés?[9]
>
> (Rousseau 1967: 263–4)

The interior imprint of the natural which gives us the rule for our actions may well have been imperceptibly corrupted by the social. This renders unreliable that supposedly reliable rule. Yet it is on the basis of this corruption that we debase contemporary culture. Rousseau must argue both that we can know nature (that it is imprinted within us) and that we cannot know nature (we are in a state of corruption such that nature's imprints may have been imperceptibly deformed). Only on the basis of this double argument can Rousseau devalue contemporary culture in opposition to and on the basis of the ideal standard of the natural.

The multiplication of legitimating 'voices'

A set of contradictions is put in play by Rousseau's multiplication of the entities or 'voices' which are considered to legitimate the prescription of sexual difference. The voices of nature, God and reason are all said to dictate sexual difference. This proliferation of legitimating terms for sexual difference is particularly strong in book 5 of *Emile*. Sexual difference is the law of nature:

> This is not the law of love, I agree. But it is that of nature, prior to love itself
>
> (Rousseau 1991: 358)

126

By the very law of nature women are at the mercy of men's judgements . . . It is not enough that they be estimable; they must be esteemed. It is not enough for them to be pretty; they must please
(Rousseau 1991: 364)

In following nature's directions, man and woman ought to act in concert, but they ought not to do the same things
(Rousseau 1991: 363);

and the law of God:

The Supreme Being . . . while abandoning man to immoderate passions . . . joins reason to these passions in order to govern them. While abandoning woman to unlimited desires, He joins modesty to these desires in order to constrain them
(Rousseau 1991: 359);

and the law of reason:

The use of reason that leads man to the knowledge of his duties is not very complex. The use of reason that leads woman to the knowledge of hers is even simpler.
(Rousseau 1991: 382)

A similar multiplication of 'terms' governing women occurs in *La Nouvelle Héloïse*. Julie prays to God on her wedding day, 'Je veux tout ce qui se rapporte à l'ordre de la nature que tu as établi, et aux règles de la raison que je tiens de toi' (Rousseau 1967: 263).[10] The law to which Julie is subject divides between God, nature and reason.

What is enabled by the proliferation of legitimating terms? The legitimation of sexual difference must be both immanent in and transcendent to culture. It must be immanent in the sense that its law is intelligible to a corrupted humanity. The law of nature cannot refer only to the transcendent, the radically exterior to culture. The fact that sexual difference is recommended by the voices of nature, reason and God facilitates the multiple demands on sexual difference to be at once immanent and transcendent. The fact that sexual difference is recommended by a divine, stably transcendent entity, God, reinforces the transcendent connotations of the recommendation of sexual difference. This grounds the legitimating force of the prescription. The fact that the 'voice of reason' also prescribes sexual difference reinforces the connotation of the law of sexual difference as immanent, as locatable within the social continuum. If sexual difference is a law of reason, there is no difficulty explaining how we can perceive the law. Nor is there any difficulty with the incoherence of a natural state of relations between the sexes. The different connotations of nature are reinforced by a multiplication of prescribing bodies: nature, reason and God. God's prescription of sexual difference reinforces the transcendent sense of 'natural' sexual relations. Reason's prescription reinforces the 'immanent' connotations. Prescription by nature, reason and God reinforces the impression that sexual difference is simultaneously an immanent and transcendent law.

That reason, nature and God all prescribe sexual difference suggests that the recommendations of these entities are compatible. But Rousseau frequently presents both reason and nature, and also reason and God as opposed rather than complementary 'voices'. Nature and reason, and nature and God, are represented as both opposed and aligned.

Reason and nature as complementary and opposed

Rousseau's devaluations of reason as unnatural (see Rousseau 1987b: 54 etc.) are notorious. Yet Rousseau sometimes offers extravagant exaltations of reason (Rousseau 1987a: 3) and often presents the dictates of reason and nature as 'complementary'. It is not only the voices of nature and God, but also the voice of reason which instructs men and women to respect sexual difference.

Reason's dictate of sexual difference should be related to the role of culture in general as supplementary to nature. Both culture in general and the cultivation of reason in particular represent degradation from nature. But reason and social conventions are also necessary supplements to nature precisely because we are in a state of degradation from nature. The cultivation of reason is unnatural, and is one of the marks of our degradation. Because we are in a state of degradation, it is to reason that we must turn, nevertheless, to decipher the dictates of nature (Rousseau 1991: 382). Reason is therefore assigned both negative and positive connotations, and the 'double' account of reason as both positive and negative does not constitute a simple inconsistency on Rousseau's part. However, the reliability of reason as a voice instructing us in our actions is more problematic. This question involves a second series of contradictions. Rousseau argues both that reason is a reliable voice that we must listen to and also that it is an unreliable voice. The use of a simple reason is said to lead woman to a knowledge of her duties (Rousseau 1991: 382). Reason also obscures our knowledge of natural relations:

Throughout the ages the natural relations do not change... Prejudices parading under the vain name of reason change nothing but the appearance of these standards.

(Rousseau 1991: 391)

The prescription of sexual difference entails a proliferation of terms legitimating that prescription. Each of those terms is considered both to be reliable and to be unreliable as a 'prescriptive voice'. A 'redivision' of each term into further, multiple meanings occurs. Reason is presented as both reliable and as unreliable as a voice which instructs the sexes about appropriate mores. The meaning, and not just the 'value' of reason, divides. Reason is devalued as a voice which pertains to culture and public prejudice. But where the voice of reason is 'valued' it is no longer a voice which speaks 'independently', but rather a voice which acts as a mediator. The voice of reason is unreliable and riddled with cultural prejudice. But the voice of reason which mediates between the auditor's 'inner conscience' and the cultural prejudices in which the auditor is bathed is a reliable voice (Rousseau 1991: 382). In the case of the dichotomy 'inner conscience/reason' or 'voice of nature/voice of reason', reason is devalued, and it signifies an autonomous, competing voice. But where the location of the 'misleading voice' is displaced to the realm of 'public prejudice', reason takes on a new meaning. Rather than a voice which is external (that of public prejudice), it is the mediator between internal and external forces. It mediates between inner conscience and public prejudice. When the competing voices multiply and where the meaning of reason changes from 'exterior' to 'mediator', its connotation changes from negative to positive. It is considered to be a reliable as opposed to an unreliable voice.

Reason and God as complementary and opposed

For Rousseau, the voices of reason and God are in contradictory tension: they are both complementary and opposed. As Robert Derathé points out, Rousseau often does present reason and religion as compatible (Derathé 1979: 1). He describes religious doctrine as thoroughly adapted to his reason, his heart and his whole being (Rousseau 1979: 56). In *La Nouvelle Héloïse* he describes the origin of reason as divine (Rousseau 1967: 263). Although the 'Profession of faith' casts an opposition between reason and natural religion, it affirms the rational faculty of understanding as endowed by God. Rousseau precedes the 'Profession' with the statement, 'The philosopher who does not believe is wrong, because he uses badly the reason he has cultivated and because he is in a position to understand the truths he rejects' (Rousseau 1991: 257–8). There is a correct use of reason by the philosopher which is compatible with theological truths. The 'Lettres écrites de la montagne' defend reason as a means of perceiving divine origin as opposed to the distortions of prejudice (Rousseau 1964b: 728–9). In that text Rousseau defends his ideas on religion by the right of one who reasons (Rousseau 1964b: 735–6). Through reason, we establish God's existence and laws. Reason is compatible with other instruments of theological interrogation (Derathé 1979: 3–4).

On Groethuysen's reading of Rousseau, rational interrogation of the nature and existence of God is not necessary. We worship God sufficiently through our worship of the universal harmony of his creation, nature

(Groethuysen 1945: 337). It is sufficient to worship nature through the faculty of sentiment, rather than analytically inferring the existence of God. Rousseau privileges nature rather than organised religion, arguing that reason is redundant in relation to religious matters. For Groethuysen, this is Rousseau's attempt to reconcile rational philosophy and natural theology (Groethuysen 1945: 337). Grimsley accords with this interpretation in proposing that for Rousseau, 'certain truths – for example, the true nature of God or the soul – might well lie beyond the range of reason, but they could never be against it' (Grimsley 1961: 133). These are accounts which understand reason as irrelevant to religious contemplation, but not incompatible with it.

However, as Derathé points out:

Tantôt Rousseau déclare que nous devons écouter la voix de la nature . . . tantôt c'est au contraire la raison qu'il nous conseille de suivre. Tour à tour la conscience et la raison sont présentées comme le guide que l'homme a reçu de Dieu pour le conduire. Tantôt elles s'opposent, tantôt leurs liens sont si étroits qu'elles paraissent se confondre. Enfin, en ce qui concerne la raison même, nous voyons Rousseau tout d'abord la récuser comme une source d'erreurs ou de sophismes, puis l'exalter comme le flambeau divin que l'Etre suprême nous a donné pour nous éclairer.

(Derathé 1979: 4)[11]

Reason is also frequently rejected as a source of error and confusion in relation to the perception of God and his directives. The Vicar of Savoy is against reasoning about the nature of God, for 'These reasonings are always rash.' The wise man knows that he is not made to plumb the depths of God's nature (Rousseau 1991: 277). Rousseau repeatedly devalues philosophical speculation about metaphysics and rarefied theological speculation as exorbitant excesses of the practice of reason, for example, in the 'Profession' (Rousseau 1991: 268, 274); in La Nouvelle Héloïse (Rousseau 1967: 532);[12] and in the 'Letter to M. Franquières' (Rousseau 1969b: 1137).

Reason is also devalued in the 'Profession' as a deceptive guide when we are confronted with the contradictory 'voices' of the passions and the divine voice of conscience (Rousseau 1991: 286). But in book 5 of Emile, reason is valued specifically as an instrument which enables us to determine between contradictory voices, in this case those of conscience and of public prejudice: 'It is important, therefore, that [women] cultivate a faculty that serves as arbiter between the two guides, which does not let the conscience go astray, and which corrects the errors of prejudice. That faculty is reason' (Rousseau 1991: 382).

Where contradictory positions occur concerning the compatibility of the voices of God and reason, we see a multiplication of the definitions of God and reason. Groethuysen discusses the 'several Gods' in Rousseau's work. Like the multiple senses of the term 'nature', multiple senses of divinity are also in play. One sense of 'God', points out Groethuysen, is that of an anonymous and radically inconceivable entity (for example, that God before whom the old woman can say nothing but 'O' (Rousseau 1953: 593). This God is the source of our nameless ecstasy, but not the source of our rational comprehension (Rousseau 1969b: 1137; Rousseau 1991: 285). God is also the object of our rational comprehension. We can infer the nature of God, his divine will or intelligence, from his creations (Rousseau 1991: 300; Groethuysen 1945: 286).[13] So, asks Groethuysen:

> Comment expliquer que l'idée de Dieu subisse tant de méta-morphoses chez Rousseau et qu'elle réunisse en elle des éléments divergents qui seraient difficilement conciliables? ... Pourquoi est-ce tantôt le sentiment qui parle, le sentiment pur, le sentiment tout personnel d'une âme qui recherche l'infini, et tantôt l'esprit constructif d'un législateur qui veut imposer un Dieu à une société? Pourquoi Dieu semble-t-il tantôt dépendre d'un raisonnement, tantôt de conceptions morales?
>
> (Groethuysen 1945: 334)[14]

Is God knowable or unknowable? Both versions are at work in the 'Profession'. This tension leads to a contradictory account of whether man is to be seen as 'like God' or as 'not like' God. The Vicar expresses his indignation at descriptions of God as spirit, and the soul as spiritual: 'As if God and my soul were of the same nature!' he exclaims (Rousseau 1991: 285). The strident rejection of similarity between man and God is connected to the Vicar's insistence on the radical ineffability of God: 'I lift and fatigue my mind in vain to conceive His essence' (Rousseau 1991: 285). Yet Rousseau sometimes does want to emphasise some link between divine nature and the essence of man. In particular, he describes our inner conscience as our 'divine instinct', and as that which makes man like unto God, again in the 'Profession':

> Conscience, conscience! Divine instinct, immortal and celestial voice, certain guide of a being that is ignorant and limited but intelligent and free; infallible judge of good and bad which makes man like unto God.
>
> (Rousseau 1991: 290)

It is unacceptable to describe God's nature as like that of man. It is nevertheless acceptable to describe man's nature as to some extent like that of God. God is presented as a radically ineffable entity, and one must not describe God and the soul with terms like 'spirit'. But man is presented as able to know with certainty the dictates of God. At this point, we are told that conscience makes us like God and is our 'certain' and 'infallible' guide.

The definitions of reason also multiply in relation to our knowledge of God's voice. On the one hand, there is 'good reason', that which is ruled by inner conscience. 'Good' reason is not incompatible with divine contemplation, but is not necessary to it. Without conscience, reason would be unprincipled. Reason is compatible with conscience if guided by it. Nevertheless, it is also redundant. The Vicar exclaims that conscience delivers us 'from all that terrifying apparatus of philosophy. We can be men without being scholars' (Rousseau 1991: 290). There is another version of 'good' reason which is again ruled by inner sentiment. This 'reason' is necessary to divine contemplation, enabling us to comprehend the divine entity so as to worship it. Third, there is also a 'bad' reason, which obscures and conflicts with a divine voice by pursuing vain metaphysical and theological subtleties.

Finally, let us return to the account of reason as deceptive in the 'Profession'. By way of contrast the conscience is presented as entirely reliable: 'conscience never deceives; it is man's true guide' (Rousseau 1991: 286). At this point in the text, we see a further proliferation of entities or 'voices' which are said to guide us. As well as the voices of nature, reason and God, there is a 'fourth' voice: that of inner conscience, in relation to which reason is devalued. Conscience is not an independent voice, but another mediating voice. Conscience is described as the 'voice of the soul'. In a further complication, 'he who follows conscience', says Rousseau, 'obeys nature' (Rousseau 1991: 286).

The various voices invoked by Rousseau are not discrete from each other. The voice of reason is not quite a third voice, or the voice of conscience a fourth, because conscience is a voice which interprets the voice of the soul. It is not clear that the 'soul' and 'nature' are separate voices. Conscience is described as the voice both of the soul and of nature as if these are indistinguishable (Rousseau 1991: 286). Where a proliferation of legitimating or guiding 'voices' (God, reason, nature, soul, conscience) occurs, we see a structure of internal redivision of the entities used to legitimate privileged accounts of human actions and mores, including sexual difference. Indeed, Rousseau further multiplies these terms. We may also rely on the inner voices of our 'heart' and our 'inner sensibility', for example.[15]

This multiplication of terms is not in itself contradictory. But it entails contradictory tensions concerning the compatibility of these voices. How might we understand this multiplication, or redivision, of voices to be operative in legitimating Rousseau's prescription of sexual difference?

Rousseau is well known for his general devaluation of mediation.[16] The Vicar of Savoy laments mediation between himself and God. The devaluation of mediation is invoked by Rousseau to devalue a variety of cultural institutions, including organised religion. The Vicar's laments 'How many men between God and me'. Mediation is analysed by Starobinski as the prime symptom of cultural degradation. The two ideal, original transcendent points projected by Rousseau, nature and God, are both understood as 'self-present' and self-coinciding.[17]

Nevertheless, mediating terms are essential to Rousseau's account of sexual difference. The transcendent status of nature and God legitimates their prescriptions. Yet humans must reliably identify those prescriptions. Rousseau must tell us both that we can know transcendent points such as nature and God and that we cannot. Rousseau both tells us that we are 'like' God (i.e., able to know divine prescriptions) and that God is in no way like us. God is described both as knowable and as unknowable. Reason is both devalued and valued as a means of 'knowing' God.

The multiplication of entities legitimating sexual difference obscures the conceptual aporia at the heart of that prescription. At any particular moment, any one of those entities seems to resolve the difficulty of how we can reliably perceive a transcendent model in a state of corruption. In one account, it is reason which allows us to do so; in another, it is conscience and not reason, and so on.

None of these individual entities resolves Rousseau's conceptual difficulty. Both reason and inner conscience operate within a state of social degradation. Degradation is defined precisely as muffling and obscuring the dictates of inner conscience, or the soul, or 'the heart' (Rousseau 1991: 264, 280, 286). No number of mediating terms will resolve this difficulty. Rousseau must tell us that inner conscience (or the soul, or the heart) has been partly stifled.

The social is devalued on the basis that it has stifled the voices of nature, conscience, soul and the heart. On this basis, Rousseau privileges the purported recommendations of transcendent nature. At one point in his argument, he is able to displace on to 'reason' an identity as unreliable, corrupted mediator, favouring 'inner conscience' as the 'valued' mediator of nature's dictates. At another point, he argues that we must use reason since inner conscience alone is not reliable. Because of the proliferation of mediating points, some can be privileged as reliable with the spectre of 'unreliability' continually being displaced.

Each mediating term further defers the location of the purported original legislative voice. If contemporary mores are said to be legitimated by 'the voice of nature' or 'the voice of God', then the conceptual problems related to those voices are immediately apparent. The voice of reason is a corrupted voice, and the voice of God is uncorrupted, but is unreliably known by a corrupt man. The voice of nature incorporates both conceptual problems. As a transcendent voice, the voice of nature entails the same problem as does the voice of God. As an immanent voice, the voice of nature entails the same problem as does the voice of reason. But with the number of mediating voices whose role it is to 'interpret' the voices of God, or nature proliferating, the conceptual aporia at the heart of those voices is deferred. Rousseau must tell us that we can know these voices of God and nature and that we cannot. This conceptual problem[18] appears to be resolved by the proliferation of mediating terms. These give the impression that given the right mediating 'instrument', we can perceive transcendent voices. The assertions that mediating instruments such as the soul, heart, the inner conscience or reason enable us to know the prescriptions of God and nature create the impression that one can know prescriptions which must also be positioned as transcendent and unknowable.

THE INTERCONNECTION OF HIERARCHICAL BINARISMS WITH TRANSCENDENT PROJECTIONS

How is the prescription of sexual difference legitimated within the Rousseauist account? Certain contradictions may be seen as textually enabling in this context. Rousseau positions transcendent terms which authorise the rigid, modern masculine/feminine opposition. Contradictions concerning transcendent authority involve two sets of phenomena. The first set is the multiplication of terms legitimating the prescription of sexual difference (for example, the voices of nature, God and reason). The second set is the multiplication of meanings of specific terms legitimating that prescription (for example, nature as both interior and exterior to the social continuum).

One effect is the proliferation of terms understood as mediating between the 'actual human' and the transcendent entity prescribing sexual difference. This involves another set of contradictory tensions, because certain terms such as reason have a status as both 'independent' and 'mediating'. Reason is considered negative as an 'independent' voice, and yet positive where it is a mediating voice. Rousseau generally devalues mediation, in a corpus which devalues contemporary culture as an obstacle to natural immediacy. Mediation by social forces between ourselves and the muffled voice of nature is the symptom and tragedy of our degradation. Rousseau devalues anything which comes 'between' ourselves and our ability to perceive the original transcendent voices of God and reason directly. But he also values a proliferation of terms which come between us and transcendent laws. A conceptual aporia lies at the heart of authorising, transcendent voices, an aporia obscured by the proliferation of mediating voices translating the transcendent.

Derrida's account of the proliferation of 'origins which divide themselves', and his account of a textual economy where points of mediation are endowed with both positive and negative status, can be related to the interpretation of Rousseau I have proposed in this chapter.

134

We have considered Derrida's description of 'the strange workings of the historical progress according to Rousseau. It never varies: beginning with an origin or a centre that divides itself and leaves itself, an historical progress is described, which is degenerative in direction but progressive and compensatory in effect. On the circumference of that circle are new origins for new circles' (Derrida 1976: 202). This reading can be used in considering the radical mobility of 'nature'. Progress can be described in terms of a constant redivision of the opposition 'nature/culture'. Contained within each positioning of the domain 'culture' is a new nature/culture opposition. For example, the institution of the family signifies 'culture' in opposition to the primitive state of nature, but evokes nature in opposition to a degraded society of sexual confusion. The radical contradictions in the definition of 'nature' can be related to the constant redivision of the term such that any particular point is capable of being presented by Rousseau as either 'natural' or 'social' depending on the 'other' to which that point is opposed.

Paradoxes sustain Rousseau's hierarchical oppositions between the 'pure' and the 'degraded', the 'natural' and 'social', the 'transparent' and the 'mediated'. These oppositions could be described as 'auto-deconstructive'. Each devaluation of a particular term (for example, writing as loss of immediacy, or the social as state of corruption) is undermined by the fact that the privileged terms to which these devalued terms are opposed contain at their heart their 'other'. In the case of Rousseau, we have seen that this means both that each valued term is in turn a 'devalued' term in relation to a 'more' original term, and also that even the terms projected as ultimately original are still not 'pure' of their 'other' insofar as they comprise the factor impelling their 'fall' into the other. The deconstructibility of the prescription of sexual difference can also be understood as the operative conditions of that prescription. As Derrida emphasises, 'effects of interiority' are produced through the paradoxical devaluation of various terms as 'exterior'.

Recall Derrida's discussion of speech/writing oppositions where writing is devalued in opposition to speech as a less mediated form of representation. The displacement of 'mediation' on to the 'face' of writing produces the effect of speech's alignment with presence. Speech is also presented as a form of mediation. This is the paradoxical condition of the hierarchy of speech over writing. Speech must also be presented as a form of mediation, because the grounds on which speech is elevated over writing (and thereby obtains its identification with 'presence') is precisely that it is apparently 'closer' to a transcendent state or point (in the case of Plato, truth, or logos. The condition of the identification of speech with presence is at the same time the condition of the impossibility of that effect. In other words, the effect is generated by an operative contradiction.

One symptom of this structure is what Derrida in the passage referred to above describes as 'redivision'. For example, in the case of the reading of Plato's speech/writing opposition, the positive/negative relationship between original truth and mediating representation is at one point organised as between truth and language. At another point, the secondary term 'language' is reorganised into (or can be said to contain) another truth/language opposition. Here, the positive term is 'good' language: speech, and the secondary term is 'bad' language: writing. In the first opposition (truth/language), language is organised as 'mediation'. But the second opposition is a redivision of the secondary pole of the first opposition. Here, only one division of the term 'language' is devalued: 'writing'. The 'bad face' of mediation is displaced on to the face of 'writing'.

The projection of a transcendent (nature, truth) legitimates the binary opposition (speech/writing) by providing grounds on which speech is valued over writing (it is closer to truth, nature). It destabilises that hierarchy since the grounds supposed by that hierarchy (that speech is closer to truth, nature) also render speech itself merely a mediation or representation in relation to a projected transcendent (truth, nature). This can be seen as an operative contradiction producing the effect of the identification of speech with 'presence'.

These points can be related to the series of nature/culture oppositions in Rousseau's work. In the example considered, Derrida's problematic concerns the condition of possibility of the legitimation of the hierarchy of the speech/writing opposition. Our problematic is the condition of possibility of the legitimation of Rousseau's hierarchical account of sexual difference. The prescription of sexual difference is supported by para-doxical nature/culture oppositions. This prescription is sustained by the textual effect of accessible transcendent voices, which we are both 'present' to and distant from. The symptom of this paradoxical structure is the phenomenon of 'redivision'.

In the speech/writing opposition, the representation of writing as mediation or representation aligns speech with (transcendent) presence. Speech is also mediation or representation in relation to transcendent truth or logos. This produces redivision: at one point all of language is 'representation' and at another, only 'writing'. 'Redivision' is also the symptom of an aporia legitimating and destabilising the man/woman opposition. At one point the positive/negative relationship is represented by the voice of nature versus the voice of reason. At another point, the otherwise devalued term 'reason' is redivided into 'good' and 'bad' reason. Good reason is 'natural', a simple and natural reason, where bad reason is philosophical reflection (Rousseau 1967: 264, 266). At one point the positive/negative relationship represents the immediacy/mediation opposition. At another point, the devalued term 'mediation' is redivided into good 'mediation' (reason helps us interpret the transcendent voices of nature and God) and 'bad' mediation (reason is part of a cultural impediment preventing us from hearing the transcendent voice of nature and God; thus reason is a 'voice' conflicting with the voices of nature and God).

These redivisions represent the operative aporia enabling the legitimation of the prescription of sexual difference. That prescription relies on an account of modern society as cut off from transcendent voices. In a state of corruption, relations between the sexes are devalued in relation to an ideal of the 'natural'. However, the prescription also relies on our being able to access transcendent voices so that we can access a blueprint for 'natural' sexual relations. In sum, Rousseau's contradictions sustain his prescription of sexual difference as natural.

This interpretation of the contradictions which riddle Rousseau's account of sexual difference is an alternative to accounts which would see the contradictions as serving no purpose except to weaken his account of women. Instead, I have suggested that Rousseau's account of women functions on the strength of its contradictory elements. We have seen that there is a wealth of Rousseauist contradictions concerning women, and a diversity of methodologies within feminist philosophy for the analysis of those contradictions. Understandably, feminist interpretation has tended to focus on Rousseau's arguments concerning women and femininity. Some critics have focused on the discrepancy between the concept of Sophie as 'natural' and the concept of the primitive state as 'natural'. Developing this direction, my position has been that the contradictions which should be analysed from a feminist perspective are not only those which concern what Rousseau says about women, but also those concerning the terms in which he legitimates his arguments. This pivots feminist analysis towards discrepancies in Rousseau's arguments concerning the voices of nature, reason and God, as well as towards the discrepancies in the account of nature.

The material in this chapter has been used both to argue that certain textual contradictions enable the operation of Rousseau's man/woman opposition and also that his conception of sexual difference should be interpreted in the broader context of a cluster of concepts projecting transcendent and legislative authority. We have seen the importance of a chimaerical exterior legitimating point for the production of the naturalised opposition man/woman and the necessity with which such a legitimating point is also positioned as 'interior' to man, or accessible to man. In Rousseau's work, we have seen that this exterior/interior point is occupied by an original or essential nature. In its 'exterior' connotations, this point is also co-extensive with the prescriptions of God. Because I have directed the focus away from arguments concerning the status of women to include the transcendent/immanent terms on the basis of which these arguments are supported, the analysis has profited from Derrida's interpretation of Rousseau. Crucial to the legitimation of the prescription of sexual difference is the rhetorical effect of voices which dictate the sexual order, located in either divine or natural origins. It is Derrida who offers an argument concerning différance as that which generates effects of pure, unmediated points of origin. Derrida argues that Rousseau's points of origin are always mediated by the 'outside', that the status of the original is unstable in his work. Where Derrida analyses 'the power of exteriority as constitutive of interiority' (Derrida 1976: 313) in the Rousseauist textual economy, I have analysed the enabling effects of this 'power' for the prescription for sexual difference. The prescriptive status of the voice designated as original, whose provenance is divine or natural, relies on the status of the original as uncontaminated by the 'exterior'. Yet the status of such points is unstable, since they are always 'contaminated' by the exterior.

One temptation, then, is to argue that Rousseau's prescription is destabilised by the unstable status of the original in his work. This argument does justice to what I have proposed is an interpretative imperative for feminism: to be attentive to the instabilities of phallo-centrism in our interpretation of the history of philosophy. However, the role of the feminist critic is not merely to *unveil* the internal trouble in Rousseau's work. This is an important project, to be sure. But I have also argued for an approach which does not see Rousseau's work as merely destabilised by its instability. This is because of connotations of destabilisation with the undone, and with the mitigated. My argument has been that the phallocentrism is not merely 'undone' by its internal instability. The phallocentrism is also rendered by the instability, and it has been my main task in this chapter to show how the phallocentrism is rendered by the instability surrounding the original legitimation of the dictate of sexual difference in Rousseau's work. With this analysis, my aim has been to combine an account of how Rousseau's text is unstable with an account of how the prescription of sexual difference is effected through that instability.

I have argued that the history of the man of reason should be narrated in such a way that the instabilities of that history are not suppressed or de-emphasised in a desire to reconstruct a consistent story. An analytical approach specifically attentive to instability, contradiction, terminological slippage and other elements of 'textual trouble' would also allow us to reconsider other accounts of woman in the history of philosophy, many of which are woven with contradictions. For example, Genevieve Lloyd points out that both Augustine and Aquinas argue that woman is 'nature' or the 'physical' whereas man is 'intellect', and yet also argue that woman is the intellectual equal of man. Plato's account of sexual equality in the Republic is famous, and yet Plato's dialogues are no less full of associations of woman with the weak, the frail, the foolish, the irrational, the disordered, the disruptive, children and slaves (see Irigaray 1985a: 152–9). John Locke defends parental equality but also describes women as subject to their husbands. The history of philosophy is a history in which descriptions of the role and nature of women are consistently unstable. Feminist commentary which focuses on such instability is confronted with the question of what methodological techniques to employ in its analysis. The interpretation of Rousseau and the readings which follow in the remainder of this book offer one possible response to this question. They constitute an attempt to combine an attentiveness to instability with an interpretation which does not only see such instability as weakening, disabling or invalidating the philosophy in question. Instead, I focus equally on the ways in which spurious accounts of women are mobilised by their constitutive instability.

In brief, my suggestion is that the interpretation of contradiction as constitutive or operative in phallocentric accounts of women and femininity which I have proposed in this chapter could be extended beyond the texts of Rousseau. In the next chapter, I turn to the comments on women in Augustine's *Confessions*. I begin with a consideration of feminist interpretation of Augustine. Again, I focus on methodologies which have been used within feminist critique in its analysis of contradictions in Augustine's work concerning the nature of women. Many of the tendencies seen in feminist interpretation of Rousseauist contradictions are also seen in feminist interpretation of Augustine. Again, we shall encounter some theorists for whom Augustine's instabilities mitigate or soften his misogyny. And again, I shall oppose what I identify as a range of devices deployed by commentators to 'stabilise' Augustinian contradiction. Opposing such stabilisation, I shall interpret Augustine's account of women as constituted by its instabilities.

I have, furthermore, begun to emphasise the importance of the projection of external/internal, transcendent or original points in the production of certain accounts of the nature of woman. The *Confessions* serve as an ideal opportunity to pursue this theme in tandem with that of operative contradiction. In the next chapter, then, I also further explore the role of the positioning of a divine identity in relation to the operation of man/woman oppositions. How do external divine or transcendent points ground man/woman oppositions? I shall suggest that this ground is constituted by contradictory tensions in the *Confessions* relating to the relationship between man and God.

In reading Rousseau, we have seen that the account of women is interconnected with concepts that are not obviously related to the problem of sexual difference. For example, we have seen that the account of women is related to the status and mobility of the Rousseauist conception of nature and the proliferation of points mediating between man and his access to the dictates of nature and God. Similarly, in reading Augustine I shall suggest that the account of woman is related to a problem that might appear to be distinct – that of man's likeness to God.

6

OPERATIVE CONTRADICTION IN AUGUSTINE'S *CONFESSIONS*

Inexplicably, Augustine must . . . affirm that Eve, too, has a rational nature, being likewise a compound of spirit and body. Yet in relation to man she stands for body *vis-à-vis* male spirit.

(Rosemary Radford Ruether)

The Western 'fathers of the church' have provided some of the most ambivalent accounts of women in history, idealising woman as virgin while denouncing the tempting seductress. This chapter addresses methodologies deployed in feminist interpretation of religious philosophy through a discussion of interpretations of Saint Augustine's views on women. There is a genre of simple critique of misogynist representations of women. Critique runs the risk of reinforcing the consistency of the tradition, rather than analysing its instability. There is also a feminist tradition of exposing the incoherence of representations of women. This can distract from interrogating the coherence of the figure to which women are subordinated: man.

Devalued representations of women and femininity generate the appearance of a stable masculine identity. Yet masculine identity can be analysed as unstable, both in relation to women and in relation to God. When we only analyse the instability of representations of women, we reinforce the impression of man's stable identity. In the reading of Augustine's *Confessions* presented in the second half of this chapter, I focus on the instability of representations of the feminine and the masculine. As in the reading of Rousseau, I focus less on the account of women's nature and role than on what legitimates this account. I analyse the constitutive instability of the appeal to the man/God relation to legitimate the subordination of women.

AUGUSTINE, WOMEN, AND FEMININITY

Many feminist scholars, including Rosemary Radford Ruether, Genevieve Lloyd and Elaine Pagels, interpret the role attributed to women and

141

femininity in Augustine's work in terms of the reason–soul/body dualism which he inherited from Greek philosophy. Prior to the incorporation of dualism into biblical exegesis:

Neither Jesus nor St Paul would have understood this separation between body and soul because Judaism at that time did not divide people up in this way. When Paul decries the 'flesh' . . . he doesn't mean the body as opposed to the soul . . . For Paul 'flesh' is not the body but man as he exists (body/soul together) unredeemed by Christ. The separation of man into body and soul came from the Greeks . . . When later Greek-trained theologians read Paul's words about the 'flesh' they naturally thought he was talking about the body . . . the salvation offered by Jesus was seen as a liberation from the body. St Ambrose . . . preached the idea of a wholly spiritual God, which was a revolutionary . . . idea to his disciple . . . St Augustine.

(Armstrong 1986: 20–1)

However, once the distinction was in place, and given its associations with gender connotations dating back to early Greek philosophy, soul signified distinction from the body, which was associated with the feminine. Dualism consolidated the symbolic connotations of femininity and women as more 'distant' from God.

Dualism can be seen in various aspects of Augustine's work, including his discussions of the original state of paradise. Augustine considers what state of embodiment we should attribute to Adam and Eve. As Hunter explains, the problems facing Augustine include: 'Were Adam and Eve created with mortal bodies even before their sin? And how are we to understand God's command to "increase and multiply" which appears to have been given to Adam and Eve (Gen 1: 28) even before the creation of their bodies?' (Hunter 1994: 165–6).[1] After early discussions in which Augustine stressed 'the spiritual character of the original creation', believing that the bodies of Adam and Eve were 'of a spiritual substance quite unlike ours today; there certainly was no sex or procreation in paradise', he eventually concluded that Adam and Eve were fully embodied, engaging in sex for the purposes of procreation, *but without lust* (Hunter 1994: 166). As he writes in the *City of God*, sexual organs would have been aroused by the will (Augustine 1972: 587; XIV. 24).[2]

Even in the context of Augustine's eventual view that Adam and Eve were always already embodied, the eating of the fruit is still understood as causing their descent into a devalued embodiment. To quote again from the *City of God*:

after their disobedience to God's instructions . . . they felt a novel disturbance in their disobedient flesh, as a punishment which answered to their own disobedience.

142

The soul . . . was deprived of the obedient service which its body had at first rendered . . . it no longer retained its inferior and servant obedient to its will. It did not keep its own flesh subject to it in all respects, as it could have kept it for ever if it had itself continued in subjection to God.

(Augustine 1972: 522–3; XIII.13)

Adam and Eve are cursed with the full gamut of lust and arousal far beyond the needs of procreation. Their will is subordinated to their bodies, and particularly to sexuality and reproduction. Adam is said to be cursed with erection difficult to control, and women with the painful rigours of childbirth.[3] In these senses, the fall is figured by a strongly devalued embodiment. On a dualist framework, 'lesser embodiedness', or subordination of body to will, signifies closeness to God. Augustine supposes that even if they did procreate sexually, Adam and Eve would have enjoyed faithful partnership, but not passion. Their wills would not have been resisted by lustful bodies (Augustine 1972: 591; XIV.26).

Women's collapse into a devalued embodiment is painted luridly. It involves the rigours of childbirth, menstruation and voracious desire. But since being under the sway of embodiment symbolises being under the sway of the feminine, man's collapse into a devalued embodiment represents the additional ignominy of being under the sway of the feminine. Furthermore, women are responsible for the unwilled arousal of the male member. As Radford Ruether writes, Augustine believes that:

the male penis . . . is the literal embodiment of that 'law in the members that wars against the law of the minds'. Augustine's horrified description of the male erection . . . usually brings embarrassed laughter . . .

But if the male erection was the essence of sin, woman, as its source, became peculiarly the cause, object and extension of it.

(Radford Ruether 1974: 162–3)

Radford Ruether emphasises the associative connection between a male body (whose emblem is an erect penis) out of control of the mind's will and the woman – the female principle – who is understood as inciting this lack of control. The connotations of woman are those of the body which must be resisted by man. Woman signifies not 'will' or 'mind' but that bodily domain which is opposed to 'man's' will.

Augustine muted the equation of godliness with perfect celibacy. Unlike ascetics such as Jerome, he did not disparage sexual intercourse in marriage. Nevertheless, he did believe that such intercourse should be free of sexual pleasure and only for the purposes of procreation (see Augustine 1988a: 400). As Peter Brown writes, couples should beget children with 'a certain, medically approved zest, as a duty to the earthly city'. And citing a stronger formulation: 'The Christian married couple must "descend with a certain sadness" to that particular task: for in the act of married intercourse itself, their very bodies spoke to them of Adam's fall' (Brown 1988: 426–7).

The biblical account of Eve as produced from Adam's rib was used in support of women's natural subservience to men. 'The first natural bond of human society', writes Augustine, 'is man and wife. Nor did God create these each by himself . . . He created the one out of the other.' There may be a 'friendly and true' union between husband and wife but the relationship is described as 'the one ruling, the other obeying' (Augustine 1988a: 399). Augustine merges this view with his dualist tendencies. He likens the subservience of women to men to the subservience of body to soul:

> The Apostle has made known to us certain three unions, Christ and the Church, husband and wife, spirit and flesh. Of these, the former consult for the good of the latter, the latter wait upon the former.
>
> (Augustine 1988b: 388)

And again: 'Your flesh is like your wife . . . Learn now to master what you will receive as a united whole' (Enarratio in Ps. 140 16.1825–6, cited by Brown 1988: 426). Women are devalued insofar as they represent the spectre of lust and an excessive sexuality, and are also considered naturally subservient to men.

Augustine takes disembodiedness (the essential state of the soul, also associated with reason) to signify closeness to God. At death, he suggested in *On Continence*, the animal body is replaced by a spiritual body:

> the flesh is said to lust against the spirit, when the soul with fleshly lust wrestles against the spirit . . . the flesh itself . . . on the departure of the soul dies . . . Then from that time the flesh will not lust after anything against the spirit . . . forasmuch as not only without any opposition, but also without any need of bodily aliment, it shall be for ever made subject unto the spirit, to be quickened by Christ.
>
> (Augustine 1988b: 386–78)

In cultivating his will, resisting lust and mastering the body man renders himself closer to God. Because the devalued body is equated with the feminine, and women with lust, women are associated with that which impedes proximity to God. What is interesting about these metaphorical associations between women, the body, and distance from God is Augustine's concurrent position: that women as rational creatures are equally made in God's image. In *On the Literal Interpretation of Genesis*, he points out that there is no male or female in the image of the Creator:

As women are not separated from this grace of renewal and this reformation of the image of God (even though their bodily sex might be a metaphor according to which the man alone is said to be the image and glory of God), so in the original condition of humanity, since the woman was a human being also, she certainly had her own mind, and a rational mind, according to which she, too, was made in the image of God.

(Augustine 1994: 251; III.22)

But this does not affect women's position as subordinate to men:

Suppose it was necessary in order to live together for one to command the other to obey . . . An order for maintaining this would not have been lacking if one were created first and the other later, especially if the second were created from the first, as was the woman.

(Augustine 1994: 252; IX.5)

Augustine establishes a hierarchy according to which woman is secondary to and subject to man's will, while both are subject to God's will. As souls, man and woman are equal in the eyes of God. But as bodies, man is made in the image of God in a sense in which woman is not. Women are considered physically tributary to man, made from his rib. As the being from which another being (woman) is derived, even man-as-body can still be said to be made in God's image, in a sense in which women cannot. Women and men are thus considered both equal and unequal. They are unequal in terms of the order of creation. They are unequal politically and socially. Augustine never questions woman's role of obedience to man. But they are equal in God's eyes as disembodied souls. God 'authorises' the earthly or worldly obedience of women to men, although in the 'City of God' women and men would be equal.

While Augustine emphasises women's equality to man, he considers the spirituality of both to involve a transcendence of the feminine principle, the flesh. In the case of men, 'godliness' amounts to a series of symbolic connotations of keeping one's distance from women, who represent lust, and loss of will over the body. But for women, this signifies the more problematic understanding that women must transcend the flesh they themselves symbolically represent. Godliness would involve women keeping distance from 'themselves'. In the most extreme form of this position, the godliness of women involves them in a 'becoming male' (Radford Ruether 1974: 161).[4]

Augustine's inconsistency on the subject of women is well known. To adopt the title of Børreson's study (1981), for Augustine women are both subordinate, and equivalent, to men. The issue for feminist theorists is one of interpretation. What methodologies are drawn upon in the interpretation of the well-known Augustinian inconsistencies?

CONTRADICTIONS IN AUGUSTINE'S ACCOUNT
OF WOMEN'S SUBORDINATION AND
EQUIVALENCE

Genevieve Lloyd's *The Man of Reason* is known as a text which traces the masculine connotations of rationality throughout the history of philosophy. Yet, I have suggested that many of the sections in *The Man of Reason* reveal something other than the masculine connotations of reason. Often, Lloyd's discussions reveal the typical ambivalence of those connotations in the work of many philosophers. A key example of this aspect of Lloyd's work is to be found in her discussion of Saint Augustine. Lloyd argues that Augustine tried to 'upgrade' female nature, in opposition to earlier accounts which saw women as a corruption of masculinity, a symbol of the fall. Lloyd takes him to be specifically opposing misogynist exegesis. Kari Børreson goes so far as to describe Augustine's exegesis (albeit in scare quotes) as 'feminist' (Børreson 1994: 144). For this reason, Augustine might seem an unexpected inclusion in *The Man of Reason*. He makes an appearance because his attempt to upgrade women's status is ambivalent. Although he sees woman as the spiritual equal of man, and therefore not irrational in nature, he also characterises women as subordinate to men. He does see woman as inferior in terms of bodily difference, although not inferior in spiritual terms. And he associates women's bodily 'inferiority', and subordination to men, with a lesser form of reason (Lloyd 1984: 30). Thus, despite Augustine's overt defence of women in terms of spiritual equality and rationality, he contributes to the history of associations of masculinity with rationality and the exercise of will over a body symbolised as feminine.

On Lloyd's interpretation, a contradiction occurs in Augustine's work between what he actually wants to say about women (that they are man's spiritual equal) and the symbolic connotations with which women are associated. He demonstrates a greater vigilance than his predecessors in distinguishing the issue of woman's nature from the issue of their symbolic connotations. He reminds us that although women might represent, symbolically, lust and the dangers of the flesh, and the realm of everyday practical matters which distract the mind from spiritual contemplation,[5] nevertheless these symbolic connotations are a different issue from the question of women's actual capacities and nature. Women might represent everyday banality and the dangers of the flesh to men, yet we should not confuse this with their rational and spiritual nature, which is equal to man's. Nevertheless, Augustine does not simply distinguish women from the history of symbolic connotations with which they are associated. As we have seen, he also reinforces and compounds those associations. In Augustine's work, Lloyd points out, just as in his predecessors', are the very symbolic connotations in question.

146

Augustine replaced the older sexual symbolism in deference to spiritual equality, but structurally the situation is much the same as before. It is by resisting being dragged down into the will's entanglements with fornications of phantasy, still associated with woman, that the soul pursues the life of Reason and virtue. Woman remains associated with bodily perturbation, in opposition to Reason. And her 'natural' subordination to man represents rational control, the subjection of flesh to spirit in the right ordering of things.

(Lloyd 1984: 33)

The result, argues Lloyd, is a contradictory tension in Augustine's work between his description of women's capacities and the symbolic role attributed to women:

Despite his good intentions, his own symbolism pulls against his explicit doctrine of sexual equality with respect to the possession of Reason.

(Lloyd 1984: 31)

How should we interpret Augustine's ambivalence regarding women's rationality? For Lloyd, the ambivalence serves a kind of 'nevertheless' function. Despite Augustine's apparent good intentions, nevertheless he does reinforce associations between femininity, irrationality and that which must be transcended by spiritual reason in the contemplation of the divine. Even in the case of a philosopher of good intentions, who espouses sexual equality in matters of rationality and declares that 'the mind has no sex', nevertheless the symbolism of that same philosopher may undermine his intentions. The masculine connotations of reason may still be reinforced by the same philosopher. Kari Børreson also qualifies her interpretation of Augustine in feminist terms with a 'nevertheless'. Augustine's 'feminist' emendations to biblical exegesis, she writes, are seen in *On The Trinity*, where he argues that:

human nature as such, which includes both sexes . . . has been made in the image of God. Consequently, the first woman (*femina*) is not excluded from creational God-likeness. Nevertheless, Augustine's insertion of Paul's *mulier* through the stratagem of attributing to her a sexless intellect (*mens*), sharpens the conflict between rational God-likeness and inferior femaleness . . . Women are not God-like *qua* females.

(Børreson 1994: 145)

Børreson and Lloyd see Augustine as effectively both 'feminist' and 'anti-feminist'. Interpreting the contradictory tensions, they deploy a neutralising interpretative strategy of the 'nevertheless'. The 'nevertheless' serves to suggest that the one conflicting tension reduces or counteracts

147

the other tension, leaving us one (mitigated) position. Augustine has some pro-feminist tendencies. His association of femininity with inferiority lessens the strength of those tendencies. Børreson isolates one tendency in Augustine as the 'real' import of his philosophy: at bottom, Augustine shows himself to be anti-feminist. This is a position also taken by Mary Daly (Daly 1975: 85) and many other commentators.

However, other feminist theorists have taken alternative positions. While acknowledging that Augustine consolidates the subjugation of women to men, Elshtain considers that 'taken all in all, [he] is one of the great undoers of Greek misogyny which dictated a separate and inferior female nature' (1981: 71, 73). To take Augustine 'all in all' is to measure all factors together and arrive at a final position: in this case, the undoing of misogyny. The contradictory tensions are neutralised by the critic, synthesised into a definitive position.

Mary Daly discusses the history of the church fathers as a 'record of contradictions' in which Augustine plays his part. 'Most observable', she writes, 'is the conflict between Christian teachings on the worth of every human person and the oppressive, misogynistic ideas . . . Intimately bound up with this dialectic there is another tension, between a pseudo-glorification of "woman" and degrading teachings and practices concerning real women' (Daly 1975: 74). For example, Daly cites Augustine as an example of ambivalent discourse on women. 'Eve', she writes, 'was balanced off by Mary . . . Augustine wrote that woman is honored in Mary. He claimed that since man (*homo*) fell through the female sex, he was restored by the female sex' (Daly 1975: 88).

Like Elshtain, Daly takes an 'all in all' approach. 'The symbolic glorification of "woman" arose as a substitute for recognition of full personhood and equal rights' (Daly 1975: 74). In this interpretation, Daly supposes that there is a hidden agenda to the contradictory tension. The hidden agenda is the misogynist attitude towards women. Daly sifts out the apparently contradictory tension – the elevation of Mary and virginal women – and argues that this contradictory refrain serves a blinding function. Whereas Elshtain synthesises the tensions to arrive at one, modified overall position, Daly supposes that the one contradictory tension conceals another, 'real position': 'The sort of polemic . . . which attempts to cover the antifeminism of the Fathers by pointing to their glorification of Mary ignores the important point that this did not improve their doctrine about concrete, living women' (Daly 1975: 88).

If one approach is to 'neutralise' the contradiction, by establishing one of the contradictory tensions as the real meaning (or synthesising the tensions into a modified, 'all in all' position), the other most typical approach to the interpretation of Augustine's contradictory tensions is an approach we have seen repeatedly in feminist commentary on Rousseau: the causal explanatory approach. Critics have found a range of devices to explain Augustine's inconsistencies. For some, Augustine has 'good intentions' towards sexuality and women, but these are mitigated by the cultural or intellectual influences on his work. Daly suggests that it is the 'cultural conditioning' of the period which might have led to an obscuring or contradiction of the basic doctrine of equality of humans before God (Daly 1975: 74). Tavard and Clark suggest that it is the reaction against the asceticism of his forebears and his day which leads an Augustine suspicious of lust, women and sexuality nevertheless to reject the ascetic position on these matters, and in particular on marriage (see Tavard 1973: 102; Clark 1986b: 40). Here, tension occurs between Augustine's asceticism and a more extreme asceticism of the period which he wished to resist. Power also explains tensions in Augustine's philosophy in terms of his cultural and intellectual milieu. However, these are tensions which pertain to asceticism per se. Augustine's work, he suggests, is riven by the fundamental tensions between the 'fragility of his chastity' and 'a philosophical and ascetical milieu that perceived sexual love as perilous'. What to make of Augustine's simultaneous belief that 'sexuality was fundamentally God-given', his view that duly controlled desire 'might' have been present in paradise? Again, Power takes the explanatory angle: 'perhaps we have his concubine to thank for this concession' (Power 1992: 60–1).

Some have attempted to explain Augustine's contradictions in terms of contradictory intellectual influences in his work. Alexander offers the same analysis as Lloyd and others about the synthesis of Platonic and Christian traditions and the relation of this synthesis to the 'gender tensions' in his work. However, for Alexander the synthesis serves as sufficient explanation of those gender tensions: 'Augustine's interpretation of sexuality was an attempt to satisfy both the biblical doctrine of creation and Platonic philosophy', he agrees (Alexander 1974: 207). Tensions arise because of Augustine's 'synthesizing of the Platonic evaluation of sex and the Hebrew-Christian view of man's sin and fall. The effect was to give woman a soul and the philosophical reason of man a body but to make them pay for it' (Alexander 1974: 197).

Others explain contradictions in Augustine's work as arising from the development of his ideas and evolution of his position over his career, as in essays by Elizabeth Clark on Augustine in *Ascetic Piety* (1986b). Others still take a psychologistic explanatory approach. For example, in Karen Armstrong's words, 'we all have neuroses and emotional complexes which often contradict our rational beliefs and make us act destructively and in opposition to our ideals' (Armstrong 1986: 19). For Armstrong, Augustine is one of a group of church fathers who were 'neurotic and highly emotional men', 'unable to come to terms peacefully with their sexual lives prior to conversion' (Armstrong 1986: 30). Armstrong claims that the contradictory psychological tensions concerning women and concerning sexual relations with women are manifest in a series of thinkers of whom Augustine is just one example:

> The Christian attitude to sex and the body has been plagued by a process of double-think . . .
>
> Theologians have often defended the dogma of the holiness of married sexuality, but then, in an off-guard moment, have shown that emotionally they feel that sex is evil and abhorrent. Thus Augustine said that marriage was a Sacrament, because it was a symbol used by St Paul to express Christ's love of the Church. However, Augustine also said: 'We ought not to condemn wedlock because of the evil of lust, but nor must we praise lust because of the good of wedlock.' It is an uneasy conundrum which shows the depth of his confusion.
>
> (Armstrong 1986: 24)

The psychologistic approach is not uncommon, and ranges from speculations concerning Augustine's possible separation anxiety (Kirkman and Grieve 1986: 64) to Daly's speculations that the elevated woman compensated for the vilified woman and may have 'unconsciously served as a means to relieve any possible guilt feelings about injustice to the other sex' (Daly 1975: 88). Critics speculate about the specificities of Augustine's individual psyche, often with reference to his strained, guilty and intense relationship with his mother Monica. Sometimes the conclusion is simply that Augustine's position is 'confused'. For Fredrikson, Augustine's views on sexuality are just confused, and ignorant (Fredrikson 1988: 88).

Either the conclusion that Augustine's contradictions can be explained, or the conclusion that he is simply a 'confused' thinker ensures that the interpreter goes no further in the exploration of the contradictory tensions. Interpretation halts, because the issue is to find possible causes for the tensions (to look behind them, as it were) rather than focussing directly on them. Another approach halts with the identification of the tensions, as in Børreson's conclusion to *Subordination and Equivalence*. Børreson presents Augustine's contradictory tensions related to women and sexuality with meticulous attention. However, offering an exposition of Augustine's position is said to constitute 'a critique in itself' (Børreson 1981: 339). Børreson takes herself to have exposed how Augustine's discussion occurs from a masculine standpoint: 'All this teaching about the nature and function of woman is worked out exclusively from man's point of view. Its foundation rests on the identifying of man with the human being. The *vir*, man, is the exemplary human being, and woman is defined as differing from this norm' (Børreson 1981: 329). Here, Børreson concludes with a banal feminist device: exposition and indictment of sex bias.

Contradictory tensions may well constitute critique in themselves. But the issue for feminist analysis is how to direct critical attention directly and analytically at those contradictory tensions, rather than simply pointing them out or looking 'behind' them. In this regard, some comments by three feminist critics will be of particular interest.

INTERPRETING THE CONTRADICTIONS

Elizabeth Clark writes that there has been a 'dual evaluation of woman by the church fathers as the "devil's gateway" and the "bride of Christ." The fathers' alternate condemnation and exaltation of the female sex is both striking and baffling.' As she continues, 'Their extreme ambivalence on the topic of womanhood has led some commentators to assert that women made progress in the early Christian centuries, and others, looking at different evidence, to conclude that they regressed. In this instance, both sides are right' (Clark 1986b: 24–5). Clark describes the contradictory tension as baffling, a refrain we have seen in many feminist commentators on the history of philosophy, such as Mary Daly: 'A study of Christianity's documents concerning women reveals a puzzling ambiguity if not an outright contradiction' (Daly 1975: 74). It is time to cease being puzzled and baffled, time to analyse less naively the contradictory tensions, ambivalences and inconsistencies encountered repeatedly.

Still, Clark does not try to synthesise contradictory positions so as to arrive at a definitive, stable, 'all in all' position. Augustine's account of woman is comprehensible – is read by Clark – as both progressive and regressive. Clark does not try to stabilise Augustine into either the one or the other position. Two further responses also read the contradictory tensions as operating in tandem. Joan Cocks suggests that the lesson of the *Confessions* may be 'a lesson in reversals . . . a great hatred of bodily pleasure can veil a great love of it'. While this lesson leans towards the intimation, resonant of psychologistic interpretation, that Augustine's true feelings can be distinguished against a duplicitous veil, Cocks adds a second suggestion: 'a lesson in disjunctures . . . a substantive repudiation of the sensuously concrete can go hand in hand with a stylistic embrace of it' (Cocks 1991: 145).

Radford Ruether is unsurprised by the combination of misogyny with high praise for women, and she does not try to stabilise the combination into one view which is more 'characteristic' than the other. Instead, she suggests that the contradictory stances operate in tandem: 'Ambivalence between misogynism and the praise of the virginal woman is not accidental . . . Both stand together as two sides of a dualistic psychology' (Radford Ruether 1974: 150). Where a woman is praised as 'virgin', Radford Ruether argues that she is praised as 'non-feminine'. The validation of virgins is consistent with the devaluation of femininity because virgins are validated as non-feminine. Women are devalued insofar as they signify embodiment and sexuality. Virginity is effectively a transcendence of the feminine (Radford Ruether 1974: 164).

In some ways, Radford Ruether acknowledges the contradiction so as to leave it standing. But she also attempts to resolve it, demonstrating how the two opposing attitudes towards women are more consistent than first appears.

> Virginal woman was thus bound for heaven, and her male ascetic devotees would stop at nothing short of this prize for her. But they paid the price of despising all real physical women, sex and fecundity, and wholly etherealizing women into incorporeal phantasms in order to provide love objects for the sublimated libido and guard against turning back to any physical expression of love with the dangerous daughters of Eve.
>
> (Radford Ruether 1974: 179)

The methodologies drawn upon by Radford Ruether proliferate in her analysis. Sometimes, she simply indicts the androcentric perspective presupposed by Augustine. At one point, she suggests that we might interpret his ambivalent account of women as a half-success. At least, as desexualised virgins, women had achieved a representation in terms of 'transcendence and spiritual personhood'. Perhaps, she suggests, we should not discard this achievement, although it should be gained 'not against the body, but in and through the body' (Radford Ruether 1974: 179).

The explanatory approach is also evident in her work. Like Lloyd, she discusses the contradictions which arise from the interconnection of Greek philosophical, and biblical traditions. Where femaleness represents the corporeal aspect of humanity, women are seen as subservient to men, yet we are told that Eve also has a rational nature. She describes this contradiction as 'inexplicable' (Radford Ruether 1974: 156). In fact, her methodological approach is oriented towards attempting to explain the puzzle. It is the 'assimilation of male–female dualism into soul–body dualism' which 'conditions' the definition of woman (Radford Ruether 1974: 158). The split between soul-reason and embodiment, combined with its symbolic gender connotations, causes the contradiction whereby femininity represents embodiment although women are seen as equally rational. According to a dualist approach, sexed embodiment cannot significantly alter one's rational capacities. In the context of the dualist framework, women will inevitably be, in Børreson's words, both subordinate and equivalent. Inevitably, we shall be told that women are equal to men in the eyes of God. Yet, as Radford Ruether writes, because of the assimilation of male–female dualism with soul–body dualism, 'woman is not really seen as a self-sufficient, whole person with equal honor, as the image of God in her own right, but is seen, ethically, as dangerous to the male' (Radford Ruether 1974: 156–7).

In sum, Radford Ruether focuses on Augustine's inconsistencies and instabilities. At times, these are said to be 'inexplicable' or 'unjustified'. At times, as we have seen, it is the gendered soul–body dualism which is taken to explain the inconsistencies:

> This assimilation of woman into bodiliness allows Augustine to explain why woman's subjugation is 'natural' within the order of creation, but it makes for some contradiction when it comes time to defend woman's redeemability and her ability, like that of the man, to . . . return to the monistic incorporeal nature.
>
> (Radford Ruether 1974: 158)

She also offers a psychologistic explanation of the interconnection of the 'anti-sex' tenor and the obsession with matters sexual: 'Modern Freudian psychology can well explain why such a mechanism of repression was bound to be self-defeating and always to produce its own opposite in obsession with sexual fantasies' (Radford Ruether 1974: 167).

And at times, rather than trying to explain the inconsistency, Radford Ruether focuses instead on how Augustine himself tried to explain it: 'Augustine attempts to explain this contradiction by distinguishing between what woman is, as a rational spirit (in which she is equivalent to the male), and what she "symbolizes" in her bodily nature' (Radford Ruether 1974: 158). Lastly, Radford Ruether also focuses on what Augustine's divided definition enables rather than attempting to explain it. That said, this analysis is particularly unsatisfying in its tautological structure. A divided definition of women, she claims, allows 'the Fathers to slide somewhat inconsistently' between the different definitions. The inconsistency enables inconsistency.

Radford Ruether moves between many different methodological approaches to interpreting contradiction. She is right that the contradictory tensions in Augustine's work are open to interpretation in many of the ways suggested. Still, we might resist elements in her approach which neutralise the contradictory tensions by analysing them as consistent, and the elements which would identify one aspect of Augustine's approach to women as positive, and try to build on to that base for feminist purposes. In particular, Radford Ruether would suppose here that the positive aspect of Augustine's approach (the element which sees woman as made in the image of God) does not interconnect crucially with the element which conceptually severs female embodiment from that image. Radford Ruether has rightly shown how these dual representations of women do operate in tandem. The suggestion that we approach the duality by focusing, nevertheless, on the positive aspects of these representations supposes that women might be valued in terms of rational disembodiment, while feminism builds on to this base a valuation of women in terms of feminine embodiment. Yet much in Radford Ruether's interpretation suggests precisely the opposite. The valuation of women as equally made in the image of God occurs precisely *as* a devaluation of materiality, which is gendered feminine. The one element cannot be separated from the other.

Instead, I shall argue that we should interpret these strains in Augustine's work as crucially interconnected. Instead of attempting to explain the contradictory tensions, the focus should be kept on considering what they enable in the Augustinian figuring of women and femininity. This keeps our interpretative focus on the reasons why the positive and negative interpretations of women cannot be separated. Last, I shall suggest that the focus should not only be on the incoherence of the devalued status of women, but also on the incoherence of the terms on which man occupies a superior position to woman. From a feminist perspective, an analysis of the contradictory tensions in the relation 'man/ God' is as important as an analysis of the relation 'man/woman' because of the interconnection between these relations.

In the remainder of this chapter, I consider the account of man and woman which is found in passages of Augustine's *Confessions*. Both Augustine and Rousseau, to recall the argument of the previous chapter, serve as case-studies of the ways in which hierarchical man/woman oppositions are legitimated by the projection of 'external' (transcendent or divine) entities and by operative contradiction. Augustine, like Rousseau, presents woman as subject to man. For both philosophers it is the projection of a transcendental entity – either nature or God – which legitimates their subordination of women. However, unlike Rousseau, Augustine also proposes that woman's mind and rational intelligence render her the equal of man. Interestingly, as we have seen, this second account is also legitimated by God, for it is in the eyes of God that woman is the equal of man. An operative contradiction enables the subordination of women by reference to God. I shall therefore consider textual contradictions relating to whether man is presented as 'like' or as 'not like' God, and contradictions pertaining to the simultaneous equality and inequality of woman which interconnect with that account.

AUGUSTINE'S *CONFESSIONS*

How does Augustine understand the relationship between man and God? Unlike philosophers who have wanted to suggest some kind of affinity or interconnectedness,[6] Augustine emphasises that God should be understood as a negation of man's characteristics and attributes, as radically 'not-man'.[7] However, this position is complicated by the scriptural account of man as being 'made in God's image' (Augustine 1961: 114; VI.3).

Augustine's explanation is that this reference must be understood in a 'spiritual' rather than a literal sense. The Bible is often contrary or illogical, and frequently needs to be understood as having this kind of double meaning. Simplistic terms are often used to render biblical meaning comprehensible to the layman as well as to the scholar sensitive to theological subtleties (Augustine 1961: 108, 289, 304; V.14, XII.12, 27). However, despite this explanation, an emphasis on man as aligned with rather than radically different from God often reemerges in Augustine's account.

This is particularly apparent in his account of the hierarchical relation between man, woman, nature and animals. While both men and women are subordinate to God, woman is further subordinate to man. Woman is said to have the weaker body (Augustine 1961: 186; XI.4); she is described as 'mere' woman (Augustine 1961: 191; IX.7), as having been made for man and as being physically subject to him, 'in the same way as our natural impulses need to be subjected to the reasoning power of the mind' (Augustine 1961: 344; XIII.32). A metaphorical connection is established by Augustine between the superiority of reason over the other faculties, and the superiority of men over women. As such, women are metaphorically aligned with those lesser creatures, animals, who are further from God than man because they lack rationality.

> the animals . . . are not guided by reason, which can sift the information relayed to them by their senses. Man, on the other hand, can question nature. He is able to catch sight of God's invisible nature through his creatures.
>
> (Augustine 1961: 213; X.6)

It is the likeness of man to God which legitimates the hierarchy according to which man rules over irrational creatures:

> We see man, made in your image and likeness, ruling over all the irrational animals for the very reason that he was made in your image and resembles you, that is, because he has the power of reason and understanding.
>
> (Augustine 1961: 344)

Reason is valued because it renders the possessor most like God and allows man to read the world as God's material scripture. When Augustine posits man as superior to woman because he is more closely aligned with reason, this superiority of reason and man's superior position are dependent on the positioning of God as akin to man by virtue of reason.[8] In explaining the superiority of the man of reason, Augustine is reliant on the image of a God to whom this man is close, in whose image he has been made. Rather than explaining away the reference to man being made in God's image, he now relies on it.

155

While Augustine presents man and God as radically opposed, he also presents them as aligned in opposition to creatures affiliated with unreason and nature. Now God forms with man a kind of continuum along which God is 'even more' than man, rather than being 'not-man':

And I know that my soul is the better part of me, because it animates the whole of my body. It gives it life, and this is something that no body can give to another body. But God is even more. He is the Life of the life of my soul.

(Augustine 1961: 213; X.6)

Sustaining the positions of God and man involves a contradiction on Augustine's part. Man is valued insofar as he is like God, but God is identified insofar he is not like man.[9] A kind of double move sustains the value of reason and the identity of man. Man owes his worldly primacy to his identification with the divine, and so that identification is asserted. Yet the divine, on which man's identity is parasitic, owes its identity to its difference from man, and so the association between God and man is also rejected. God is represented doubly: both in alignment with man in opposition to woman, the animals and nature, and also in opposition to man as 'not' everything that man is.

Since God's relation to man is dual and self-contradictory, man's identity is similarly structured. God guarantees man's position as the privileged man of reason, ruling over all the irrational creatures because of that power of understanding by virtue of which he is made in God's image. Nevertheless in relation to God, man is also humble, submissive, lowly, weak, a child, despised, mere dust and ashes. Here is Augustine speaking of his relationship, as a man, to God:

I do your bidding in word and deed alike. I do it beneath the protection of your wings, for the peril would be too great if it were not that my soul has submitted to you and sought the shelter of your wings and that my weakness is known to you. I am no more than a child . . . in your sight, I despise myself and consider myself as mere dust and ashes.

(Augustine 1961: 210–11; X.4, 5)

Not only is man devalued, and cast in a lowly position in relation to God, but he is also 'mere dust and ashes'. He is considered a kind of human *clay*. Since it is God who provides his animation, man is identified not with reason but with materiality. Man is both like God, as privileged reason, and 'not like God', as devalued matter.

While identities are revolving about, it may seem that at least woman is the one constant, fixed point: more devalued, and aligned, metaphorically, with the animals over which man also rules. Is woman not firmly positioned on the lowest rung of the divinely ordered ladder? Just as there are divided representations of God's relation to man, and of man's identity in relation to God, there are also divided representations of women. While woman is represented as subordinate to man, she is also represented as equivalent to man:

> In her mind and her rational intelligence she has a nature the equal of man's.
>
> (Augustine 1961: 344; XIII.32)

> For you created man male and female, but in your spiritual grace they are as one. Your grace no more discriminates between them according to their sex than it draws distinction between Jew and Greek or slave and freeman.
>
> (Augustine 1961: 333; XIII.23)

Where Augustine casts woman as irrational, her position as inferior is rendered with reference to God. God legitimates the standard by which man is superior by virtue of being more aligned with the rational faculty that allows humans to approach God. Yet it is also with reference to God that men and women are equal. It is God who does not discriminate 'according to their sex'.

In sum, dual and a self-contradictory identities are attributed to God, man and woman. God is both 'like man' and 'not like man'; man is identified with reason (and valued) in opposition to materiality, and yet he is also identified with materiality (and devalued) in opposition to God; and woman is both subject to man as a natural impulse is subject to reason, and equal to man since she is equal in reason.

ENABLING CONTRADICTIONS

The first section of this chapter reviewed feminist analyses of Augustine. I focused in particular on methodologies deployed in the interpretation of Augustine's contradictions. Feminist focus tended to be directed on the divided account of woman as subordinate and equal to man. I am suggesting that this account should be interpreted insofar as it interconnects with divided accounts which Augustine offers of man, and of the man–God relation. Further, I wish to suggest that these self-contradictions can be understood as necessary, and not incidental to the identity of each. I have already suggested that God must be both 'like man' and 'not-man'. God's identity is established via his position as 'not-man', an identity with which man at the same time identifies in his own capacity as 'like God'. Inevitably, man is both aligned with the feminine and opposed to the feminine. Man is identified with the material (dust and ashes, the mere mortal), while he is also aligned with the immaterial (with reason, and its transcendence of materiality).

Where God is identified as 'not-man', man gives this content by being rendered the equivalent of the feminine, and the dichotomy between man and woman must be forsaken. In other words, where we are told that God is 'not-*man*', we are told that God is not-material, not-embodied, not-emotional, not-passionate, not-feeble. It is necessary (if paradoxical) for man to be the equivalent of the feminine in order to be masculine. It is as feminine that man negatively gives God the identity he identifies with as masculine.

The concept of God both ensures man's identity as masculine and renders him the equivalent of the feminine. God therefore both ensures and undermines the basis for man's superiority over woman. While ensuring the subordination of woman as feminine, God yet renders her equal as the equivalent of the masculine. Augustine associates man with mind, and woman with body or nature. Mind is valued over body or nature because it allows one to approach God through the reading of his message. Yet the legitimation provided by God involves a contortion. By that standard, Augustine invokes the primacy of mind over body. Yet in so doing, he is led into an account of the subordination of body to reason: mere bodily difference does not affect the quality of the mind 'within'. Augustine considers that the difference between man and woman is merely a difference of alternate body shells.

This is why Augustine must tell us, paradoxically, that woman is inferior 'by body', and yet also that her bodily difference cannot render her inferior and that the male and female are 'created as one'. It is via the claim that man and woman are 'created as one' in terms of their reason that reason gains its position as the trait significant where body is not. Only through having so used woman to help establish the primacy of reason will Augustine disassociate woman from it. Woman has been included with man as 'reason' to be devalued in opposition to him as 'not-reason'.

The 'man of reason' has always been acknowledged to be a bodily, material man, insofar as the soul or reasoning mind is located in a mortal body. However, the fact of embodiment is seen as extrinsic to man's crucial reasoning faculty, and so does not destabilise the identity of the man of reason. I have suggested that Augustine's man of reason is not accidentally but necessarily represented as material man, his irrational woman not accidentally but necessarily represented as rational, and his 'unlike man' God not accidentally but necessarily represented as 'like man'. These dual, paradoxical identities are not accidental, but are functional and operative in enabling the identity of the man of reason.

We might rethink our understanding of the relationship between the representation of the 'man of reason' and anomalies whereby man is considered to be material and feminine. Via the structure discussed here, it is *only* by *not* being the man of reason (for example, by being positioned as material and equivalent to the feminine in relation to God, and by conceding that woman's rational intelligence makes her equal to man) that man is established as the man of reason. It is not 'despite' but *because* of the dual and self-contradictory identities of God, man and woman that the identity of the 'man of reason' is established.

Attempts to describe the man/woman opposition in isolation from this complicated structure of interrelated identities are misleading. Justice needs to be done to the complexity of these interdependent terms. For example, how might we represent God's role in relation to the man/woman opposition? I have suggested that God needs to be represented doubly: both in opposition to the masculine side, and in alignment with it. However, doing justice to this complexity informs our understanding of man/woman dichotomies and sexed oppositions such as mind/body and reason/emotion. The difficulties involved in our 'pinning down' God relate to the fact that neither man nor woman is any the easier to pin down. None of these terms are discrete, separate or fixed: they are constitutively confused. Indeed, their representation as aligned, fixed and rigid binary oppositions is inappropriate. The masculine side, rather than pertaining to man while the feminine side pertains to woman, has to incorporate the feminine. Woman must sometimes be aligned with the masculine, while also being aligned with the feminine.

This is a series of relations which the representation in terms of polarised binary dichotomies 'misses', or elides. What is effaced is the degree of slippage of terms necessary to the effect of binary dichotomies. For example, man is aligned with reason in opposition to body only if both woman and man also represent both mind and body. If we discuss only the history of stable binary dichotomies (man = reason; woman = body), we suppress the degree of terminological slippage constituting that history. In Augustine's text, the non-coincidence of man and masculinity is operative. It allows a *slippage between* 'man' and 'masculinity', via which the identities of man and God, and the devaluation of the feminine, are rendered.

In the *Confessions*, Augustine does not discuss a distinction between man and masculinity. Nevertheless, there is in this text a difference between 'man' and what 'man' is identified with which is crucial to the identity of 'man'. On the basis of the self-contradictions of God, woman and man, how is it that the identity of the man of reason is effectively produced? The implicit distinction, or difference, between man and masculinity (that with which man is identified) is crucial in this regard. In general, masculinity is a most facilitating and flexible concept because of the slippage by which it defines man *by not coinciding with*, indeed by being different from, the term 'man'. This distinction enables man to be accounted for as *in excess of that with which he is identified*. We have seen that man must share the attributes associated with the feminine

159

– emotions, passions, the embodied – if the divine is to be the ideal point on which man's masculinity is parasitic. It is the man/masculine distinction which is able to account for, or encapsulate, the fact that man must be 'contaminated' by the feminine to be distinguished from it.

This distinction divides off and displaces on to the feminine whatever of man exceeds that with which man is identified. Accordingly, where the relationship between 'man' and the masculine is shifting and flexible, the feminine also has an extreme flexibility. Masculinity, man's identity, or that with which man is identified, defines man by being different from man, deferring that identity. Where man does not coincide with that with which he is identified, his identity is a receding, vanishing point. Masculine identity is 'evanescent'.

To follow this recession, let us start by examining the mind/body opposition which is usually, and simply, represented as aligned with the man/woman opposition. The problem with the simple binary representation is that it does not adequately describe the way in which, where man is aligned with mind, mind/body is a division of, or split between, masculine and feminine *within* the term 'man'. Here, it is as body that man exceeds the masculine and so body is displaced on to the feminine. However, it would also be incorrect to represent mind as the fixed term identifying man. For example, Augustine describes mind as infiltrated by its bodily housing, filled with passions, desires, everyday matters and incorrect thoughts; a muddled storehouse of images is delivered to the mind, or to the memory by the senses (Augustine 1961: 220, 214, 238; X.14, 8, 33). Materiality reoccupies that mind with which man is identified. At the 'point' of mind, man also exceeds rather than coinciding with that with which he is identified. The kernel of man recedes yet a little further. What is essential to man recedes to a moment of 'undistracted' reason that can be extracted out of, and which sorts through, the everyday mental morass. But man's reasoning mind joins body on the side of material discarded in relation to the soul, which survives beyond the earthly confines of the body and so achieves a greater disembodiment than reason.[10] So the ideal point with which man is identified moves towards the divine, involving a progressive displacement on to the feminine of that which pertains to man but falls short of this ideal point. Indeed, there is a point in Augustine's text where in relation to the soul, the feminine has become a category inclusive of mind and reason.

In relation to the soul, mind, inclusive of reason and inferior mental content, is part of man's materiality, abandoned at death. Yet not even the soul guarantees man's coincidence with the point of God which it approaches. Man must always fall short of God, and this is how Augustine specifically accounts for the relationship. As the soul we shall dwell in God's heaven of heavens – but never *entirely* coincide with God (Augustine 1961: 286–8; XII.9–11).

Since Augustine associates women with nature and materiality, we may say that the material excess, by which man is constantly exceeding the masculine point which identifies him, is feminised. This material excess is the extent to which man does not coincide with God. Yet within Augustine's terms it is impossible that man should coincide with God, for the necessary difference between man and God (upon which God's identity is based, upon which man is parasitic) would then be lost. But, in effect, this means that the point of pure masculinity, which defines man and by which the feminine as 'not-man' is devalued, must be positioned as a point inaccessible to man. Despite the fact that God has been defined as 'not-man', man is only truly masculine insofar as he approximates God. So for all that God is 'not-man', paradoxically it is God who is positioned as the ideal point with which man is identified. So the recession, while rendering an illusion of masculine identity as mind, or reason, does so by moving towards a point never arrived at. All that is progressively isolated from man and devalued as 'not-man' is displaced on to the feminine. Man is defined by a term he nevertheless is not, and is never at one with, defined by a term which is but a shifting recession to a point it never coincides with. So the feminine, being the extent to which man falls short of God, is thereby a term flexible enough to include *all that we typically define as masculine*: reason, mind, man.

In summary, discussing the self-contradictory identities of God, man and woman, I asked how they act to produce an identity that has been termed the 'man of reason'. I have made the following suggestions:

First, man and man's identity must be dislodged so that man does not coincide with that with which he is identified. This allows man to be identified with a shifting 'vanishing point'. In this receding movement, the feminine is a devalued category in relation to man, who himself also always falls short of the identity which the feminine is devalued for not being.

Second, Augustine is only able to value the privileged masculine term in each shift, and devalue all that the privileged term is opposed to, because of the illusion of and identification with a point not attainable. To sustain the effect of man's identity, there must be the positioning of a divine point which is nevertheless incoherent as the ultimate point of man's identity.

Third, there must be a field of feminised materiality, which, far from coinciding with the term 'woman', must be a term elastic enough to encompass every aspect of man displaced in the recession to his illusory, ideal identity. In this sense, we can say that enveloped within the conceptual field of the feminine-material will be body, of course, but also mind and even, at a certain point, reason.

I have considered slippages between man and man's identity in Augustine's *Confessions*. I have suggested that there is a movement of

161

deferral at work in the production of a theological account of man's identity. A deferring slippage produces the effect of man's identity and the hierarchy between man and woman. This structure depends not so much on the projection of an ideal, supernatural personage, 'God', but rather on the deferral of masculinity towards a transcendent ideal that it both must and must not be identifiable with. As part of such a structure, man and that with which man is identified are interdependent but blurred and chimerical. Man's identity defines man without coinciding with him, while receding from him.

Reason, or whatever man is identified with and valued in terms of, is never intrinsically valuable – it always relies on a legitimating prop. The hierarchy of man/woman oppositions must always be supported. Even if it is not in terms of the reading of God's message, such hierarchies often rely upon and are legitimated by the projection of some kind of transcendent point, entity, voice, field or ideal. The primacy of man and reason defers towards the realm of logos, nature or the realm of truth. The man/woman hierarchy relies on the pursuit of and recession towards some transcendent point which the masculine both does not coincide with and yet is identified with.

It is the very non-coincidence of man with his ideal identity which enables the effect of man seeming to coincide with that identity. Since it is via the dislodgement of man and his identity that the illusion of their coincidence is rendered, we can say that the terms are separate, yet not separable, interconnected, but not at one. It is because man's ideal identity is dislodged from, is different from man, and yet is not separable from man, that man is associated with an illusory ideal which he does not arrive at, at the expense of women.

AUGUSTINE AND FEMINISM

Feminist theorists have offered a host of reasons for the critique of 'fathers of the church' such as Augustine. It is argued that 'old prejudices die hard', and that their influence is unconsciously reproduced, even in a post-Christian era. The Christian view on women, argues Armstrong, 'still continues to affect us at a deep level', and for this reason she emphasises the importance of continued critical analysis of the traditions grounding that view (Armstrong 1986: xi–ix). Judith Plaskow and Carol Christ agree: 'If religion, myth and symbol have outlived their usefulness, then one should be no more than irritated at the quaint archaism of traditional religious sexism. But, once one recognizes the importance of religion, then an enormous sense of injustice must follow the discovery that religions are sexist and that they continue to exert a powerful influence on society' (Christ and Plaskow 1979: 3). Similarly, Mary Daly claims that 'the Judeo-Christian tradition has served to legitimate sexually imbalanced patriarchal society' (Daly 1979: 54).

Feminist critics suggest that canonical thinkers continue to exert an influence on contemporary ideas about women and femininity, and that sustained critique of the history of philosophy continues to be valuable for this reason. From this perspective, the political stakes involved in re-reading the views of Rousseau and Augustine are much the same. For example, introducing *Woman and the History of Philosophy*, Nancy Tuana comments on the way in which Rousseau's texts continue to alienate women (Tuana 1992: 4). Tuana explains the continued need for feminist critique of canonical philosophers: 'the gender system in their writings reveals a pattern of depreciation of woman and the feminine that is still prevalent in much of contemporary Western philosophy' (Tuana 1992: 8). The reasons why Tuana thinks we should sustain feminist critique of Rousseau are the same as those cited by Plaskow, Christ, Daly and Armstrong for why we should sustain feminist critique of a figure such as Saint Augustine.

But, in another sense, the political stakes of interpreting Augustine are different from those of interpreting Rousseau. Augustine is part of a Christian tradition which continues to oppress women, excluding them from reproductive rights and from certain roles within the church, and alienating women with a misogyny recognised as retrograde in most other spheres of contemporary Western culture. For example, Elaine Pagels criticises the extreme influence that Augustine's treatment of original sin has had on Christian attitudes towards sexuality and femininity: 'Adam, Eve and the serpent . . . continue, often in some version of its Augustinian form, to affect our lives to the present day' (Pagels 1988: 150). The issue, she claims, is to try to reassess and qualify Augustine's singular dominance in much of Western Christian history (Pagels 1988: 153). Many feminist theorists involved in critique of sex bias in the history of philosophy of religion are also trying to renegotiate concepts of divinity. Destabilising Augustine's biblical exegesis is likely to have religious significance for such critics.

Feminist critiques of the history of philosophy of religion have involved every approach already seen in this work, from a simple critique of sex bias to arguments for the eradication of sex bias.[11] Eradicating sex bias can involve a series of strategies, including revalorising feminine figures in the Bible, or forgotten women in early Christian tradition. Arguing that women's history has been stolen from them, Schüssler Fiorenza might reconstruct 'the scant information we have about a leading woman in early Christianity' such as Phoebe of Cenchreae (Schüssler Fiorenza 1987: 35). Other feminists might revalorise 'feminine principles' in the Christian tradition (perhaps Christ's femininity, or early feminine connotations for Spirit, or maternal connotations for God).

Feminists resist the masculine-paternal imagery for divinity, in what Radford Ruether calls a 'feminist reconstruction of God/ess' (Radford Ruether 1989: 159). Elements in biblical history might be found which undermine dominant biblical interpretation, as when Phyllis Trible locates elements in Genesis which undermine the subordination of women to the masculine (Trible 1979: 74–5). Some argue that sex bias is so deeply entrenched that the Christian tradition must be abandoned in favour of attempts to revalorise early female-oriented deities or generate 'new feminist spiritual visions' (Christ and Plaskow 1979: 10).

Feminist interpretation which simply exposes sex bias, or which abandons the tradition, runs the risk of reinforcing the impression of a consistent, indomitable tradition of sex bias. For this reason, the feminist critic does better to expose the instability of sex bias in the history of philosophy of religion. For one thing, feminist critique needs to beware of reinforcing misogynist textual effects. Women have not been consistently excluded from the privileged relationship with the figure God which man seems to have occupied. The exclusion of women has been consistently inconsistent and ambivalent. Woman has been both subordinate and equal to man in the eyes of God. This does not mitigate the devaluation of women. Emphasising this ambivalence is not to argue that the subordination of women has only been moderate. It is to emphasise the necessary instability of the terms on which woman is excluded from godliness.

She is excluded on the basis of a feminine embodiedness. Women's equality in the eyes of God only occurs in terms of their becoming 'virile'. But what is it to become virile? I have argued that the virile is always already the feminine, for in relation to God the virile is rendered the equivalent of the feminine: dutiful, submissive, weak, childlike, mere dust and ashes (Augustine 1961: 210–11; X.4).

This should not be seen as simple 'confusion'. Feminists have often analysed Augustine's inconsistencies as the product of confused thinking. Should the subordination of women to men on Augustine's model be seen as the product of accidentally muddled ideas? Instead, I have suggested that feminists should focus on the conceptual impossibility with which man is sustained in a hierarchically elevated position, with a consistent identity, in relation to God, at the expense of women. Feminists have focused on the incoherence of women's subordination to man. But the conceptual basis of masculine dominance, and man's identity, is equally unstable. The instability is neither accidental nor a curious phenomenon to be explained. The instability is necessary to the very terms upon which women are devalued, men valued, and the identities of man and woman established.

A constant reference for the readings of the history of philosophy offered in this work has been Genevieve Lloyd's overt argument that reason has been associated with masculinity, and with a transcendence of the feminine. While this point is somewhat less signposted by Lloyd, women have been repeatedly associated *both* with reason *and* with the antithesis of reason (that which disrupts or impedes reason), frequently within the work of the same philosopher. If reason is understood as a transcendence of the feminine, then philosophers who attempt to present reason as 'sex-neutral' are bound to present internally contradictory arguments. The representation of women as rationally capable will inevitably present woman in terms of her own transcendence of the feminine. The connotations of woman as both 'equally reasonable' and 'that which is transcended in the pursuit of reason' are in that sense intertwined. Furthermore, we might recall that Simone de Beauvoir simultaneously aligns women with embodiment and with a transcendence of the body; she simultaneously rejects and reinforces dualism, and simultaneously argues that women are responsible, yet not responsible, for their oppression.[12] In the next chapter, I shall consider the intertwining of these tensions in her work. Again, I shall argue that such instabilities are neither accidental nor a curious phenomenon to be explained. If Augustine's instabilities are necessary to his phallocentrism, Beauvoir's instabilities are, I shall argue, necessary to her feminism.

I have suggested that 'double' and contradictory versions of woman have persisted throughout the history of philosophy. My interpretation has been guided by an emphasis on the operative role of contradiction. For example, I have suggested that we interpret the alignment of reason and masculinity as the effect of (rather than as undermined by) contradictory versions of woman as both irrational and rational.

First, the representation of reason as a higher faculty, rather than a bodily faculty, should be seen as *enabled* by the association of women with reason. That association reinforces the connotations of reason as a transcendence of the bodily. In other words, if women, occupying sexually different bodies, are represented as less capable of reason, then reason is seen as subservient to bodily difference. This is a logic we can locate both in Plato and Descartes, for example.[13]

Second, the masculine connotations of reason are produced in terms of the opposition to, and devaluation of, that which is associated with the feminine: the body, the emotions and the passions. This is another representation of woman which must be seen as enabling the identity of the 'man of reason', since the feminine acts as the other, or negative face of philosophy. Woman supports the identity of the man of reason insofar as she represents that which he transcends in the pursuit of reason.

Thus, we are confronted with the fact that contradictory representations of woman enable the identity of the 'man of reason'. Indeed, the combination of these contradictory accounts is not accidental, nor indeed 'incoherent', but interrelated with and essential to the identity of the 'man of reason'. The very same account of reason as a transcendence of the feminine is sustained both by representations of woman as reason and by representations of woman as the body, or unreason. The very argument that woman is 'reasonable' relies on the devaluation of the body in opposition to reason. In other words, it relies on a philosophical other which is represented by woman. Thus, it is *only* insofar as she also represents body that woman represents reason's transcendence of body. The former possibility is premised on the latter, although it is also undermined by it.

The point is not only that the representation of the man of reason tends to be accompanied by contradictory representations of women. Rather, these contradictory versions of women are the *condition* of an effect which we call the 'masculine connotations of reason'. The terms by which man is associated with reason involve *both* the alignment of the feminine with the passions and *also* the alignment of women with reason because of the argument that bodily difference is not relevant to rational capacities.

This argument is also implied in Michèle Le Dœuff's well-known discussion of philosophy's other-ing of women and the feminine in 'Long Hair, Short Ideas'. She interprets the historical devaluation of women's philosophical abilities by arguing that one of the conditions of the identity of philosophy is the role of woman as 'other'. She points out that when women have gained access to philosophy, they have only done so by occupying certain (very limited) roles, which seem to sustain simultaneously their role as the philosophical 'other'. Thus, women remain the philosophical other despite their entrance into the domain of philosophy (Le Dœuff 1989: 100–28).

An implicit concept of operative contradiction may be drawn from Le Dœuff's argument. The contradictory versions of women (as both 'equally capable of philosophy' and as 'philosophy's other') are not only possible within philosophy, but indeed sustain the identity of philosophy. It is not just 'woman' who (as Le Dœuff suggests) sustains philosophical identity, but specifically *contradictory* representations of woman which have this effect. The very domain of 'philosophy' which women enter is sustained by the projection of woman as philosophy's other. Thus, the representation of woman as *both* appropriate and inappropriate to the domain of philosophy is not a curious paradox dogging philosophy and those women attempting to enter the philosophical domain. It is a paradox essential to the generation of the identity of philosophy.

In suggesting in this chapter that the association of woman with rationality paradoxically enables a hierarchical relationship whereby man is associated with reason and woman with the physical and natural impulses, I have resisted a feminist reading of the history of philosophy which is only interested in a narrative of woman's association with the devalued, the emotions, the passions, the formless, the disordered and the irrational. I have argued that feminist analysis must not suppress, in its narratives about the history of philosophy, the complications and contradictions with which those associations have been intertwined. An emphasis of the complications and contradictions is the most enabling reading for feminist purposes. If we downplay these textual elements, we reinforce the effect of a stable history of the man of reason. What needs to be emphasised is the constitutive trouble of this history.

This suggests a direction in feminist interpretation of the history of philosophy angled towards an interpretation of the contradictions of that history as more than surprising, curious or puzzling. Attempts to 'explain' contradictions are extremely speculative. In directing attention towards 'why' they might arise, my concern is that they direct attention away from the constitutive role played by contradictions. Finally, analysing the constitutive role of contradictions requires that contradiction be seen as performing a textual role not reducible to destabilising accounts of the man of reason. Contradiction needs also to be understood as sustaining the effect of the man of reason. For example, I have argued that contradictions whereby woman is represented both as rational and as irrational should be seen as sustaining the identity of the 'man of reason' rather than merely confusing or destabilising that identity effect.

In the introduction, I began with the question of subversion of women's naturalised identity. I asked whether the account of woman as an 'always already destabilised' discursive effect constituted a substantial subversion of that effect. While the effect is sustained by internal trouble, it is real and material. The trouble is operative, to the point where its overt 'unveiling' does not inevitably constitute a destabilising intervention.

I demarcated a field of anglophone feminist commentary on Rousseau, asking to what extent contradiction is analysed in terms of its textual effects. I considered some of Rousseau's contradictions which had been discussed by anglophone feminist critics, and focused on a particular set of contradictions involving the relationship between the identity of man and the dictates of nature and God. To sustain the subordination of women, I argued that these dictates must be both immanent in and transcendent to man. As in the case of Augustine, I considered contradictions between whether man is like, or continuous with, or can know, or on the other hand is radically opposed to or severed from transcendent terms: Rousseau's nature, or Augustine's God. I argued that these contradictions are neither 'incoherent', nor merely 'apparent', nor 'resolvable'. Through being 'unresolved', I argued that they are operative, and produce the account of women as subordinate in both accounts.

One way of saying this is that the subordination of women in the work of Augustine and Rousseau is invalid. That articulation, however, belies the tenacity of the textual trouble through which accounts of women as subordinate are sustained. To describe them as 'invalid' suggests that they need concern us no longer, that they are undone, that they are not 'effective'. This is not the implication I wish to draw from the location of textual trouble. However, I have argued that both the man of reason and the subordination of women are sustained in philosophical arguments through the rhetorical effects of considerable textual trouble, such as incoherence, instability, contradiction, slippage in definition, and so on. My point is not to 'unveil' such textual elements, as if to 'unveil' is to disrupt, to trouble. But my point is to resist any narrativising of the man of reason and the subordination of women in the history of philosophy which de-emphasises the instability of that history in the interests of constructing a coherent narrative. If the work of textual trouble sustains a narrative of the man of reason and the subordination of women, as I have argued, feminist re-readings should not reconsolidate the coherence of that narrative.

We usually think of man as associated with reason, and woman with the emotions in the history of philosophy. I have suggested a structure according to which it is through man *not* being associated with reason (and rather being associated with the bodily and material, in opposition to God) that his association with reason (through a contradictory alignment with God) is possible. We may better understand the production of the entity named as the 'man of reason' if we consider the constitutive role of operative contradictions. We should not *simply* conclude of the history of philosophy that man has been associated with reason and women with materiality and the emotions. The conditions of that association are, I have argued, that man be aligned with woman as well as opposed to her, and that woman be aligned with man as well as opposed to him.

7

THE NOTORIOUS
CONTRADICTIONS OF
SIMONE DE BEAUVOIR

The French existentialist does not speak with a single voice. Either she wishes to have it both ways, or she takes with one hand that which she gives with the other.

(Céline Léon)

Is any feminist philosopher of the twentieth century better known for her contradictory arguments than Simone de Beauvoir?[1] She is well known for her declaration that one is not born, but becomes, a woman. She argues that female embodiment is no handicap to women's freedom. If it seems to be, this is only because of the cultural meaning with which it is imbued. But Beauvoir also offers lurid and negative accounts of female embodiment which do suggest that it is a handicap to women's freedom. She argues that a status of otherness is imposed on women. Nevertheless, she describes women who are complicit with the status of otherness imposed upon them in tones of moral condemnation. In the words of Jean Elshtain, 'De Beauvoir launches volleys against her subjects in the name of liberating them' (Elshtain 1981: 307).

EMPHASISING BEAUVOIR'S INCONSISTENCIES

Just as we have seen in commentary on Rousseau and Augustine, there is a tendency on the part of critics to find the contradictory tensions in Beauvoir's work a puzzling mystery. Says Mary Evans, 'Curious contradictions remain a puzzling part of *The Second Sex* . . . a curious ambivalence about female-ness and femininity runs throughout' (Evans 1985: 67). For Evans, it is surprising that Beauvoir does not demonstrate a rigorous clarity of thought about the topic of her own study. Yet consistency of argument in discussions of women and femininity is found in few thinkers in the history of Western thought.

Like Jean-Jacques Rousseau, Beauvoir has animated debate amongst feminist commentators about how the tensions in her work should be understood. And as with Rousseau again, a dominant theme of these debates is whether Beauvoir should be understood as in control, or out of control, of the instabilities in her philosophy. An important difference from debate surrounding the work of Rousseau, however, is that Simone de Beauvoir's work has been repeatedly interpreted in terms of the influence of another intellectual figure: Jean-Paul Sartre. This factor alters the terms of the debate about Beauvoir's control over her work. For some, instabilities in Beauvoir's work have been caused by her attempt to turn to feminist purposes an existentialist philosophical framework shared with Sartre. According to this framework, subjects are always free. This causes a contradictory tension with Beauvoir's feminist position that women are not free. According to a feminist existentialism, women are not free, but are also always free.

Interpretations which ask how Beauvoir's inconsistencies may be explained can contribute to an infantilisation of Beauvoir. She is repre-sented as under the influence of her philosopher lover, and as 'unable' to control entirely the unstable, conflicting theoretical elements with which she is dealing. Tina Chanter presents Beauvoir as a thinker who 'deprives herself – or perhaps she suffers from the fact that she wrote in the early stages of twentieth-century feminism – of the resources that she needs in order to complete the project', who 'falls short of' the rethinking of woman as other which will occur later in the century with French feminists such as Luce Irigaray. She continues:

> *The Second Sex* . . . remains limited both by the intellectual legacy Beauvoir inherits from her philosophical mentors, and by her refusal, or inability, to fully inhabit the role of a woman . . . we see Beauvoir's reluctance to embrace her womanhood . . . Beauvoir explores women's situation by fusing together the philosophical perspectives of Sartre and Hegel in an account that never quite manages to overcome the problems that such a marriage of minds produces.
>
> (Chanter 1995: 13)

Points of theoretical tension which are to be found in *The Second Sex* lead critics to construct a portrait of a thinker who is deprived, suffering, inadequate, limited, reluctant. One is reminded of the phenomenon we have seen in relation to Rousseau. This is what de Man, it will be recalled, describes as 'the commentators . . . ha[ving] to apologize or to offer a cure for something that went astray in their author' (de Man 1971: 112). Where Rousseau's lack of control is often attributed to his unique 'psychological case', Beauvoir's lack of control is often attributed to the unique circumstances of her relations with an intellectual partner. Where Rousseau is under the influence of his particular psychology, Beauvoir is under the influence of Sartre.

We see here the different political ramifications of interpreting textual instability. The cases of Rousseau and Beauvoir demonstrate the different implications of the critic's causal-explanatory approach. Interpreting Rousseau in terms of a unique, tortured psychology contributes to a normalisation of the myth of the rigorous, rational philosopher entirely in control of the text.[2] By contrast, interpreting Beauvoir as under the influence of another has different political implications. The interpretation feeds into a tradition of how women philosophers have repeatedly been interpreted. Harriet Taylor is interpreted as influenced by Mill, Mary Wollstonecraft in terms of her debt to Rousseau, and so on. Women philosophers have often been seen as appendages to male partners or mentors, and seen as merely extending given theories such as liberalism, Marxism or psychoanalysis to feminist purposes.[3]

This tradition overdetermines feminist interpretations of Beauvoir. One style of feminist interpretation of female philosophers such as Taylor, Wollstonecraft and Beauvoir would rebut the suggestion that they merely apply pre-existing theories not of their own invention to the analysis of women's condition. We shall consider some feminist interpretations in which Beauvoir does more than apply a Sartrian existentialism to analyse the condition of the women. The aim is to recuperate Beauvoir as a philosopher in relation to Sartre. However, this tactic can take many different expressions, not all of them compatible. Some feminist theorists resist the view of Beauvoir as an 'appendage' to Sartre, while others reinforce this view for strategic purposes.

Emphasising the influence of Sartre runs the risk of implying that Beauvoir lacks intellectual autonomy. However, emphasising the influence of Sartre may also be a means of recuperating Beauvoir as a philosopher. For example, if the tensions in her work are said to arise from her use of an existentialism identified as 'Sartrian', then the cause of Beauvoir's textual tensions can be attributed by the critic to 'Sartre', not to Beauvoir. Sartre's existentialism is a philosophy for gender-neutral existents. Thus, it should be appropriate for an analysis of women's condition. If it is not, does this not suggest the limitations of existentialism, more than Beauvoir's limitations?

> I do not here mean to suggest that de Beauvoir explicitly sets out to demonstrate the inadequacies of existentialism. Quite the contrary, it is by taking seriously its own claims to be a universally applicable theory of human being, that she, albeit inadvertently, exposes its masculine bias and limitations.
>
> (Gatens 1991: 51)

Gatens' problematic is how the inconsistencies of Beauvoir's account may be explained. Presenting Sartre's views on feminine embodiment, she claims that 'Sartre's influence on de Beauvoir's conception of the female body and femininity is quite clear' (Gatens 1991: 56). This is the best example of how the instabilities in Beauvoir's work are taken by the critic to demonstrate the limitations not of Beauvoir's work but of Sartre's work. The problems in Beauvoir's account of woman's being are used to cast doubt 'on the explanatory power of existentialism in the field of social analysis – problems that eventually came to trouble Sartre himself' (Gatens 1991: 50). Locating tensions in Beauvoir's philosophy, Gatens reroutes the critical reading of Beauvoir into a critical reading of Sartre. Beauvoir is recast as an inadvertent, implicitly critical reader of Sartre:

> Existentialism allows de Beauvoir to examine . . . the situation of women, whilst, at the same time, such an examination demonstrates the inadequacies of existentialism as a theory of *human* or social, rather than male or individual, being.
>
> (Gatens 1991: 50–1)

For Gatens, the overriding reason why tension and inconsistencies are to be found in Beauvoir's work is that Sartre's work harboured bias against women. Sartre had associated transcendence with transcendence of materiality and embodiment, to which he gave feminine associations.[4] In adopting the Sartrian framework, Beauvoir inherited the implicit sex bias. Arguing that women were the other, Beauvoir neglected to empha- sise the way in which within Sartrian existentialism, femininity, materiality and embodiment were also 'the other' – of freedom. Beauvoir's work thus becomes the site of tensions between her feminist intentions and a philosophical baggage loaded with sex bias. What emerges from her work is the repeated suggestion, shared with Sartre, 'that the female body and femininity quite simply *are* absolutely Other to the human subject, irrespective of the sex of that subject' (Gatens 1991: 58). This sex bias emerges from Beauvoir's work. But Gatens attributes the bias less to Beauvoir than to Sartre. The error made by Beauvoir lay in supposing that a sex-biased framework was sex-neutral, and so more appropriate to the analysis of women's condition than was the case.

Here, the critic must focus on Beauvoir's textual tensions, must identify her philosophy as limited, and must also emphasise her intellectual connection with Sartre. But that done, the limitation can then be displaced from Beauvoir to its true source, existentialism. Paradoxically, Beauvoir is thereby recuperated as a thinker, since the intellectual problem is diagnosed as pertaining to existentialism more than to Beauvoir. Critics taking this tack include Moira Gatens and Toril Moi. Moi suggests, 'it is in the very passages where Beauvoir unconsciously seeks to pay tribute to Sartre that she betrays his philosophy' (Moi 1994: 164).

DE-EMPHASISING BEAUVOIR'S INCONSISTENCIES

Other feminist critics direct their energies towards denying, or acknowledging only a minimal presence of, inconsistencies and instabilities in Beauvoir's work. As in the case of Jean-Jacques Rousseau, some critics demonstrate that apparent tensions in Beauvoir's work prove on closer inspection not to be inconsistent. For example, Lloyd argues that Beauvoir does not describe the meaning of the female body 'in-itself' (for embodiment has no meaning 'in-itself'). Beauvoir describes the experience of a female body 'which has been culturally objectified by exposure to the male look' (Lloyd 1984: 99). Lloyd acknowledges, 'it seems that women must struggle not only with their own bad faith and male power, but with their own bodies, if they are to achieve true selfhood and freedom'. Such passages are disconcerting. But we can partly recuperate Beauvoir by understanding that they manifest only a language into which she 'slips' because of the influence of a Hegelian concept of species-life in which transcendence involves transcendence of immersion in life, matter and reproduction (Lloyd 1984: 101).

Some critics acknowledge the contradictory tensions in Beauvoir's work, while de-emphasising them in the interests of examining the functional, successful aspects of her philosophy. For example, Toril Moi agrees that Beauvoir's rhetoric 'tends to devalorize the female position, regardless of her own arguments to the contrary', but still emphasises 'that Beauvoir's overvaluation of masculinity does not prevent her from developing a strikingly original theory of female subjectivity under patriarchy' (Moi 1994: 164). Here, Moi de-emphasises the contradictory tensions not because she thinks them unimportant, but because she considers it more important to emphasise what is achieved by Beauvoir's text despite those tensions.

Other feminists also resist overly emphasising the failure of Beauvoir's philosophy. For Michèle Le Dœuff, we should also emphasise its curious success. Beauvoir manages to make a feminist philosophy out of Sartrian existentialism, the most unlikely philosophical framework for analysing sex oppression. 'The philosophical referential which Beauvoir holds to be absolutely true is', Le Dœuff points out, 'the one least adequate of all to explain the phenomenon' (Le Dœuff 1987: 152). Le Doeuff does not deny that there are tensions and inconsistencies in *The Second Sex*, particularly between Beauvoir's feminist intent and the existentialist conceptual grid. And existentialism surely has its drawbacks. For example, it leads to Beauvoir's moral condemnation of women, her excessive focus on the individual's freedom, and even a strange leaning towards liberalism. Nevertheless, Le Dœuff still proposes that we might analyse Beauvoir's work in terms of the 'operative', rather than the dysfunctional. 'Beauvoir', she suggests, 'made existentialism work "beyond its means" because she got more out of it than might have been expected' (Le Dœuff 1987: 152).

Notice that Le Dœuff is not proposing that the tensions and inconsistencies are themselves 'operative'. Instead, without de-emphasising the tensions, Beauvoir's work should be interpreted insofar as it is operative despite its problems. Having argued that the ethic of authenticity is an unlikely ethic to put to feminist purposes, Le Dœuff therefore declares:

> My object here will be to show how the ethic of authenticity functions as a pertinent theoretical lever, an operative viewpoint for exposing the character of women's oppression.
>
> (Le Dœuff 1987: 145)

How does the ethic of authenticity function as an 'operative viewpoint'? True, it leads to Beauvoir's argument that women are complicit with their own oppression. Nevertheless, Le Dœuff argues that it also allows Beauvoir to emphasise that the 'otherness' of women should not be taken as a matter of course (Le Dœuff 1987: 145).

Taking a similar tack, Moira Gatens acknowledges that 'it is to de Beauvoir's credit that she manages to introduce the structural or social element into existentialist theory without thereby having to abandon it altogether' (Gatens 1991: 50). The tensions in Beauvoir's work should not diminish one's appreciation of the tour de force involved in her very generation of a feminism out of existentialist premises. Nevertheless, we have seen how Gatens focuses also on the problems incurred by Beauvoir. As she points out, 'the introduction of the notion of oppression gives rise to several confusions and inconsistencies in her account of woman's being' (Gatens 1991: 50). In contrast to Le Dœuff, Gatens' emphasis is less on the way in which Beauvoir's feminism is operative, more on the ways in which it is dysfunctional. Beauvoir both ascribes the negative experience of female embodiment to the material effects of female oppression and yet also suggests that female biology limits women's transcendence.

In sum, as with some interpretations of Rousseau, we see interpretations of Beauvoir which defend the coherence of her thought, and other approaches which acknowledge incoherence in her thought, but attempt to shift 'responsibility' for this incoherence away from Beauvoir to influences on her work. This includes attempts to explain problems in her work as arising from the influence of Jean-Paul Sartre.

CAUSAL-EXPLANATORY APPROACHES TO INTERPRETING INSTABILITY

We have considered feminist approaches which de-emphasise instabilities in Beauvoir's philosophy, and approaches which emphasise those instabilities. One version of the latter can also be seen as a variation on an 'explanatory' approach, since Beauvoir's textual tensions are explained in terms of her intellectual debt to Sartre. This leads us into a third category of feminist approach to Beauvoir, analyses which attempt a 'causal' or 'explanatory' approach to Beauvoir's inconsistencies and ambivalence. Such instabilities are interpreted in terms of influences on Beauvoir's work – intellectual (as in the case of Sartre's influence), or personal or psychological influences.

Given the methodologies considered in my discussion of feminist commentary on Saint Augustine and Rousseau, the reader will not be surprised to encounter psychologistic explanations again. For example, Moi suggests that the 'deeply ambivalent' relationship with Beauvoir's mother might be the explanation of some of her most hostile accounts of women's sexuality (Moi 1994: 168). As with Augustine, there are some who suggest that tensions arise in Beauvoir's work because of the influence of contemporary attitudes, and the limited knowledge of the day:

in de Beauvoir's defence it must also be said that she was writing in a generation in which some of the 'facts' of human physiology were not fully understood . . . For example, until the mid-1950s accurate information about the physiology of conception did not exist . . . [Beauvoir] reflects many contemporary attitudes and misconceptions about women's biology, and too rapidly assumes that male biology is some sort of norm, from which women deviate.

(Evans 1985: 65)

After initial work on Beauvoir which attempts to resolve Beauvoir's position,[5] Judith Butler changes tack so as to acknowledge its contradictory tendencies: 'Despite my own previous efforts to argue the contrary, it appears that Beauvoir maintains the mind/body dualism, even as she proposes a synthesis of those terms.' But Butler immediately turns away from the contradiction to its possible explanation. It can be read, she suggests, 'as symptomatic of the very phallogocentrism that Beauvoir underestimates' (Butler 1990: 12). Implicit sex bias in Beauvoir's work is displaced to the domain of the causal, since it is attributed to a mind/body philosophical tradition seen as influencing Beauvoir.

For Gilda Lerner, as for Tina Chanter, Beauvoir is hampered by the limited development of feminist theory in the 1940s: 'One may well quarrel with her biological determinism as well as with the negative weight she places on female biological function. She was a pioneer; much of the feminist scholarship refuting such deterministic assumptions was not yet available to her' (Lerner 1987: 156). Yet another approach would see Beauvoir as the victim of the times in which she lived: 'Beauvoir's contradictory statements', suggests Léon, particularly those relating to feminine essence, 'reproduce the power structure by which Western civilization has been shaped' (Léon 1995: 155). Such interpretative strategies direct critical attention away from an analysis of the rhetorical work performed by the contradiction. We are asked not to look at Beauvoir's contradictions, but 'away from', or behind, them to possible causes or explanations for their occurrence. I next examine a series of feminist interpretations of one particular site of contradictory tensions in Beauvoir's work, those surrounding feminine embodiment. I find a critical bias towards downplaying or resolving those contradictory tensions.

CONTRADICTIONS RELATING TO FEMININE EMBODIMENT

One of the most disturbing aspects of *The Second Sex* is the painting of feminine embodiment in negative tones. Notoriously, Beauvoir declares the following in a chapter entitled 'The Data of Biology':

> Woman is weaker than man, she has less muscular strength, fewer red blood corpuscles, less lung capacity, she runs more slowly, can lift less heavy weights, can compete with man in hardly any sport; she cannot stand up to him in a fight. To all this weakness must be added the instability, the lack of control, and the fragility already discussed: these are facts.
>
> (Beauvoir 1988: 66)

Because of such passages, critics suggest that biological essentialism emerges in her work despite her overt denunciation of it. Beauvoir argues that childbirth is painful and difficult, breastfeeding involves soreness and fever and saps the resources of the mother's vitality, maternity renders women dependent, and the menopause is a difficult crisis (Beauvoir 1988: 62–3). Puberty makes a young girl's body 'more fragile than formerly'; 'for the future, her muscular power, endurance, and agility will be inferior to those qualities in a man':

> Menstruation is painful: headaches, over-fatigue, abdominal pains, make normal activities distressing or impossible; psychic difficulties often appear; nervous and irritable, a woman may be temporarily in a state of semi-lunacy; the control of the nerve centres over the peripheral and sympathetic systems is no longer assured.
>
> (Beauvoir 1988: 353)

The feminine sex organs are evoked as mysterious, sullied with fluids, a domain in which women do not recognise themselves. We are told that heterosexual intercourse is experienced as violation. Argues Beauvoir, woman always feels passive in intercourse: 'she undergoes coition whereas the man exerts himself actively'. The heterosexual erotic experience leads to feeling of disgust, denial and revolt against 'her sexual destiny' (Beauvoir 1988: 406–7).

Beauvoir's account of feminine embodiment is disturbing not only because of its negativity, but also because it takes for granted that female embodiment simply is a limitation. Beauvoir presents these facts with the explanation that she is adopting the perspective 'of Heidegger, Sartre, and Merleau-Ponty', for whom the body is 'a limiting factor for our projects' (Beauvoir 1988: 66). This is an extremely contentious representation of Heidegger, Sartre and Merleau-Ponty. Even were it adequate, one would still be left with the fact that Beauvoir presents masculine embodiment as far less of a limitation on male freedom than is feminine embodiment for women. As Catriona Mackenzie writes, women's bodies are represented as somehow standing 'between the female human being and her quest for subjectivity and transcendence' (Mackenzie 1986: 147). The implication is that if women were more like men physically and psychologically, then they would be less limited or restricted existents. Indeed, Beauvoir does place a premium on technological developments which might level the playing field between men and women. There are overt passages in Beauvoir's work which suggest that women should take as their goal being more like men. As Mary Evans has argued, the account seems to suggest that what is wrong with women is that they are women at all: 'she is sometimes very close to asking, Why can't a woman be more like a man?' (Evans 1987: 176).

Critics have been particularly disturbed by Beauvoir's devaluation of feminine embodiment because it occupies a contradictory status in her text. As Kristina Arp summarises the problem: 'Beauvoir does offer a rather harsh description of female biological functions. But she also goes out of her way to deny that biological facts determine the way that one experiences one's body' (Arp 1995: 161). The tension is seen in the 'Data of Biology' section, where Beauvoir enumerates women's weaker muscles, lungs, bones, blood corpuscle level, nervous system, and proneness to hysterical fits, directly following this by the declaration that these are bodily facts which cannot be denied. She then continues, 'but in themselves they have no significance' (Beauvoir 1988: 66). She argues repeatedly that there is a list of locatable, biological facts which are not to be denied. She argues just as repeatedly that there are no biological facts, since humans establish the truth of such facts by the ways in which they are dealt with. As Butler glosses the position, 'The formulation does not dispute the biological or physiological facticity of the body, but is concerned, rather, with the meaning that the body – in all its facticity – comes to assume within the context of historical experience' (Butler 1989: 254).

In this sense, to enumerate any list of biological 'facts' could only be an abstraction from their synthesis with economic, historical, moral and social contextualisation. The abstraction is seriously misleading since 'facts' arise only in context. Yet the abstraction is one which Beauvoir repeatedly appeals to, all the while insisting on the invalidity of doing so. There should be no intrinsically devalued female biology in *The Second Sex*. And yet Beauvoir is convinced and nearly convincing about the fact that female embodiment constitutes a physical limitation to women's freedom.

This dilemma will constitute the object of every imaginable stratagem for analysing contradictions. Many critics have taken the causal-explanatory approach. The devaluation of female embodiment may be regarded as resulting from the influence of Sartre. To this end, reference will be made to passages from works such as *Being and Nothingness* in which a revolted Sartre gives accounts of feminine embodiment.[6] Critics have also attempted to give psycho-biographical explanations for Beauvoir's views about the female body.[7]

Methodological principles

Taking a different tack, other critics have responded to contradictions concerning feminine embodiment by suggesting that one aspect must be de-emphasised, the other emphasised as Beauvoir's 'real meaning'. This entails discounting some aspects of Beauvoir's argument. Karen Vintges, for example, is sympathetic with the view that Beauvoir's rejection of the female body is an expression of Sartre's influence. Accordingly, she attempts to distinguish Beauvoir's real view from textual tensions seen as arising from Sartre and also as *fundamentally extraneous* to Beauvoir's main argument:

> We occasionally hear some echoes of Sartre's influence, but it is clear they are not the main 'sound' of the work . . . My conclusion is that criticisms of Beauvoir that claim she is in opposition to the female body as such ignore the main thesis in *The Second Sex*.
>
> (Vintges 1995: 57)

Kristina Arp agrees, suggesting that we should 'mainly discoun[t] her remarks on female biology, as she in fact almost invites us to do' (Arp 1995: 162). What is noteworthy about these comments is their deliberate avoidance of a more sustained engagement with the contradictory elements of Beauvoir's text. Arp concertedly refuses to interpret Beauvoir's text as the site of contradictory tensions:

> I belong to the second camp, which does not take Beauvoir's statements about female biology at face value. Biology alone cannot determine how a woman experiences her body. For Beauvoir to assert otherwise would contradict the philosophical basis of her thought.
>
> (Arp 1995: 164)

Arp deliberately interprets Beauvoir's contradictions so as to find a meaning other than those of the split, explicit statements, so as to avoid the conclusion that Beauvoir contradicts her own ideas. Beauvoir aligns herself with existentialism and, Arp points out, it is contrary to existentialism to see biology as destiny. This then 'could not be' the argument which Beauvoir is really espousing.

For some commentators, it is only because of the reader's bias that contradiction is incorrectly perceived in Beauvoir's description of the body. Arp offers an argument with which many critics concur, that the reader should not suppose too quickly that the body described by Beauvoir in 'The Facts of Biology' is a description of the body 'from biology alone'. Arp takes Beauvoir to be describing a feminine biology which is always already a social construction. Because Beauvoir devalues feminine embodiment, the reader supposes that she is making an invalid reference to biological 'facts'. But it is only the reader who supposes that a reference to feminine embodiment must amount to an invalid claim about an ahistorical, decontextualised bodily truth:

> a number of statements . . . appear to be ahistorical and essentialist, such as that in intercourse, as in fertilization, woman experiences a 'profound alienation', and that since the embryo requires the woman to become 'other than herself', she becomes alienated from her body . . . Or, again, we find that in morning sickness we see 'the revolt of the organism against the invading species'. I suggest, however, that it is unnecessary to read these claims as essentialist . . . After all, it is only if we expect Beauvoir to be making ahistorical claims that we find this is the only possible interpretation. If, on the other hand, we acknowledge that she is not limited to describing the body as a *thing*, there is no need to read these statements as essentialist.
>
> (Ward 1995: 233)

Certainly, Beauvoir does describe the way in which female embodiment is alienating in the context of the cultural significance of woman as other. But the critic's attempt to render this position entirely consistent is less a reading of Beauvoir than a declaration of methodological principles. What is expressed is presuppositions about how to interpret apparent contradictions. Let us look again at Ward, for whom Beauvoir only 'looks to be making essentialist statements about women's bodies; in fact, this is not true. For, as Beauvoir points out, one cannot make neutral, aperspectival claims about female biology . . . she must reject the idea of the body as a purely biological mechanism, contrary to her critics' charge' (Ward 1995: 225). This is an example of how, when Beauvoir does refer to the facts of biology, the critic's response is to read against the letter of the text and suppress the contradiction. Since Beauvoir's reference to

179

biological facts undermines her own argument, Ward supposes that the onus is on the reader to suppress her reference to them, thereby suppressing the textual tension in accordance with the overt refrain. When Beauvoir lists the biological facts, the onus is therefore on the reader to suppose that she is referring to enculturated facts. If this is not a matter of giving the author the benefit of the doubt, it is a matter of performing reconciliatory work on the text:

> In coming to general conclusions about Beauvoir's view of woman's body, I have followed two heuristic principles. The first is that when confronted with apparent contradictions among an author's claims, one needs to look deeper for some means of reconciling them.
>
> (Ward 1995: 226)

I disagree with this critical bias against acknowledging contradictory tensions in texts. This is a bias which is overtly expressed in methodological declarations about the need to isolate one position as the real, intended meaning, or the need for the critic to reconcile contradictory tensions. I propose an alternative approach to presuppositions that we should look 'behind' Beauvoir's contradictions to their 'causes', or that we should deny or resolve them: instead, why not read Beauvoir's contradictions to the letter? Beauvoir describes certain facts of biology, and also identifies that description as an invalid abstraction.

I suggest that we try reading the text without the distinction between which elements are meant by Beauvoir and which are not. This is not to argue that Beauvoir was entirely in control of her text, nor is it to suggest the contrary. Rather than (implicitly or explicitly) positing an authorial *hors-texte* taken to be either in, or out of, control, I hazard a reading which brackets this distinction. Rather than attempting to resolve or explain Beauvoir's contradictions, I ask what they enable in her work. In the case of her argument concerning female embodiment, I take Beauvoir literally when she both argues (a) that there are biological facts which can be enumerated; and (b) that there are no biological facts which can be enumerated out of social context. I want to interpret Beauvoir precisely in and with the very moment she says: there are no facts, and, these are the facts.

Beauvoir is so palpably, in one and the same paragraph, referring to biological facts while declaring that one cannot do so. It is an intriguing gesture. Too much is lost when the contradiction is stabilised, resolved or explained away by the commentator. Critics who explain, deny or stabilise Beauvoir's contradictions may be underestimating the almost *inevitable* inconsistency with which Beauvoir distinguishes the category of a 'biological, real' body in the very gesture of saying that the body is always already acculturated and that there is no such body. The condition of Beauvoir's arguing that 'there are no facts' may be precisely her concurrent statement: 'these are the facts'. In considering this possibility, I turn to a consideration of the status of the 'in-itself' in the work of Beauvoir and Sartre.

The paradox of the in-itself

Like the tensions about embodiment, a similar series of textual tensions occur more generally with the category of the 'in-itself' or 'facticity' in the work of Beauvoir and Sartre. The category of the 'in-itself' can refer to anything from an object in the world (a table, a mountain) to given facts about ourselves (our biographical history, our embodied state). For Beauvoir and Sartre, it is the 'for-itself', human subjectivity, which gives meaning to the in-itself. Thus the mountain does not exist for us except insofar as it is already synthesised with our aims and attitudes. The rocky crag only exists for me *as* 'easy to climb', distant landscape, proof of my weakness, etc. (Sartre 1958: 482, 489). One cannot separate 'the mountain' from my aims and attitudes or the in-itself from the for-itself: these form an inseparable, synthesised unity:

> In itself – if one can even imagine what the crag can be in itself – it is neutral; that is, it waits to be illuminated by an end in order to manifest itself as adverse or helpful. Again it can manifest itself in one or the other way only within an instrumental-complex which is already established . . .
>
> Of course, even after all these observations, there remains an unnamable and unthinkable *residuum which belongs to the in-itself*.
>
> (Sartre 1958: 482)

Of course, one can posit, in abstraction, the residuum which belongs to the in-itself. But this is a misleading abstraction, since such a residuum is both *unnameable* and *unthinkable*. Sartre names a residuum in order to say that it cannot be named.

Similarly, my biographical history only exists as synthesised with implicit aims and attitudes. This might include such factors as: suppositions that my history limits my opportunities, that my period in prison fruitfully made me what I am or that vows made in the past are the test of my honour. My wronged past might be the spur to seek revenge on those who wronged me or the spur of my self-understanding as a forgiving pietist. 'The meaning of the past is strictly dependent on my present project' (Sartre 1958: 498). The past and its meaning for us form an inseparable synthesis. Like the world with which I interact, the past stripped of its given meanings is unnameable and unthinkable.

My body stripped of its meaning for me is equally unthinkable. With Sartre, Beauvoir argues that in-itself and for-itself, facticity and freedom constitute an inseparable synthesis. The in-itself is unnameable except insofar as it is always already rendered meaningful. There is no *nameable*, pre-meaningful body. We should place in this context Beauvoir's argument that biological or physical facts have no meaning. As Ward glosses, 'it is only within the context of certain social norms and values that differences in lung capacity and muscular mass have any significance' (Ward 1995: 232). In the words of Beauvoir:

> Woman is weaker than man . . . Certainly these facts cannot be denied – but in themselves they have no significance. Once we adopt the human perspective, interpreting the body on a basis of existence, biology becomes an abstract science; whenever the physiological fact (for instance, muscular inferiority) takes on meaning, this meaning is at once seen as dependent on a whole context: the 'weakness' is revealed as such only in the light of the ends man proposes, the instruments he has available, and the laws he establishes.
>
> (Beauvoir 1988: 66–7)

In this passage, Beauvoir names what she designates as unnameable. She indicates a fact, so as to state that it has no significance in-itself. But she occupies a philosophical position according to which facts without significance *cannot be named*, and cannot be thought. One might posit that there is an in-itself distinguishable from its synthesis with the for-itself. But one cannot name or think the in-itself as distinct from that synthesis.

In making the point, therefore, in-itself and for-itself are thought as separable by the same theorists who want to argue that they cannot be so thought. The gesture is invalidated by the theoretical framework in question, because it does suppose that we can distinguish the in-itself from the different ways in which it is interpreted, in order to demonstrate that 'it' can be interpreted in different ways. This is a gesture repeated in all the above examples, in relation to the mountain, and the past, as well as in Beauvoir's examples about female embodiment. As against all the above critics who would deny it, I argue that this is a contradictory position of the form: 'I cannot make this gesture I am making right now'; 'One cannot name the unnameable I am here naming.' Beauvoir's argument is well known because of its emblematic statement: 'these facts cannot be denied – but in themselves they have no significance'. For the position to be stable, the philosopher would have to theorise the possibility of 'naming' or 'thinking' a 'fact' which has no significance: a fact *not* in synthesis with the for-itself. The philosophical position occupied by Sartre and Beauvoir deems this unthinkable. In-itself and for-itself constitute an inseparable unity.

Many critical glosses argue that Beauvoir's position is not contradictory. Consider Ward's statement: 'the physical capacities of either sex gain meaning only when placed in a cultural and historical context'. Ward supposes that this is a non-contradictory position. Indeed, she offers this gloss precisely to *resolve* the apparently contradictory status of Beauvoir's seeming biologism. It will be recalled that Ward's explanation is that Beauvoir only 'appears to make neutral statements about females and biology in women's bodies'. We saw her rejoinder: 'the physical capacities of either sex gain meaning only when placed in a cultural and historical context' (Ward 1995: 225). Here, the critic denies that Beauvoir gestures towards an unnameable, pre-meaningful biology. Yet the critic avows that Beauvoir does that very thing. The critic tells us that Beauvoir gestures towards an unnameable, pre-meaningful biology in order to tell us that such a biology can only be named in social context. This explanation pretends to resolve the paradox, but in so doing repeats it. Critics suppose that Beauvoir's position can be stabilised with explanations of the kind 'that the physical body is a social artifact'. In so doing, they suppress the intrinsically paradoxical status of this very position. Sartre and Beauvoir repeat the paradox because the position cannot be sustained without paradox.

They should make no reference to an unthinkable in-itself such as a 'mountain' which takes on meaning, a 'body' whose facts have no meaning. A more consistent philosophy might *refuse* the very statement: 'the mountain has no meaning except in synthesis with that which renders it: easy to climb, beautiful landscape etc.'. It might do so because the mountain should not be nameable except *as* easy to climb, beautiful landscape, etc. Similarly, a more consistent philosophy might refuse the statement: these are the biological facts, but in themselves they have no meaning. Instead, a more consistent position might say: no 'facts' can be named or thought except as meaningful.

However, what is key to the philosophy of Sartre and Beauvoir would be lost without this paradoxical naming of the unnameable. The arguments of both are based on the contestability of meanings, and thus on human and social responsibility for meanings. Both theorists gesture impossibly towards an '*x*' (a mountain, a biological body) *so as* to declare that 'it' can take on one meaning, or another. Sartre argues that 'a mountain' can mean challenge or impediment, landscape or sport. This argument relies on the concept of the synthesis of in-itself and for-itself, a synthesis which renders the 'mountain' unnameable and unthinkable. But the argument also relies on being able to 'think' the mountain, so as to say: it can take on the one meaning or the other. In other words, the argument relies both on the conceptual distinguishability and the conceptual indistinguishability of mountain and meaning.

Similarly, critics repeatedly suppose that Beauvoir makes a simple slip in declaring that there are biological facts, and that these facts have no meaning. Alternatively, critics argue that by biological facts, she really means lived, enculturated facts. Since, by her own argument, she should not refer to the 'biological facts', critics suggest that we ignore or reinterpret the reference. The reference is incoherent. However, what is overlooked is the operative nature of the incoherence in relation to the argument. Beauvoir's argument, like that of Sartre, is founded on the simultaneous demarcation of specific in-itselfs which 'take on' this or that meaning, and on the philosophical position that specific, 'pre-meaningful' in-itselves are unthinkable, unnameable. It is fundamental to Beauvoir's philosophy that there be no biological facts. However, it is also fundamental to Beauvoir's philosophy that she designate (paradoxically, incoherently) biological facts, so as to say: in themselves these have no meaning. These facts may take on this or that meaning. This paradox is fundamental to her feminism. This is what is overlooked by the critic who would suppress the apparent contradiction as a slip or reinterpret it as a consistent position. Consider the statement:

> Woman is the victim of no mysterious fatality; the peculiarities that identify her as specifically a woman get their importance from the significance placed upon them. They can be surmounted, in the future, when they are regarded in new perspectives.
>
> (Beauvoir 1988: 736)

Beauvoir's point relies on an impossible gesture. She must conceptually separate 'the peculiarities which identity woman' (the physical and biological facts) from the 'the significance placed on them', in a philosophical context according to which that separation is unthinkable. It is precisely this contradiction which gives Beauvoir her feminism. She gestures at a woman's body so as to say that 'it' can be regarded 'in new perspectives'. 'It' is capable of signifying differently based on whether 'it' occurs in synthesis with misogynist meaning, or in synthesis with an affirmation of women's freedom. This position enables Beauvoir both to indict misogynist culture and speak in the name of other interpretative possibilities for women. This is an operative contradiction in Beauvoir's work. Beauvoir wants to argue that she cannot make the very gesture she is making. A paradoxical gesture grounds what is key to the feminism. This is neither a defence nor a critique of Beauvoir's position, but a highlighting of the key, operative elements of that position.

THE PARADOX OF FREEDOM

We negate or affirm our circumstances of place, past, physicality and context. We defy them, or believe we are determined by them, and in different modes interpret and respond to them. In bad faith, I might see myself as determined by my circumstances. This is bad faith, because it denies that the denial itself is an expression of my freedom. What is denied is that I am free to defy, or see myself as determined by my circumstances, and in this sense, I am at all times free. This is the existentialist concept of freedom, adopted by Beauvoir, who states that her perspective is one of existentialist ethics (Beauvoir 1988: 28).

This position involves another series of contradictory tensions in Beauvoir's work. Beauvoir argues both that women are radically free and that they are oppressed. She is ambivalent on the topic of women's responsibility for their situation. Woman 'finds herself living in a world where men compel her to assume the status of the Other' (Beauvoir 1988: 29). For Beauvoir, this is a real loss of freedom. 'All the main features of her training combine to bar her from the roads of revolt and adventure' (Beauvoir 1988: 730); 'it was neither a changeless essence nor a mistaken choice that doomed her to immanence, to inferiority. They were imposed upon her' (Beauvoir 1988: 726). Yet one can never lose one's freedom. Accordingly, Beauvoir also rails against women for their complicity with their oppression. 'She cheerfully believes these lies because they invite her to follow the easy slope' (Beauvoir 1988: 730). That women are compelled by men to 'assume the status of the Other', we are told, 'spells frustration and oppression' if it is inflicted on women. But it represents 'a moral fault if the subject consents to it' (Beauvoir 1988: 29). Competing refrains in *The Second Sex* suggest that women are oppressed, and also in moral fault.

The problem lies with the definition of freedom to which these issues of responsibility and moral fault are attached. Beauvoir's position that women are less free is precluded by her concept of radical freedom:

> to compare the use which, within their limitations, men and women make of their liberty is *a priori* a meaningless attempt, since precisely what they do is use it freely . . . inner liberty is complete in both.
>
> (Beauvoir 1988: 638–9)

Women are locked into a position as 'other', and yet Beauvoir is committed to the position that no human individual can be locked into such a role. The tensions turn around the definition of freedom, and equally around the elastic concept of 'facticity'. In approaching this issue, the extent to which oppression can be theorised within a philosophy of radical freedom should be considered.

Sartre argues that a temporary loss of freedom does occur when I am rendered 'object' in relation to another, becoming a 'being-for-others'. An existent constantly flickers backwards and forwards from a state as a 'being-for-itself' to a state as a 'being-for-others', and back again. For example, my state might flicker from being entirely absorbed in an activity such as eavesdropping at one moment (as a being-for-itself) to a temporary mode of self-consciousness, shame, or embarrassment (as a 'being-for-others') if caught in the act. In modes such as shame, the subject is said to be reduced to his/her facticity, and their freedom is said to be temporarily limited. This phenomenon is the only sense in which

Sartre theorises the limit of freedom. 'The Other's existence', he acknowledges, 'brings a factual limit to my freedom' (Sartre 1958: 523, 525). 'Being-seen constitutes me as a defenceless being for a freedom which is not my freedom' (Sartre 1958: 267).

But Sartre's discussion in 'The Look' recognises the limit to one's freedom as a temporary phenomenon only. One retains one's freedom to objectify others in the next moment, or to lose one's shame as one becomes absorbed again in projects. Beyond the sudden, fleeting moment in which one is reduced to a being-for-others, one always retain one's ability to 'return' the look, as it were: 'I can turn back upon the Other so as to make an object out of him in turn since the Other's object-ness destroys my object-ness for him' (Sartre 1958: 363). For this reason, an existent who sees him/herself as determined by being rendered a being-for-others is in bad faith.

Sartre's discussion of the Look as a real, but only a fleeting, loss of freedom is substantially modified by Beauvoir. She describes the way in which women internalise a social status as beings-for-others: 'Woman is determined . . . by the manner in which her body and her relation to the world are modified through the action of others than herself' (Beauvoir 1988: 734). Because it is sustained by an inequitable social and economic structure, women do not have an equal ability to shrug off their being-for-others by 'returning the look'. Beauvoir's theory of sex oppression is generated partly through her expansion of the concept of being-for-others. Sartre is usually taken to be unable to theorise oppression, partly because his concept of the loss of freedom in being-for-others is temporally so limited, and partly because he does not theorise the way in which social and economic circumstances render one more prone to the state of 'being-for-others'.

Yet although it does not receive emphasis in *Being and Nothingness*, Sartre does make some gestures towards theorising oppression. One such gesture occurs in the following passage, where Sartre discusses the example of one's construction as 'Jewish' and 'other' in the context of an anti-semitic culture:

> by means of the upsurge of the Other there appear certain determinations which I *am* without having chosen them. Here I am – Jew, or Aryan, handsome or ugly, one-armed, etc. All this I am *for the Other* with no hope of apprehending this meaning which I have *outside* and, still more important, with no hope of changing it . . . I learn of it and suffer it in and through the relations which I enter into with others, in and through their conduct with regard to me. I encounter this being at the origin of a thousand prohibitions and a thousand resistances which I bump up against at each instant: Because I am a *minor* I shall not have this or that privilege. Because

I am a Jew I shall be deprived – in certain societies – of certain possibilities, etc. . . .

We must recognize that we have just encountered a real limit to our freedom – that is, a way of being which is imposed on us without our freedom being its foundation.

(Sartre 1958: 523–4)

This description occurs in just a few lines, as opposed to the book-length study of sex oppression in *The Second Sex*. Nevertheless, in some ways the theoretical treatment offered by Beauvoir and Sartre is structurally not dissimilar. Both are willing to acknowledge that there are factors in the world capable of constricting freedom of movement, of expression, of circumstance, of identity. Both acknowledge that such factors do not arise only on the level of one-to-one encounters. There are indeed social factors which collectively contribute to a social construction of the identity of a woman, or a Jewish individual, as 'other'. *Being and Nothingness* and *The Second Sex* were works capable of theoretically accommodating a description of extensive, determining, oppressive social conditions, and the ways in which they affected individuals.

However, on both models, 'freedom' has been defined as that which one has *on the strength* of one's facticity, whatever that might be. *Being and Nothingness* emphasises that concept of freedom.[8] *The Second Sex* theorises the construction of women as other. The rhetorical weight of emphasis is placed by Beauvoir on women's oppression. Yet Beauvoir does repeatedly argue that women are still free – either to be complicit with their oppression, or not. As we have seen, extreme moral condemnation is made of those women described as complicit.

What is the theoretical relationship between freedom and facticity in the work of Beauvoir and Sartre? Every kind of oppression, whether fleeting objectification or structural or sustained oppression, can be 'recognised' by them. However, in both theories that oppression is placed within the conceptual boundaries of the facticity of a subject. Facticity and freedom are always the two sides of the coin which is the existential subject. Given facticity, freedom is then defined in terms of one's facticity. According to this model, my handicap can be 'recognised'. But it is defined as my 'facticity'. A handicap cannot 'subtract' from my freedom, because facticity and freedom are not defined in a subtractive relationship. Instead, the category of facticity comprehends whatever restrictions, givens, oppressions, etc. may be true of a subject. Freedom will then be defined as whatever options, avenues, attitudes, emotions, etc. are available to a subject under these circumstances. For example, we shall not say that my handicap lessens my freedom. Rather, we shall articulate freedom in terms of what I am free to do, be and think on the strength of my handicap.

By definition, facticity is therefore a category elastic enough to accommodate any instance of oppression which I might cite. The theoretical position of Sartre and Beauvoir acknowledges the oppression, but acknowledges it *as part of my facticity*. Freedom will always be an 'untouchable' residual category: that freedom which I am *on the strength of* all that amounts to my facticity. 'This *residue* is far from being originally a limit for freedom; in fact, it is thanks to this residue – that is, to the brute in-itself as such – that freedom arises as freedom' (Sartre 1958: 482). Notice how, within such a model, the very definition of the categories of freedom and facticity is such that there is no oppression which could be cited as 'reducing' one's freedom. This is not a denial of oppression. Both theorists are perfectly prepared to acknowledge that options of movement or thought available to me might be extremely limited. But because of the definitional structure of freedom, I shall still be defined as free. This is because there is only freedom 'thanks to' facticity. Freedom is a negation of the given; thus the given cannot 'reduce' freedom as it is not, by this definition, a quantifiable property.

If I am being tortured, I might only have options of attitude, or emotion. The only option available to me might be to look my torturer in the eye. But, by definition, I shall still be free under such circumstances, because one is free on the strength of one's facticity. Freedom and facticity are inseparable, the one a negation or interpretation of the other. Consider how Sartre acknowledges oppression, but factors it into the 'facticity' of a human subject in his discussion of anti-semitism. Sartre recognises that anti-semitism causes a total alienation of my person. He recognises that this alienation *is not fleeting*, as in 'The Look', but occurs in 'a thousand prohibitions and a thousand resistances which I bump up against at each instant', and he recognises the 'collective techniques' of alienation involved in encountering public signs such as 'No Jews allowed here' (Sartre 1958: 524). Nevertheless, he then defines freedom as the options of attitude and response which I have open to me on the strength of these given conditions:

> this prohibition can have meaning only on and through the foundation of my free choice. In fact according to the free possibilities which I choose, I can disobey the prohibition, pay no attention to it, or, on the contrary, confer on it a coercive value which it can hold only because of the weight which I attach to it. Of course the prohibition fully retains its character as an 'emanation from an alien will'; of course it has for its specific structure the fact of *taking me for an object* . . . Still the fact remains that . . . it loses its peculiar force of compulsion . . . within the limits of my own choice and according to whether under any circumstances I prefer life to death.
>
> (Sartre 1958: 524–5)

Beauvoir and Sartre share the definition of freedom discussed so far. Beauvoir's argument that women is the other is *not* a departure from that definition. Sartre can theorise a Jewish subject as structured as the 'other' in the context of anti-semitic social forces.[9] However, Beauvoir departs from this framework with her argument that women's *freedom* is actually decreased by the facticity of her role as other. Thus, in Beauvoir's work there are the contrary refrains discussed above, where women are both described as limited in freedom and yet in terms of a freedom which cannot be limited. Beauvoir argues both that women are fixed by social forces in a position as 'other' and that no human individual *can* be so fixed.

What, then, is the nature of Beauvoir's intervention into the framework shared with Sartre? First, we have seen that whereas Sartre theorises the only limit to freedom as a fleeting being-for-others, Beauvoir amplifies being-for-others so that it is theorised as a more sustained structure of human existence. Second, Sartre acknowledges the determining, structuring work of oppressive social forces. But we have seen that Sartre can only locate these forces within the category of facticity, on the strength of which we are always free. Unlike Beauvoir, he does not place these forces within the category of that which limits our freedom. Beauvoir resituates the conceptual 'place' of oppressive social relations. Since the only limit to freedom recognised by Sartre is a fleeting being-for-others, and since Beauvoir recognises oppressive social relations as a limit to freedom, we could say that Beauvoir relocates oppressive social forces to the field which Sartre articulates as the only limit to freedom: the phenomenon of 'being-for-others'. Being-for-others is no longer a fleeting phenomenon. It is seen as persistently determining women as 'other', so that women's loss of freedom is more than temporary.

We have already seen the similar account which Sartre and Beauvoir offer of the relationship between freedom and facticity, and the way in which the category of freedom could be described as having a 'receding' role in that relationship. No matter how much the circumstances of the individual are defined as oppressive or constricting, the category of freedom recedes while the category of facticity elastically expands in relation to those circumstances. The category of facticity expands to encompass whatever determining conditions are true of an individual. Held back, always over and above this category, freedom is always what is 'also' true of the individual. But something more complicated occurs in the work of Beauvoir.

We can divide Beauvoir's treatment of freedom into two components. *One*: departing from the above 'recessive'-style definition, she allows determining social circumstances (here, sex oppression) to bleed into the category of 'freedom', so that an individual's freedom can be said to be lessened. Yet, *two*: she also persists with the receding definition of freedom.

The two definitional approaches to freedom are deployed simultaneously. One result is that women's lessened freedom (according to the first conceptual structure) becomes the equivalent of a new facticity (according to a simultaneous, second conceptual structure). Thus, women are also said to be *always free* in relation to their *lessened freedom*. Beauvoir tells us that women's freedom is lessened, and yet that they can still choose to be complicit with this circumstance – or not.

On Beauvoir's model, freedom remains, as it is with Sartre, a constantly receding concept. Freedom remains projected as that which a woman yet has, no matter how much women are also defined in terms of a loss of freedom (according to the first conceptual structure). Freedom is still, as it is with Sartre, always the other side of the boundary line of facticity. The difference from Sartre is that because of the double, contradictory concepts of freedom in play in Beauvoir's work, facticity has the conceptual elasticity to encompass, paradoxically, even the loss of freedom. As freedom retains a receding capability, a subject is seen as 'always free' even when facticity is defined in terms of loss of freedom.

We have seen that critics make reference to Beauvoir's relationship with Sartre to explain the inconsistencies in her argument. Beauvoir argues that women are not equally free. If she also condemns women for complicity with their oppression, this is seen as a symptom of the influence of that existentialist moralist, Sartre. Critics often suppose that Sartre is unable to account for sustained oppression. When Beauvoir attempts to use a framework shared with him to theorise women's oppression, it is thought that contradictions accordingly ensue. My position is that while Sartre does not theorise oppression, to do so would not be inconsistent with his conceptual framework. The tensions in Beauvoir's feminism need not be seen as the result of her occupation of a Sartrian existentialist framework. They can be understood as related to her deployment of two incompatible concepts of freedom, only one of which she shares with Sartre.

My objection to the view that the inconsistency arises from the excessive influence of Sartre is partly related to the problematic narrative of the authorial subject who can't quite control the elements in her text, the infantilised persona discussed at the outset of the chapter. My objection is also related to its implication that the contradictory refrains only weaken Beauvoir's philosophy. If only Beauvoir could have perceived how inappropriate the Sartrian concept was for her purposes, she might have relinquished it, and simply deployed, consistently, the more appropriate 'subtractive' concept of freedom. I resist this interpretation, because its tendency is to overlook the rhetorical work that the contradictory definitions of freedom are doing for Beauvoir's feminist project.

What are the components of this project which relate to definitions of freedom? For Beauvoir, if women are the other, they have been 'barred'

190

from roads of revolt and adventure, denied their status as 'free and autonomous being[s] like all human creatures' (Beauvoir 1988: 29). Crucial to Beauvoir's denunciation of the oppression of women is her appeal to woman's true status as 'a free and autonomous being'. If Beauvoir does not make this appeal, she loses the terms on which she denounces the compulsion which women are under, the terms on which to define and denounce what has been inflicted on women. Within Beauvoir's conceptual framework, then, it is fundamental that she defines women as free. The 'receding' concept of freedom allows her to do this. However, by the same argument, she defines women's oppression in terms which impinge on the very definition of freedom which allows her to articulate the nature of her oppression. Whenever Beauvoir's refrain is that immanence and inferiority are imposed on women, the category of facticity has exceeded itself, since it is seen as 'lessening' freedom. The category of freedom is no longer that which a subject has on the strength of his or her facticity. This is less a paradox which requires causal explanation than a paradox which needs to be interpreted as fundamental to Beauvoir's feminism. It is thought that the combination of Beauvoir's feminism with the terminology of Sartrian existentialism is the cause of the 'trouble' in her argument. And indeed it is. But what would the argument be without that trouble? The trouble grounds the whole position, and for this reason, to analyse it as if it were the accidental result of extraneous influences is misleading.

Beauvoir must argue that women are 'free and equal transcendent existents'. It is in terms of this reference that she defines the subjection of women insofar as they are compelled to assume the status of 'other'. This reference allows the key aspect of her philosophy: her very desire to inspire women to affirm themselves as free and equal transcendents. But Beauvoir defines the 'otherness' of woman so that her own category of woman as free and equal transcendent is in question. For this argument, women both must be free and equal transcendents, and they must not be. Woman's 'becoming other' must be confined to her facticity, so that her freedom can be affirmed in a feminist project. However, women's 'becoming other' must also be defined as extending 'beyond' her facticity, so that this can be denounced in a feminist project. Beauvoir must both argue that woman's being-as-other does not affect her freedom, and that it does.

Should we conclude that Beauvoir's philosophy is limited by the constraints of her conceptual apparatus? This kind of suspicion seems to ground Chanter's feeling that Beauvoir 'suffers from the fact that she wrote in the early stages of twentieth-century feminism' (Chanter 1995: 13). Similarly, as Toril Moi points out, for some critics 'Sartre's and Beauvoir's metaphors suggest a radical *limitation* of their own original theory of freedom.' Moi replies that this 'amounts to saying that these specific images represent neither the necessary consequence nor the intrinsic "meaning" of their philosophy: they might always have chosen others' (Moi 1994: 153).

Obviously, Beauvoir's work has its limitations. But to see it as limited by its own conceptual apparatus means to adopt seriously some strange view of a virtual Beauvoir which Beauvoir almost was – but not quite. It involves cutting up the work into intrinsic and superficial elements, 'limited' elements which are embryonic forerunners of later theory, as if these are not all interconnected in Beauvoir's work.

Moi leans instead towards a causal explanatory approach. Rather than arguing that Beauvoir and Sartre should have chosen other metaphors, she argues that 'the reasons why they did not – as well as the reasons why they did not perceive the problem in the first place – are to be found in their own specific historical and intellectual circumstances' (Moi 1994: 153). Sharing Moi's wariness of the concept of the author who might have chosen otherwise, I favour, in place of the causal-explanatory, a different emphasis. Rather than looking at how Beauvoir's feminism is destabilised by its own most contradictory and apparently felicitous elements, or at how those elements might be explained, I focus on what those unstable elements enable in her work.

The Second Sex is an extremely unstable text, and critics generally agree that the existentialist and feminist tendencies sit in uneasy tension with each other. Yet it is in terms of the existentialist framework that Beauvoir kickstarts her feminism, with all the instability thereby entailed. Michèle Le Dœuff is a commentator primarily committed to examining the ways in which Beauvoir's text is functional. Moira Gatens a critic primarily interested in identifying breakdown in Beauvoir's work as grist towards an argument that textual tensions in feminist work are generated by the adoption of supposedly sex-neutral philosophical frameworks which encompass implicit sex-bias. Whether they are emphasising or de-emphasising the troubles caused in *The Second Sex* by the existentialism, for both, there would be no *Second Sex* without the existentialism. Gatens reminds us: 'Part of what makes it possible for de Beauvoir to ask this open question concerning woman is the philosophical perspective which she employs: existentialism' (Gatens 1991: 48). And Le Dœuff espouses this position:

> If many readers today skip those passages most imbued with existentialist doctrine . . . they are giving *The Second Sex* an ordinary fate . . . we'll take this and not that, says posterity. However, it is fairer, and far more instructive, to read Simone de Beauvoir's essay as it is and to try to connect its two aspects.
>
> (Le Doeuff 1991: 56)

Le Dœuff's approach to Beauvoir is particularly interesting because of its overtly political nature. Le Dœuff highlights the inconsistencies of Beauvoir while saying that, as a feminist reader, she reads Beauvoir's work as operative, rather than dysfunctional, philosophy. One can easily interpret Beauvoir's work as dysfunctional. Instead, Le Dœuff slants her reading of Beauvoir towards what it curiously manages with its unpromising elements. Yet Le Dœuff does not pretend that Beauvoir's text is more stable than it appears, as in the case of many other feminist readings. Le Dœuff does not attempt to efface or explain away Beauvoir's difficulties. Indeed, she emphasises those difficulties in her reading. It is a reading which does not suppress the complexity of Beauvoir's ambivalent, self-contradictory work in a mistaken and unnecessary politics of recuperation.

Throughout this work, we have seen multiple ways in which textual instability can be interpreted. The multiple interpretations of Beauvoir's inconsistent arguments highlight the different stakes grounding differing approaches. Emphasising the influence of Sartre may work to weaken Beauvoir's credibility as a philosopher, or may serve to weaken the credibility of Sartre. One can analyse in many ways the instability of Beauvoir's arguments. Yet it may be as important to emphasise how the instability facilitates Beauvoir's arguments. I have argued against a methodology which attempts to discount, de-emphasise or stabilise textual tensions. Such a methodology supposes that the work of the traditional philosopher is textually stable, free of instability, ambivalence or conflicting elements, and contributes to the normalisation of that myth.

CONCLUSION

> Contradictions are not . . . necessarily something to be resolved.
>
> (Judith Still)

Philosophically sound texts are assumed to be free of unstable contradictions. Accordingly, the desire to establish Beauvoir's city-rights as a philosopher leads to certain approaches to the unstable textual elements in her work. They might be deflected away from her text in an analysis of their possible causes or origins. They might be resolved through arguments that they are only apparent, or that they are marginal or accidental elements of the text, or that they are elements to be disregarded since clearly not in accordance with the author's intentions or with the main tenor of the text.

I have resisted this kind of approach for a range of reasons. For one, the approach serves a normalising function. The critic's intention is to defend Beauvoir. Wary of acknowledging contradiction in her work, the critic accepts that the good philosopher is the philosopher whose text is stable. Yet surely the same critic would acknowledge that accounts of women and femininity in the history of philosophy have frequently been unstable, troubled and self-contradictory. The critic's embarrassment at locating such elements in Beauvoir's work downplays this fact, and serves to reinforce the impression that such elements are aberrant in the philosophical canon. Beauvoir's instabilities should be placed in the context of our recognition of how common such invalidity is in the history of philosophy. We should not reinforce the impression that the history of philosophy has mostly succeeded in offering stable accounts of women and femininity. Resisting, rather than reinforcing, this impression is critical for contemporary feminist commentary.

I have resisted some aspects of the 'man of reason' thematic in feminist philosophy. I have resisted any tendency to stabilise phallocentrism overly in the history of philosophy, arguing against any downplaying by feminist commentators of the ambivalence, incoherence or contradictions involved in associations between masculinity and reason. This is not to deny that an earlier imperative for feminist philosophers was to expose the masculine connotations of reason. But such an imperative is lessened once the argument becomes conventional. From this perspective, the issue is one of timing, of keeping theory on the move. Now the imperative for feminist philosophers is to emphasise the constitutive instability of those connotations.

Of course, any critic in offering any interpretation always stabilises a text. In offering a particular interpretation, I bring to the fore aspects of texts which support my argument, and neglect others which seem irrelevant to, or complicate, or distract from my argument. To do justice to all the elements of a text is impossible. In offering any interpretation, the critic must stabilise the text in terms of a certain refrain or tenor, thereby de-emphasising certain elements which complicate that tenor. Interpretation must, in this sense, stabilise texts. Rather than questioning interpretative stabilisation per se, I have resisted the particular stabilising and normalising function which the man of reason narrative performs in de-emphasising the constitutive role of instability and contradiction in sustaining the effect of the man of reason. Further, it is not sufficient to expose instability in the man of reason tradition, for it needs to be theorised in terms of *how it sustains* that tradition.

One of the most common criticisms of deconstructive philosophy is that it is prone to contradictory positions. In a well-known critique of Irigaray, Monique Plaza argues that Irigaray's work contains contradictory views of women. For Irigaray, Plaza argues, phallocentrism emphasises sexual difference but also excludes sexual difference (Plaza 1978: 13–14). Many critics argue that Derrida is relativist about the interpretation of texts, but is not relativist about the interpretation of his own texts. For John McGowan, one cannot both say that nothing escapes from culture's signifying processes and also that a capitalist social order is not inclusive enough (McGowan 1991: 21–3). A good case can be made against these criticisms. But they bear witness to the critic's presupposition that to have caught out a theorist in a contradictory position is to have exposed and invalidated his or her position.

This raises the question of the status of constitutive contradictions in texts. The asserted invalidation of the thinker whose position is contradictory reinforces the supposition that philosophical positions are not regularly riddled with constitutive instability. Deconstruction could be characterised in terms of the alternative picture it paints of philosophy. The analysis of logocentrism, phonocentrism, the nostalgia for presence and the work of différance is an analysis of the constitutive instability of numerous metaphysical positions in the history of philosophy. The philosopher who devalues writing in favour of speech also tells us that speech is a form of writing. The philosopher who sees representation as secondary in relation to original truth also tells us that truth requires

supplementation by representation. The philosopher who devalues civilisation in favour of nature also tells us that nature requires civilisation,
necessarily collapses into civilisation and is already a form of civilisation. Metaphysical philosophies, philosophies which reify points such as
nature, truth and divinity as transcendent, original, self-present, and not
dependent on supplementation, are unstable, contradictory philosophies:
they inevitably tell us that the origin needs the supplement.

One argument in this book has been against any approach to contradiction in philosophy which reinforces the impression that the history
of philosophy, particularly in its accounts of women and femininity, is a
stable, non-contradictory history. Such approaches might include the
continual expression of surprise at the contradictory status of a particular
philosopher's arguments on such issues, surprise which we have seen
expressed in commentary on Augustine, Rousseau and Beauvoir. It
might also include the embarrassment and attempts to de-emphasise
such elements in a philosopher's texts, as if they were philosophically
aberrant. And it also includes the supposition that the philosopher whose
position is contradictory is clearly a philosopher whose argument has
been invalidated. Of course, by the criteria of stable, coherent reasoning,
this is true. However, the problem is the normalising function of the
supposition that the philosopher whose position is contradictory is therefore invalidated. This tends to reinforce the impression that there is an
otherwise stable history of sound and consistent positions on women and
femininity, to which the philosopher in question is the aberrant exception. This is a supposition I have called into question in this work, both
through the readings of Augustine, Rousseau and Beauvoir offered and
also through the insistence that even the critical works which tell of the
consistency with which reason has been associated with masculinity also
tell, implicitly, of the inconsistency and instability of those associations
in the history of philosophy.

Contradictions may be a valid, or an inevitable, negotiation of a sound
theoretical position.

> Perhaps contradictions are necessary when thinkers are trying
> to think against the grain, and yet have nothing apart from the old
> standards because they are caught (as we are) in logocentrism,
> embedded in the language of normative judgements, for this language
> is all that we have – we cannot step outside it.
>
> (Still 1994: 155)

The *point* of some positions is their contradictory status. A crucial
contradiction deployed in Irigaray's work concerns Irigarayan sexual
difference, which she argues is both 'inside' and 'outside' contemporary
culture. As seen in chapter 3, it is outside insofar as phallocentric culture
is based on its exclusion. However, it can be described as enveloped

within phallocentric culture for the same reason. This is not a contradiction which one might 'expose' in Irigaray's work, but a contradiction on which her political philosophy is premised. It is precisely because Irigarayan sexual difference occupies this paradoxical status that Irigaray can try to articulate 'what has been excluded' while arguing that it has been excluded. Derrida has described how he marks out a text which is 'simultaneously almost identical and entirely other' between the lines of the works he interprets (Derrida 1981: 4). The potency of a deconstructive reading is its account of what is both entirely within a text and entirely other to it.

This raises the question of the relationship between the status of contradictions in philosophers such as Augustine, Rousseau and Beauvoir and those of philosophers such as Irigaray and Derrida. Contradictions are revealed in interpreting the former trio as part of a politics of 'destabilising through exposing instability'. Yet the arguments of Irigaray and Derrida are grounded in a kind of instability, indeed a kind sometimes triumphantly seized upon by critics to expose the invalidity of their philosophical position (as seen in the examples of Irigaray's and Derrida's critics). Furthermore, Derrida has argued repeatedly that the deconstructive reading cannot be free of deconstructibility, and that deconstruction cannot offer the promise of a stable, consistent position, free of metaphysics. This suggests that the philosophical position of theorists such as Irigaray and Derrida will never be stable, and raises the question of whether we can distinguish between the deconstructibility of Augustine, Rousseau and Beauvoir, Irigaray and Derrida. The arguments of all, it seems, are premised upon instability, and the reader may wonder if a certain levelling of these philosophers does not occur. Perhaps it weakens the sense that there is important critique involved in exposing the instability of Augustine, Rousseau or Beauvoir, although the argument of widespread instability in phallocentric arguments is not a justification of such textual elements.

There is, however, a world of difference between contradiction in an argument which attempts to maintain a stable, non-contradictory position and contradiction in arguments whose position is that stability is not a realistic ideal, or in arguments which specifically attempt to articulate well an unstable, contradictory position. In the first case, to expose the contradiction of the philosopher in question is to undermine the text. In the second case, to expose the contradiction of the thinker in question is to fail to acknowledge the nature of the philosophical project in question. It is a neutral gesture to argue that deconstruction, or Irigarayan feminism of difference, is grounded in constitutive instability, because these are not philosophies premised in a denial of this fact. It is an intervention to expose the instability of a position which would assert its own stability. This is the difference between arguing that the positions of Derrida or

Irigaray are self-contradictory and arguing that the position of Rousseau is self-contradictory.

Deconstruction has provoked a history of sustained debates about the politics of exposing the constitutive instability of texts. These allow us to reflect both on the risks of interpreting textual instability as 'troubling' in some sense which overly downplays the constitutive role of instability, and on the risks of interpreting textual instability as constitutive, in some sense which exaggerates the subversive potential of such a reading. As a feminist intervention, this book exposes instability in arguments concerning the nature and role of women in the history of philosophy. However, since instability is understood as rendering possible phallo-centric arguments, the subversive potential of exposing their instability may be limited. Instability can be read as simultaneously destabilising and stabilising, consolidating and subverting the tradition.

NOTES

1 GENDER TROUBLE/CONSTITUTIVE TROUBLE

1 Sedgwick herself also discusses constitutive instability in homophobic law: see Sedgwick 1990: 69–86. Butler too analyses the contradictory logic of homophobia, as when a United States senator simultaneously declares that he is ignorant about homosexuality and expresses his homophobia through an asserted knowledge about homosexuality (Butler 1994: 34).

2 In *Feminist Contentions*, Seyla Benhabib and Nancy Fraser take some care in their responses to Butler to emphasise that Butler is speaking of gender 'performativity' rather than gender performance (Fraser 1995: 162; Benhabib 1995: 108–9). Since Benhabib had first taken Butler to mean that women enact gender like actors on a stage, she subsequently recognises: 'by performativity Butler does not mean a theatrical but a speech-act model' (Benhabib 1995: 109). Butler has stated, 'It is important to distinguish performance from performativity: the former presumes a subject, but the latter contests the very notion of the subject' (Butler 1994: 33). However, despite her later clarifications that she means performativity rather than performance (see Butler 1995: 134; 1993: 224–42), Butler does use the expression 'gender performance' in *Gender Trouble*, as seen at 1990: 141, for example. But she does not use 'performance' to imply that there is a doer behind the deed, the pre-gendered actor who acts a gender, or conscious deliberate performance where there is 'a "one" who precedes that "putting on"' of a mask or persona (Butler 1993: 230).

3 Butler further explains the infelicity of this interpretation of her argument: 'The problem with drag is that I offered it as an example of performativity, but it has been taken up as the paradigm for performativity. One ought always to be wary of one's examples. What's interesting is that this voluntarist interpretation, this desire for a kind of theatrical remaking of the body, is obviously out there in the public sphere . . . But no, I don't think that drag is a paradigm for the subversion of gender. I don't think that if we were all more dragged out gender life would become more expansive and less restrictive' (Butler 1994: 33).

4 By the time Butler published *Bodies That Matter*, much of the debate about her work centred on concepts of embodiment (see Butler 1993: ix–x). Butler had moved from reputedly arguing for the proliferation of drag performances to reputedly having forgotten about the materiality of the body (Butler 1993: ix; 1994: 33–4). Debate has also turned around the political implications of speech-act theory and performativity, and on assertions by some that feminist

politics should be grounded in concepts of ethics or agency which critics believe are challenged by Butler (see Huffer 1995: 20 and essays by Benhabib and Fraser in Nicholson 1995).

2 DECONSTRUCTION IN A RETROSPECTIVE TIME

1 'The "young conservatives" . . . claim as their own the revelations of a decentered subjectivity . . . To instrumental reason they juxtapose in Manichean fashion a principle only accessible through evocation, be it the will to power or sovereignty, Being or the Dionysiac force of the poetical. In France this line leads from Georges Bataille via Michel Foucault to Jacques Derrida' (Habermas 1985: 14).
2 Comparing him to Heidegger, Habermas has also stated that Derrida's orientation is 'rather more subversive': 'Derrida', says Habermas, 'stands closer to the anarchist wish to explode the continuum of history' (Habermas 1987: 181–2).
3 For his discussion of those critics, such as Walter Jackson Bate and René Wellek, who have accused deconstruction of 'negativity' and 'nihilism' see Miller 1987: 9, and for his critical response to Bate, see de Man 1982: 1355–6.
4 See, for example, McCarthy 1991: 98. McCarthy takes seriously Derrida's claims that his work has important ethical and political implications, and his is a useful piece for this reason. In the end, though, he does not consider that these claims are sustainable. For an alternative view, see Bernstein 1987.
5 For his critical comments concerning interpretations of Derrida's project as 'relativist', see Dews 1987: 5, 25.
6 See, for example, Crossan's interpretation: 'what Derrida is saying leads straight into a contemporary retrieval of negative theology' (Crossan 1980: 11, cited in Hart 1989: 184) and, for his critical discussion of this interpretation, Hart 1989: 184–6 and x.
7 For Verges, Derrida contradicts himself insofar as he both criticises sweeping metanarratives and invents his own by arguing that the phonocentric bias of history goes back to Plato (Verges 1992: 391). For Habermas, there is a paradox lurking in Derrida's work given that the critique of reason must use the tools of reason in order to perform the critique (see Habermas 1987: 185). For Ellis, Derrida repeats the either/or logic he criticises. For example, he opposes to the argument that words refer to the real world the argument that words refer to other words (see Ellis 1989: 139).
8 For example, see John Searle's comments: 'The proof that speech is really writing . . . becomes trivially easy since writing has been redefined to encompass them both.' He adds, 'The proof . . . is based on a redefinition. By such methods one can prove anything. One can prove that the rich are really poor, the true is really false, etc.' (Searle 1983: 76–7). Merquior similarly argues that Derrida's interpretation of speech as a form of writing is meaningless because of the redefinition it presupposes. Rorty, of course, is a critic who interprets Derrida as a particularly trivial philosopher, but Rorty's twist is to approve Derrida for this. Derrida is included by Rorty along with that other 'non-Kantian' Heidegger as one of those philosophers who 'do not *have* arguments or theses' (Rorty 1982: 93). '[Derrida] is not writing a philosophy. He is not giving an account of anything; he is not offering a comprehensive view of anything' (Rorty 1982: 97). 'Lack of seriousness, in the sense in which I just attributed it to Derrida, is simply this refusal to take the standard rules

seriously' (Rorty 1982: 98). To whatever extent Derrida does have a constructive side, Rorty takes this to be Derrida's 'bad side', Derrida not at his best: see Rorty 1982: 99. This interpretation is repeated in Rorty 1989: 'Accepting [my] suggestion means giving up the attempt to say, with Gasché and Culler, that Derrida has demonstrated anything or refuted anybody' (Rorty 1989: 134).

9 See, for example, Graff 1979: 39, who, in Kevin Hart's words, 'takes Derrida to argue the pluralistic thesis that in "the absence of any appeal to . . . a coercive reality to which the plurality of interpretations can be referred, all perspectives become equally valid"' (cited and discussed in Hart 1989: 144).

10 I am thinking of interpretations such as that of Frank Verges, for whom Derrida emphasises the polysemy of the text, that 'signifiers are always subject to contradictory interpretations' (Verges 1992: 389). Here, deconstruction is said to affirm what Barthes called the *jouissance* of the text, the 'free play of signifiers' (Verges 1992: 392–3). Similarly, see M. H. Abrams: 'Derrida proposes . . . that we deliver ourselves over to a free participation in the infinite free-play of signification opened out by the signs in a text' (Abrams 1977: 431).

11 For Abrams again, Derrida reverses traditional hierarchical oppositions. In giving privilege to 'writing' in favour of speech, he is thereby 'graphocentric' in place of 'phonocentric' (Abrams 1977: 431).

12 Another common argument from those who maintain that Derrida only deconstructs what analytic philosophy no longer believes in, for example, correspondence theories of truth or realist accounts of the world: see Ellis 1989: 138. The most witty exemplar is Rorty's account: 'the kind of reading which has come to be called "deconstructionist" requires . . . a macho professional philosopher who is insulted by the suggestion that he has submitted to a textual exigency . . . The philosopher had thought of himself as speaking a sparse, pure transparent language . . . There is something suspiciously old-fashioned about this way of setting up one's subjects. It is . . . considerably more difficult than it used to be to locate a real live metaphysical prig' (Rorty 1991a: 86).

13 See Ellis 1989: 140–2 and John Searle: 'There is in deconstructive writing a constant straining of the prose to attain something that sounds profound by giving it the air of a paradox' (Searle 1983: 76).

14 This is Rorty's well-known interpretation of Derrida: see Rorty 1982, Rorty 1991c and, for a critical discussion of this interpretation, Norris 1989.

15 Well-known examples include the interpretations of Rodolphe Gasché, and to a lesser extent, Irene Harvey and Christopher Norris. This version is discussed at length below.

16 That each of these interpretations has certainly been found plausible enough in certain contexts is evidenced by the fact that Irene Harvey begins her book on Derrida thus: '(Deconstruction is not) (a) metaphysics, as per the Western tradition; (b) "philosophizing with a hammer", as per Nietzsche; (c) "the destruction of metaphysics", as per Heidegger; (d) dialectics, as per Hegel; (e) semiology, as per Saussure; (f) structuralism, as per Lévi-Strauss; (g) archaeology, as per Foucault; (h) textual psychoanalysis, as per Freud; (i) literary criticism, as per the "New Critics"; (j) philosophy or epistemology, as per Plato and Socrates; (k) a theory/logic/science of textuality, as per Barthes; (l) hermeneutics, as per Gadamer . . . [Harvey continues on to 'z']' (Harvey 1986: 23).

17 See Rorty 1991c: 125 and Rorty 1989: 123–5.

18 For example, Habermas refers to Derrida's concept of writing thus: 'The archewriting takes on the role of a subjectless *generator of structures* that, according to structuralism, are without any author . . . all linguistic operations are to a certain extent *set in operation* by an archewriting not itself present' (Habermas 1987: 180, my italic). For Habermas, one reason Derrida is in an untenable position is that his archewriting is simply another origin, another foundation: 'It is important to note that in the course of pursuing this line of thought *Derrida by no means breaks with the foundationalist tenacity* of the philosophy of the subject; he only makes what it had regarded as fundamental dependent on the still profounder . . . basis of an originative power' (Habermas 1987: 178–9, my italic). And so on.

19 Habermas is also particularly close to the Rorty-Derrida-fly in his comments on Nietzsche: 'As soon as we take the *literary* character of Nietzsche's writings seriously', he writes, 'the suitableness of his critique of reason has to be assessed in accord with the standards of rhetorical success and not those of logical consistency' (Habermas 1987: 188).

20 Richard Rorty has opposed this interpretation in several essays: see Rorty 1991b: 112, for example.

21 See chapter 1, n. 1.

3 LE DŒUFF, KOFMAN AND IRIGARAY AS THEORISTS OF CONSTITUTIVE INSTABILITY

1 ('I don't accept that there's a writing somehow "proper to women". I'm a partisan of clarity, of rational, well-constructed texts', author's translation.)

2 Two sections of this text have been translated and published in American journals: see Kofman 1988 and Kofman 1982b.

3 ('Seductive and destructive object, whom I adore and whom I detest . . . abyss of good and evil', author's translation.)

4 See, for example, Margaret Canovan (1987) and Lynda Lange (1979), both of whom I discuss in chapter 4.

5 ('The division at the heart of the feminine sex is not the effect of social distance, but of a cut effected by the masculine sex, which, because of the needs of its sexual economy, denigrates, despises certain women while raising others on a pedestal, sullies some and tries to maintain the purity of others, while holding them at a distance which renders them untouchable', author's translation.)

6 See the discussion of Okin's interpretation of Rousseau in chapter 4.

7 ('This economical function . . . of respect – more or less dissimulated behind the mask of the moral – can be traced back to a general law', author's translation.) Kofman particularly presents Kant as *concealing* the 'economical function' of the account of respect behind its façade as a moral sentiment. Insofar as Kant presents respect for women as simply one example of respect for the other, she argues that he 'conceals' the fact that respect for women is 'the necessary condition of morality, necessary if men are at all to be educated in the sentiment of respect in general'.

8 In *Dissemination*, Derrida asserts that 'Plato–Rousseau–Saussure', who try 'in vain' to master 'supplementarity' (see the section on Derrida in chapter 5), all entangle themselves in logical contradiction. Derrida explains the use of the term 'kettle logic' in this context:

One would have to recognise here an instance of that kind of 'kettle-logic' to which Freud turns in the *Traumdeutung* [*Interpretation of Dreams*] in order to illustrate the logic of dreams. In his attempt to arrange everything in his favour, the defendant piles up contradictory arguments: 1. The kettle I am returning to you is brand new; 2. The holes were already in it when you lent it to me; 3. You never lent me a kettle, anyway. Analogously: 1. Writing is rigorously exterior and inferior to living memory and speech, which are therefore undamaged by it. 2. Writing is harmful to them because it puts them to sleep and infects their very life which would otherwise remain intact. 3. Anyway if one has resorted to hypomnesia at all, it is not for their intrinsic value, but because living memory is finite, it already has holes in it before writing ever comes to leave its traces. Writing has no effect on memory.

(Derrida 1981a: 110–11)

In this passage Derrida specifically suggests that one *point out* this kind of logical contradiction, rather than 'meditating on the structure that makes such supplementarity possible'. In the remarks on Derrida in this chapter, I argue that Derrida is oriented more towards the question of how textual contradiction is operative or effective, as opposed to the question of what causes it and how it can be explained.

9 Freud argued that there are no rules of non-contradiction in the unconscious dreamwork's 'grammar' (Freud 1976: 755), and also that the unconscious typically transposes a theme or emotion into its opposite (love and hate, subject and object, etc. – see, for example, Freud 1977: 81).

10 For example, the masochistic pleasure of being punished and humiliated by a woman.

11 It is partly, she states, for this reason that she juxtaposes the readings of respect in the texts of Kant and Rousseau – so that Rousseau's own account is not taken as an isolated pathology. Instead, the repetition of these themes in the work of both Rousseau and Kant leads her to suspect of Kant that: 'son économie sexuelle, malgré tout ce qui le sépare de lui, possède peut-être les mêmes exigences que celles de Rousseau; exigences communes à tous les hommes, ou à un certain type d'hommes' (Kofman 1982a: 19).

12 Indeed, if we can glean some hints from Kofman about how to be alert to ambivalences in an author's text, we might be alert to the symptoms of her own ambivalence about the role of psychoanalytic theory in her own text. Kofman both constructs and disavows the approach which reconstructs 'le cas Rousseau'.

13 I do not suggest that any interpretation, insofar as it is psychoanalytic, is necessarily oriented towards a causal or explanatory rather than a functional or operative interpretation of textual contradiction. I suggest that this is the effect of the particular way in which Kofman deploys a psychoanalytic perspective in *Le Respect des femmes*.

14 For this account of man's fragility, see in particular 'Any Theory of the "Subject" Has Always Been Appropriated by the "Masculine"', in *Speculum*: 'her possession by a "subject" . . . is yet another of his vertiginous failures . . . even as man seeks to rise higher and higher – in his knowledge too – so the ground fractures more and more beneath his feet' (Irigaray 1985a: 134). Here, the (feminine) ground 'fractures' because where man constitutes his 'ground', his 'mirror to catch his reflection' he simultaneously constitutes an other which resists and dodges his projects of representation (Irigaray 1985a:

133–6). Irigaray also isolates an element of the feminine in reserve or in excess of her role as negative mirror insofar as women has to exercise 'effort' to masquerade as negative mirror (Irigaray 1985b: 84).

15 See, for example, the account of matter as feminine in Plato's *Timaeus* discussed by Derrida 1981a: 160–1.

16 Irigaray makes clear her strategy of mimicry in 'Powers of Discourse', thus: 'There is, in an initial phase, perhaps only one "path", the one historically assigned to the feminine: that of *mimicry*. One must assume the feminine role deliberately. Which means already to convert a form of subordination into an affirmation, and thus to begin to thwart it . . . To play with mimesis is thus, for a woman, to try to recover the place of her exploitation by discourse, without allowing herself to be simply reduced to it' (Irigaray 1985b: 76). Margaret Whitford emphasises this aspect of Irigaray's project: see Whitford 1991: 71.

17 In her comments on Freud's account of femininity, she does not argue that Freud misrepresents women, but rather locates the 'internal contradictions' interrupting the coherence of Freud's own account. She states explicitly that Freud is 'describing an actual state of affairs', rather than having to reject Freud's description as false, in favour of an account of the truth of women (Irigaray 1985b: 70).

18 According to this Irigarayan paradox, the exclusion of sexual difference is a simultaneous 'indication' or marker of that exclusion, and thus destabilises itself. Critics such as John McGowan are mistaken in thinking that they have located a dilemma for so-called 'postmodern theory' which attempts to articulate the exclusion of difference. For McGowan, one cannot say both that nothing escapes from 'culture's signifying processes' and also that a capitalist social order is not inclusive enough (McGowan 1991: 21–3). This kind of interpretation, applied to Irigaray, would suggest that it is incoherent to argue that patriarchal culture excludes sexual difference. If it has been excluded, how can we indicate the concept at all? But Irigaray argues, as I make clear in this chapter, that patriarchal culture is based not so much on the exclusion of sexual difference as on a paradox by which sexual difference must be both excluded and, by virtue of that exclusion, included. Thus, the exclusion of sexual difference *both* 'reinforces' and 'destabilises' patriarchal culture.

19 For example, she locates an example of such a gesticulation in Freud's confrontation with and interrogation of the 'mystery' of femininity within a context of positioning women as a (lacking) variation of masculinity. Freud represents woman in terms of 'passive aims' in relation to the 'active aims' of man; represents the little girl as just a little boy; and represents woman's sex in terms of an atrophied masculine sex. Yet Freud *also* represents woman as a great mystery, an obstacle to scientific penetration (Freud 1973: 146–7, 149, 151, 160). Irigaray suggests that Freud's confrontation with woman as an 'impenetrable mystery' is an implicit avowal on his part that woman is more than an atrophied masculinity. Thus, Irigaray destabilises Freud's account of femininity through locating tension points at which the text would seem to undermine its own overt account of femininity (Irigaray 1985a: 13–14, 17, 19).

20 This problem is discussed in chapter 6.

21 As Derrida writes: 'To repeat: the disappearance of the good-father-capital-sun is thus the precondition of discourse . . . The disappearance of truth as presence, the withdrawal of the present origin of presence, is the condition of all (manifestation) of truth' (Derrida 1981a: 168).

4 JEAN-JACQUES ROUSSEAU AND THE INCONSTANCY OF WOMAN

1 As Derathé and Baczko emphasise, Rousseau glorifies reason and civilisation at certain points, despite also seeing in them the symptoms of degradation from the natural. While Rousseau thinks that agriculture and land ownership are symptoms of degradation (Rousseau 1987b: 47, 60), he also devalues corrupt urban communities in opposition to the idylls of pastoral communities (Rousseau 1991: 389, 474). Still, Rousseau's overall claim is that the symptoms of an extreme degradation can be located in civilisation.

2 This last point is complicated by Rousseau's argument that women do nevertheless govern men in natural relations between the sexes: 'I expect that many readers, remembering that I ascribe to woman a natural talent for governing man, will accuse me of a contradiction here. They will, however, be mistaken. There is quite a difference between arrogating to oneself the right to command and governing him who commands. Woman's empire is an empire of gentleness, skill and obligingness; her orders are caresses, her threats are tears' (Rousseau 1991: 408). Woman's empire is compatible with man's mastery over her.

3 As Groethuysen points out, it is also true that Rousseau praises 'femmes d'esprit'. These are the only women who can appreciate 'les finesses de cœur' of a work like *La Nouvelle Héloïse* which the Genevoise, for example, could not grasp (see Rousseau 1953: 504–5 and Groethuysen 1949: 396). We can add that Rousseau himself admires certain women writers such as Sappho (Rousseau 1960: 103). Nevertheless, for Rousseau one must make a choice. The Genevoise would certainly lose her naturalness in cultivating an appreciation of *La Nouvelle Héloïse*. One cannot both take pleasure in feminine literature and maintain proximity to nature.

4 As Starobinski argues, for Rousseau both children and the hypothetical primitives of the state of nature are authentic. Exterior appearance is considered no obstacle to our understanding of the inner hearts of children and 'primitive' peoples.

5 It seems to be specifically women's desire which presents the threat of immoderation. Rousseau does also argue that man's reason acts as a restraint to immoderate sexual activity, and at one point suggests that the desire of both men and women would be insatiable if not for the natural safety mechanism of women's modesty. Still, he emphasises the threat of man's destruction at the hands of women's insatiability.

6 For an analysis of Rousseau's 'economy of the veil' see both Kofman 1982a: 61–70 and Starobinski 1988: 65–80.

7 Similarly, Rousseau cites the example of Galatea, who in order to provoke the encounter with the shepherd lover pursuing her, resists and flees him (Rousseau 1991: 385).

8 There is a crucial difference between the economy of resistance pertaining to the 'bad' Parisienne and the 'good' Sophie. The Parisienne uses the artifice of modesty in order to dominate and emasculate man. Sophie feigns a more extreme modesty than is in fact 'authentic' in order to produce the 'masculinisation' of man by stimulating his virility.

9 As Jean Starobinski explains this essentialism, Rousseau argues both that the human soul has degenerated and that primitive nature persists, hidden, 'veiled, shrouded in artifice – yet intact'. The themes of a lost nature and a concealed inner nature thus interconnect in 'an optimistic and a pessimistic

version of the myth of origin: Rousseau believes sometimes in one, sometimes in the other, sometimes in both simultaneously. He tells us that man has irrevocably destroyed his natural identity, but he also says that man's original soul is indestructible and hence that it survives unchanged beneath the mask of artifice' (Starobinski 1988: 15).

10 A point also made by Jean Elshtain in *Public Man, Private Woman* (1981: 164–5).

11 For a discussion of this tendency in Rousseauist criticism, see Starobinski's introduction to the French edition of Ernst Cassirer's *The Question of Jean-Jacques Rousseau,* Cassirer 1987: III–XVII).

12 ('Man of contradictions, Rousseau has been treated with condescension: one could pardon much in him because he was a magician of words [or because his] case belonged to the field of psychiatry', author's translation).

13 Robert Bernasconi and Paul de Man have misgivings about whether Derrida entirely 'evades' this question insofar as he invokes the notion of the textual 'blind spot'. See de Man 1971: 102–41, and Bernasconi 1992: 143.

14 There is some ambiguity about whether Derrida uses his evocation of the 'supplementary logic' as a means of articulating the contradictory structure of Rousseau's text, or uses it as a means of resisting the view that Rousseau's text is contradictory. This ambiguity is due to his references to the 'strange unity' of Rousseauist contradiction, and his comments about Rousseauist statements being 'contrary' without being 'contradictory'. But this ambiguity can be ascribed to his argument that it is the supplementary logic itself which has a 'strange unity'. So, there is an interesting ambiguity about whether Derrida is saying that Rousseau 'contradicts' himself. Rousseau does contradict himself in a way analysed by Derrida as necessary. It is because of his interest in the way that Rousseau's contradictions work together to generate effects of presence that he sometimes also says of the contradictory elements that they are 'contrary without being contradictory' (Derrida 1976: 179). Robert Bernasconi gives this problem the following formulation: 'The contradictions remain only so long as one's reading of the text is governed by what Derrida calls the logic of identity. They can be resolved if another logic, which Derrida . . . calls the logic of supplementarity, is taken into account' (Bernasconi 1992: 144). Thus, Bernasconi's interpretation of the slippage between whether Derrida describes Rousseau's contradictions *as* contradictions or as contraries without being contradictions is related to Derrida's description of Rousseau's text as organised by a 'supplementary logic'. Nevertheless, we might differ with Bernasconi's use of this distinction to suggest that Derrida 'resolves' Rousseau's distinctions. Rather, I shall argue that what is crucial about Derrida's approach (as opposed to that of the many commentators committed to 'resolving' Rousseau's contradictions by arguing that some of Rousseau's statements are to be ignored as not the 'real' argument) is that Derrida does not attempt to resolve Rousseau's contradictions. Not engaging in the assertions about what Rousseau meant to say, Derrida directs his attention to the ways in which the contradictions operate and produce effects of presence, according to what he terms a 'supplementary logic'.

15 Furthermore, when Derrida asserts that the Rousseauist contradictions are strangely 'coherent', and 'strangely unified' (Derrida 1976: 142), there is no suggestion that Rousseau was 'in control' of the text. Compare this to the way in which Jean Starobinski retreats before the inference that Rousseau's contradictions are 'coherent'. It seems that Starobinski could only consider Rousseau's contradictions to be 'coherent' or 'unified' if Rousseau could be

interpreted as 'completely conscious' (to use Starobinski's term) of his text. Starobinski considers such claims extravagant because of his own supposition that such claims amount to assertions about Rousseau's original consciousness of, and control over, his own texts (Starobinski 1988: 114–15).

5 CONSTITUTIVE INSTABILITY IN ROUSSEAU'S DEFENCE OF NATURAL SEXUAL DIFFERENCE

1 Rousseau originally uses the expression 'that dangerous supplement' in his *Confessions* in relation to his discovery of masturbation. Derrida extends the concept of the supplement in his discussion of a series of privileged terms in Rousseau's work including 'nature' and 'speech'. In relation to literal masturbation, Derrida's point is that there is an aporia at the heart of the opposition between literal heterosexual intercourse and devalued masturbation. Although, in that opposition, masturbation is devalued as a 'supplement' in relation to heterosexual intercourse, heterosexuality is also always already 'supplementary'. For Rousseau, Derrida suggests, women are a substitute for the absent maternal, and the absent maternal is itself already a 'substitute' in a substitutive chain of desired 'objects'. Derrida interprets Rousseau's account of masturbation in terms of a particular economy of desire, suggesting that a structure of supplementarity parallels that which organises the nature/ culture opposition. What is crucial to that structure is the notion of the original 'object' as absent and chimerical, such that one can say of the structure of supplementary mediations that they 'produce the very thing they defer: the mirage of the thing itself, of immediate presence, of originary perception. Immediacy is derived. That all begins through the intermediary is what is indeed "inconceivable to reason"' (Derrida 1976: 157). Derrida uses the parallel between masturbation, writing and culture to argue that, in what he will call 'the chain of supplements', or 'supplementary logic', the original is always already a supplement (Derrida 1976: 156).
2 This is a flexibility whose most extreme manifestations are seen when we juxtapose the account of the radically pre-domesticated, pre-familial 'natural' creatures of the 'Discourse on the Origin of Inequality' with the account of the domestic pastoral ideal elsewhere evoked as 'natural' by Rousseau.
3 The same point can be made in many ways. We can say that exteriority simultaneously renders interiority possible and impossible. Alternatively we can state: *that which produces interiority simultaneously undermines it*. It is certainly possible to express this point as 'there is no such thing as interiority'. But Derrida, although he sometimes use such phrases, is also insistent on the fact that although exteriority, producing interiority, renders it 'non-interior', this is still the operation which *produces the effect* of interiority.
4 These comments can be related to those made in relation to Platonic truth by Derrida in *Dissemination*: 'The disappearance of truth as presence, the withdrawal of the present origin of presence, is the condition of all (manifestation) of truth. Non-truth is the truth. Non-presence is absence. Différance, the disappearance of any originary presence, is *at once* the condition of possibility *and* the condition of impossibility of truth' (Derrida 1981a: 168). To say that 'the condition of truth is non-truth' is not the same thing as to say that 'there is no truth'. Rather it is to say that the structure by which the 'condition of truth is non-truth' is the structure by which that which constitutes the *effect* of truth, the *production* and *operation* of truth, is (paradoxically) non-truth.

5 The 'Discourse on the Sciences and Arts' and the 'Discourse on the Origin of Inequality' will be referred to respectively as the 'first' and 'second' 'Discourses'.

6 Rousseau argues for the 'innocence' of original humans, as opposed to endorsing the doctrine of an original fall from grace. Nevertheless, he considers that humans have undergone a different kind of 'fall'. This is the fall to social organisation, which is responsible both for man's enlightenment and for his corruption and degradation.

7 Rousseau argues that our primitive nature persists, as Starobinski writes, 'shrouded in artifice' but nevertheless intact. He also argues that this nature is virtually unrecognisable. He maintains that humans have destroyed their natural identity, irremediably. Yet he also claims that our original soul is indestructible, and remains eternally 'self-identical' under the external social which masks it. Starobinski proposes that this contradiction be understood as 'only apparent', because Rousseau only claims that our original soul is rendered *virtually* unrecognisable (Starobinski 1988: 15).

8 This is apparent where Rousseau attempts a description of the passage from nature to culture in texts such as the 'Discourse on the Origin of Inequality' and the 'Essay on the Origin of Languages'. He is confronted with the 'choice' of which (hypothetical) moment in human development to identify as pre-social. He can choose the moment preceding the origin of language, or the moment preceding human reception of the 'word of God', or the moment preceding the perception of the other qua other, or he can attempt to trace the human back to animal origins.

The problem faced by Rousseau is conceptual, rather than one of the empirical limitations on scientific and historical investigation into human origins. We can articulate this problem thus: is such a point to be conceptually considered as *continuous* with our contemporary state of social relations (thus, as the first step in such a continuum: the first moments of language, and the first moments in the perception of the other), or as radically *prior* to the continuum of development leading to our contemporary state of social relations?

Rather than making this conceptual choice: either positioning the state of nature as prior to the continuum of social relations or positioning the state of nature as the first point in that continuum, we see Rousseau intertwining both ideas in his œuvre. An example occurs in the opening to the second 'Discourse'. Rousseau tells us that to trace man's origins would require a scientific capacity to trace the development of the human back to a primordial animal state which anatomical science does not 'currently' allow (Rousseau 1987b: 39–40). But he also states that such a tracing would not be relevant since the origin of man must be considered to be the advent of language and the ability of man to receive God's word (Rousseau 1966: 38). We see this archetypal Rousseauist coordination of the ideas that the natural is both exterior and radically prior to the social and also the original moment of the social. Culture is both exterior and interior to nature.

9 ('Finally, since the character and love of beauty has been imprinted by nature in the depths of my soul, I shall be regulated by it for as long as it does not become disfigured. But how to be assured of conserving in its pure state this interior effigy which does not have, among the living beings, any model to which it can be compared. Don't we know that disordered affections corrupt our judgement as well as our will, and that conscience becomes altered and modified imperceptibly in each people, each individual, according to the inconsistency and variety of prejudice?', author's translation.)

10 ('I hope for all which pertains to the order of nature established by you, and to be ruled by the reason with which you endowed me', author's translation.)

11 ('At one moment, Rousseau declares that we must listen to the voice of nature ... at another it is instead reason that he advises us to follow. In alternation, conscience and reason are presented as the guidance that man has received from God. At one moment conscience and reason are opposed, at another they are so closely interconnected that they seem to be indistinguishable. Finally, with regard to reason itself, we see Rousseau firstly reject it as source of error and sophism, and then elevate it as the divine torch that the supreme Being has given us to enlighten our path', author's translation.)

12 ('Voulons-nous pénétrer dans ces abîmes de métaphysique ... ?'). As Grimsley points out, Saint Preux, while educated, is specifically not a philosopher: see the discussion of this point, Grimsley 1961: 36.

13 As Groethuysen asks, 'Mais alors pourquoi faut-il donc un Dieu? (Groethuysen 1945: 291).

14 ('How to explain the fact that the notion of God undergoes so much metamorphosis in the work of Rousseau, and that it comprehends divergent elements which would be difficult to reconcile? ... Why is it sometimes sentiment which speaks, pure sentiment, the entirely personal sentiment of a soul which seeks the infinite, and sometimes the constructive spirit of a legislator who wants to impose God on society? Why does God seem sometimes to depend on reason and sometimes on moral conceptions?', author's translation.)

15 For example, see Rousseau 1991: 270, 275, 286, 289, etc.

16 See in particular Jean Starobinski's complex account of the Rousseauist ideal of transparency. This ideal is manifest in Rousseau's vision of a primordial childhood unmediated by the regard of the other; in his vision of a primordial historical time where man's relationship with nature is unmediated by the social; in his vision of ideal communities in which there is no mediation between the 'truth' of man and the way in which he appears to his fellow man, etc. (Starobinksi 1988: 11–12).

17 Again, see Starobinski 1988: 11–12 for his analysis of the concept of original nature as transparent and unmediated. See the 'Profession de foi' for the account of God as an independent being 'active in itself', a 'single intelligence', etc. (Rousseau 1991: 277).

18 I employ a distinction between 'conceptual' and 'technical' obstacles to the development of an author's argument. Such a distinction arises in relation to why Rousseau cannot trace the origin of humanity back to its hypothetical beginnings in the realm of the animal kingdom. Rousseau effectively suggests that the problem is 'technical' where he argues that 'comparative anatomy has as yet made too little progress; the observations of naturalists are as yet too uncertain' (Rousseau 1987b: 39–40). But the problem is at the same time 'conceptual'. It involves a choice of the point which is situated conceptually as the 'origins' of the human. Such a point could be the hypothetical origins in the animal kingdom (even if one is limited in one's technical ability to trace human origins back so far), or the origins of humanity could be situated conceptually at the point where one understands man as first distinct from the animals. One can decide that the origin of 'man' is the moment of passage from 'animal' to 'human', or from 'natural' to 'social', or from 'primeval' to 'civilised', or one can decide that one will understand the 'origins' of humanity as being that state which succeeds these passages. I have suggested that Rousseau's texts hover between these different meanings, that the

hovering is 'operative', and also that comments about technical restrictions on tracing origins obscure the aporia which is conceptual, not technical.

6 OPERATIVE CONTRADICTION IN AUGUSTINE'S CONFESSIONS

1 As Hunter points out in his discussion of Augustine's *Literal Commentary on Genesis*, such questions as to whether Adam and Eve are intrinsically souls, of which we may ask whether they are attached to bodies, and whether they are attached to bodies in the same way in which we are so attached, are only intelligible within a dualist framework.

2 By contrast, the mark of sin is the advent of the uncontrollable erection into paradise. Augustine speaks of 'that rebellion of the members which brought the accusing blush on those who after their sin covered these members with the fig-tree leaves' and 'the sin of that disobedience which was followed by the penalty of man's finding his own members emulating against himself that very disobedience which he had practised against God' (Augustine 1971: 251; II.39).

3 (Whereas childbirth before the fall would have been painless. See Augustine 1971: 252; II.40, 41.)

4 Radford Ruether discusses the problem concerning 'the sexual character of the risen body. If woman was essentially body and had sensual and depraved characteristics of mind, then it followed (according to a dualistic view of redemption) that either she was irredeemable or else she was redeemed only by transcending the female nature and being transformed into a male . . . Since it was normal to speak of the virgin who lived the "angelic life" as having transcended her female nature and having become "male" (*vir*), this led to a belief that in the Resurrection there would be only male bodies, all females having been changed into males. Both Augustine and Jerome must inconsistently deny this conclusion, insisting that humanity will rise as "male and female", but in some incomprehensible way that will spiritualize the body' (Radford Ruether 1974: 160).

5 With regard to the latter, see again 'On the Literal Interpretation of Genesis': 'Of course, it might be most subtly argued that the mind of the human being – that is, the rational life through which the human being was made according to the image of God – divides into a part directed toward the truth of eternal contemplation and a part directed toward the administration of temporal things, and that the mind was thus, in a sense, made male and female, with the one part considering and the other part obeying' (Augustine 1994: 251; III.22).

6 For example, the monist account by which every part of the whole of Creation is a mode of God, in Spinoza's *Ethics*.

7 An account to be found throughout the *Confessions* – for example, in the discussion of the Manicheans, who are regarded as heretical both insofar as they understand God as like man (Augustine 1961: 104; V.10) and insofar as they understand man as like God (Augustine 1961: 86; IV.15).

8 Similarly, although Plato attributes primacy to speech over writing, this is not because of some 'intrinsic' primacy (internal to the speech/writing opposition), but because of an apparently external reference point: that of the Forms. The purported primacy of speech and knowledge refers to this divine origin. As we have seen, Derrida's reading of speech as itself a writing relates to the

fact that speech is only held superior to writing because of its constant deferral to a transcendent reference. It is at the point of this deferral that Derrida finds the leverage position from which he begins to unravel the speech/writing opposition, arguing that even divine origin is not self-identical since it must '*add to itself* the possibility of being repeated as such' (Derrida 1981a: 76–81, 88).

9 Although this point should be complicated by the fact that sometimes the account of God as not-man is put in terms of God's *identifiability*. This is a point about man's insufficiency, his inability to comprehend God in any but negative terms.

10 See book XII for the multiplication of terms which occurs with the inter-changeable references to 'soul' and 'mind', a multiplication which also occurs in Descartes' *Meditations*. Rather than making a sharp distinction between soul and mind, Augustine alternates between referring to the soul, and to the mind as that which 'moves' man and sorts through the muddled messages from the senses. However, at the point at which he refers to the heaven of heavens, that which survives the body is no longer interchangeably mind and soul, and is, rather, definitively soul.

11 Two anthologies which give a good sense of different feminist interventions into theology and philosophy of religion, from critique, through reconstruction, to creating new traditions, are Christ and Plaskow 1979 and Plaskow and Christ 1989.

12 See Gatens 1991: 48–60; Mackenzie 1986: 144–57; Butler 1990: 12.

13 See the argument in the *Republic* that it would be just as ridiculous to suggest that the difference of a man's baldness or hairiness affects the quality of his soul as to suggest that sexual difference affects the difference of a man's or a woman's soul (Plato 1961: 693). Descartes' letter to Vatier of 22 February 1638, in which his view is that 'even women' might understand something of his work, is discussed in Lloyd 1984: 44.

7 THE NOTORIOUS CONTRADICTIONS OF SIMONE DE BEAUVOIR

1 Throughout this chapter I shall refer to Beauvoir as a feminist philosopher and to *The Second Sex* as a feminist project, although Beauvoir did not name herself a feminist until the 1960s. That said, I shall also locate elements of a phallocentric account of women and femininity in Beauvoir's philosophy.

2 As Jean Starobinski points out, Ernst Cassirer's *Le Problème Jean-Jacques Rousseau* was particularly controversial when first presented in 1932 to French philosophers precisely because it presented Rousseau's work as a coherent whole (Cassirer 1987: III). The question at that time, in a French context, was whether or not Rousseau was to be accorded legitimacy as a philosopher, and one can consult in this regard the debate that takes place among the members of the Société française de philosophie in 1937 in the discussion following Cassirer's presentation of his work, published in the *Bulletin de la société française de philosophie* (Cassirer 1932 cited in Cassirer 1987: 67ff.). For example, Raymond Lenoir objected to Cassirer's presentation of his work with the following comment: 'La méthode de Cassirer consiste ici à accorder un statut de pleine légitimité philosophique à un discours chaleureux que Rousseau n'a pas organisé selon les normes exigibles d'un philosophe "de métier". ('Cassirer's method here consists in attributing a status of full philosophical

legitimacy to an impassioned discourse that Rousseau did not organise according to the norms required of a "professional" philosopher') (cited by Cassirer 1987: v).

3 For a discussion of this phenomenon, see Gatens 1991: 1, and Le Dœuff 1989: 100–28.

4 An argument also put forward by Genevieve Lloyd (1984: 87), and many other theorists.

5 In an earlier piece, 'Variations on Sex and Gender', Butler acknowledges that Beauvoir's work on gender is ambivalent about the Cartesian mind/body dualism. However, she argues that Beauvoir's ambivalence is less serious than Sartre's, that she 'takes him at his non-Cartesian best', and that her work 'argues the limits of a Cartesian version of disembodied freedom' (Butler 1987: 129–33).

6 See Sartre's notorious passages on 'holes and slime' in 'Quality as a Revelation of Being' (Sartre 1958: 600–15). For a discussion of this passage, see Collins and Pierce 1976, and for a discussion of expressions of Sartre's revulsion at embodiment and the feminine in his work and in letters, see Le Dœuff 1991: 180–93.

7 Arp relates the tenor in Beauvoir's work to the experiences which she and her acquaintances might have had: 'Perhaps Beauvoir herself, as well as many of the women of her time and place, did experience her body in this way' (Arp 1995: 164).

8 For this reason, the work is taken to task for its failure to place a political or ethical priority on theorising the ways in which we could be described as 'not free' rather than the ways in which we could be described as free.

9 Sartre and Beauvoir use the terminology of the other in an inverse sense. For Beauvoir, woman is the other. For Sartre, the 'Other' is s/he who *renders* me a being-for-others.

BIBLIOGRAPHY

Abrams, M. H. (1977) 'The Deconstructive Angel', *Critical Inquiry* 3, Spring: 425–38.

Alexander, W. M. (1974) 'Sex and Philosophy in Augustine', *Augustinian Studies* 5: 197–208.

Armstrong, K. (1986) *The Gospel According to Woman: Christianity's Creation of the Sex War in the West*, London: Elm Tree Books.

Arp, K. (1995) 'Beauvoir's Concept of Bodily Alienation', in M. A. Simons (ed.) *Feminist Interpretations of Simone de Beauvoir*, University Park, PA: Pennsylvania State University Press.

Augustine, St (1961) *Confessions*, trans. R. S. Pine-Coffin. Harmondsworth: Penguin.

Augustine, St (1971) 'On the Grace of Christ, and on Original Sin', in P. Schaff (ed.) *A Select Library of the Nicene and Post-Nicene Fathers of the Christian Church*, Grand Rapids, MI: Wm. B. Eerdmans Publishing Company.

Augustine, St (1972) *Concerning the City of God Against the Pagans*, trans. Henry Bettenson. Harmondsworth: Penguin.

Augustine, St (1988a) 'On The Good of Marriage', in P. Schaff (ed.) *A Select Library of the Nicene and Post-Nicene Fathers of the Christian Church*, Grand Rapids, MI: Wm. B. Eerdmans Publishing Company.

Augustine, St (1988b) 'On Continence', in P. Schaff (ed.) *A Select Library of the Nicene and Post-Nicene Fathers of the Christian Church*, Grand Rapids, MI: Wm. B. Eerdmans Publishing Company.

Augustine, St (1994) 'On the Literal Interpretation of Genesis', in E. L. Fortin and D. Kries (eds) *Augustine: Political Writings*, Indianapolis: Hackett.

Baczko, B. (1974) *Rousseau, solitude et communauté*, trans. C. Brendhel-Lamhaut. Paris and The Hague: Mouton.

Barthes, R. (1972) 'The Structuralist Activity', in *Critical Essays*, trans. R. Howard, Evanston: Northwestern University Press.

Barthes, R. (1977) *Roland Barthes*, trans. R. Howard, New York: Hill and Wang.

Barthes, R. (1984) 'Introduction to the Structural Analysis of Narratives', in *Image Music Text*, trans. S. Heath. London: Fontana.

Barthes, R. (1988) *The Semiotic Challenge*, trans. R. Howard. New York: Hill and Wang.

Bate, W. J. (1982) 'The Crisis in English Studies', *Harvard Magazine* 85, 12: 46–53.

Beaulavon, M. G. (1937) 'La Philosophie de Jean-Jacques Rousseau et l'esprit cartésien', *Revue de Métaphysique et de Morale* 44, 1: 325–52.

Beaver, H. (1981) 'Homosexual Signs', *Critical Inquiry* 8, Autumn: 99–119.

Beauvoir, S. de (1988) *The Second Sex*, trans. H. M. Parshley. London: Pan.

Benhabib, S. (1995) 'Subjectivity, Historiography, and Politics: Reflections on the "Feminism/Postmodernism Exchange"', in L. Nicholson (ed.) *Feminist Contentions: A Philosophical Exchange*, New York and London: Routledge.

Bernasconi, R. (1992) 'No More Stories, Good or Bad: de Man's Criticisms of Derrida on Rousseau', in D. Wood (ed.) *Derrida: A Critical Reader*, Oxford, UK and Cambridge, MA: Blackwell Publishers.

Bernstein, R. (1987) 'Serious Play: The Ethical–Political Horizon of Jacques Derrida', *Journal of Speculative Philosophy* 1, 2: 93–117.

Børresen, K. E. (1981) *Subordination and Equivalence: The Nature and Rôle of Woman in Augustine and Thomas Aquinas*, Washington, DC: University Press of America.

Børresen, K. E. (1993) *Women's Studies of the Christian and Islamic Traditions: Ancient Medieval and Renaissance Foremothers*, Dordrecht, The Netherlands: Kluwer Academic Publishers.

Børreson, K. (1994) 'Patristic "Feminism": The Case of Augustine', *Augustinian Studies* 25: 139–52.

Brown, P. (1988) *The Body and Society: Men, Women, and Sexual Renunciation in Early Christianity*, New York: Columbia University Press.

Butler, J. (1987) 'Variations on Sex and Gender: Beauvoir, Wittig and Foucault', in S. Benhabib and D. Cornell (eds) *Feminism as Critique*, Minneapolis: University of Minnesota Press.

Butler, J. (1989) 'Gendering the Body: Beauvoir's Philosophical Contribution', in A. Garry and M. Pearsall (eds) *Women, Knowledge, and Reality: Explorations in Feminist Philosophy*, Boston, MA: Unwin Hyman.

Butler, J. (1990) *Gender Trouble*, New York and London: Routledge.

Butler, J. (1993) *Bodies That Matter: On the Discursive Limits of Sex*, New York and London: Routledge.

Butler, J. (1994a) 'Gender as Performance: An Interview with Judith Butler', *Radical Philosophy* 67: 32–9.

Butler, J. (1994b) 'Against Proper Objects', *differences A Journal of Feminist Cultural Studies* 6:2 and 3: 1–26.

Butler, J. (1995) 'For a Careful Reading', in L. Nicholson (ed.) *Feminist Contentions: A Philosophical Exchange*, New York and London: Routledge.

Butler, J. with Rubin, G. (1994) 'Sexual Traffic', *differences A Journal of Feminist Cultural Studies* 6, 2 and 3: 62–99.

Cadava, E., Connor, P. and Nancy, J.-L. (eds) (1991) *Who Comes After the Subject?*, New York and London: Routledge.

Canovan, M. (1987) 'Rousseau's Two Concepts of Citizenship', in E. Kennedy and S. Mendus (eds) *Women in Western Political Theory*, Sussex: Wheatsheaf Books, Harvester Press.

Cassirer, E. (1987) *Le Problème Jean-Jacques Rousseau*, trans. Marc B. de Launay. Paris: Hachette.

Chanter, T. (1995) *Ethics of Eros: Irigaray's Rewriting of the Philosophers*, New York and London: Routledge.

Christ, C. P. and Plaskow, J. (eds) (1979) *Womanspirit Rising*, San Francisco: Harper and Row.

Clark, E. (1986a) '"Adam's Only Companion": Augustine and the Early Christian Debate on Marriage', *Recherches Augustiniennes* 21: 139–62.

Clark, E. A. (1986b) *Ascetic Piety and Women's Faith*, Lewiston, NY, Queenston, Ontario and Lampeter, UK: Edwin Mellen Press.

Cocks, J. (1991) 'Augustine, Nietzsche and Contemporary Body Politics', *differences A Journal of Feminist Cultural Studies* 3, 1: 144–58.

Cohen, T. (1994) *Anti-mimesis from Plato to Hitchcock*, Cambridge: Cambridge University Press.

Collins, M. and Pierce, C. (1976) 'Holes and Slime: Sexism in Sartre's Psychoanalysis', in C. C. Gould and M. W. Wartofsky (eds) *Women and Philosophy: Toward a Theory of Liberation*, New York: Perigee.

Crossan, J. D. (1980) *Cliffs of Fall: Paradox and Polyvalence in the Parables of Jesus*, New York: Seabury Press.

Culler, J. (1982) *On Deconstruction: Theory and Criticism After Structuralism*, Ithaca, New York: Cornell University Press.

Daly, M. (1975) *The Church and the Second Sex*, New York: Harper and Row.

Daly, M. (1979) 'After the Death of God the Father', in C. P. Christ and J. Plaskow (eds) *Womanspirit Rising*, San Francisco: Harper and Row.

Derathé, R. (1979) *Le Rationalisme de Jean-Jacques Rousseau*, Geneva: Slatkine Reprints.

Derrida, J. (1976) *Of Grammatology*, trans. Gayatri Chakravorty Spivak. Baltimore and London: Johns Hopkins Press.

Derrida, J. (1978) 'Structure, Sign and Play', in *Writing and Difference*, trans. A. Bass, London: Routledge and Kegan Paul.

Derrida, J. (1981a) *Dissemination*, trans. Barbara Johnson. Chicago: University of Chicago Press.

Derrida, J. (1981b) *Positions*, trans. A. Bass. Chicago: University of Chicago Press.

Derrida, J. (1986) *Memoires for Paul de Man*, trans. C. Lindsay, J. Culler and E. Cadava, New York: Columbia University Press.

Derrida, J. (1988) *Limited Inc*, trans. S. Weber and J. Mehlman, Evanston, IL: Northwestern University Press.

Derrida, J. (1991) 'Letter to a Japanese Friend', in P. Kamuf (ed.) *A Derrida Reader: Between the Blinds*, New York: Columbia University Press.

Derrida, J. (1995a) '*Honoris Causa*: "This is *also* extremely funny"', in E. Weber (ed.) *Points . . . Interviews, 1974–1994*, Stanford: Stanford University Press.

Derrida, J. (1995b) 'The Time is Out of Joint', in A. Haverkamp (ed.) *Deconstruction is/in America: A New Sense of the Political*, New York and London: New York University Press.

Deutscher, P. (1992) 'The Evanascence of Masculinity: Deferral in Saint Augustine's Confessions and Some Thoughts on its Bearing on the Sex/Gender Debate', *Australian Feminist Studies* 15, Autumn: 41–56.

Deutscher, P. (1994) '"The Only Diabolical Thing about Women . . . ": Luce Irigaray on Divinity', *Hypatia* 9, 4: 88–111.

Dews, P. (1987) *Logics of Disintegration: Poststructuralist Thought and the Claims of Critical Theory*, London and New York: Verso Press.

Eisenman, P. (1995) 'Presentness and the "Being-Only-Once" of Architecture', in A. Haverkamp (ed.) *Deconstruction is/in America: A New Sense of the Political*, New York and London: New York University Press.

Ellis, J. M. (1989) *Against Deconstruction*, Princeton, NJ: Princeton University Press.

Elshtain, J. B. (1981) *Public Man, Private Woman: Women in Social and Political Thought*, Princeton, NJ: Princeton University Press.

Evans, M. (1985) *Simone de Beauvoir: A Feminist Mandarin*, London and New York: Tavistock.

Evans, M. (1987) 'Views of Women and Men in the Work of Simone de Beauvoir', in E. Marks (ed.) *Critical Essays on Simone de Beauvoir*, Boston, MA: G. K. Hall & Co.

Fiorenza, E. S. (1987) 'The "Quilting" of Women's History: Phoebe of Cenchreae', in P. M. Cooey, S. A. Farmer and M. E. Ross (eds) *Embodied Love: Sensuality and Relationship as Feminist Values*, San Francisco: Harper and Row.

Foucault, M. (1980) *Herculine Barbin, Being the Recently Discovered Memoirs of a Nineteenth-Century Hermaphrodite*, trans. R. McDougall, New York: Colophon.

Fraser, N. (1995) 'Pragmatism, Feminism and the Linguistic Turn', in L. Nicholson (ed.) *Feminist Contentions: A Philosophical Exchange*, New York and London: Routledge.

Fredriksen, P. (1988) 'Beyond the Body/Soul Dichotomy: Augustine on Paul Against the Manichees and the Pelagians', *Recherches Augustiniennes* 23: 87–114.

Freud, S. (1973) 'Femininity', in A. Richards (ed.) *New Introductory Lectures on Psychoanalysis*, trans. J. Strachey, Harmondsworth: Penguin.

Freud, S. (1976) *The Interpretation of Dreams*, trans. James Strachey. Harmondsworth: Penguin.

Freud, S. (1977) 'Three Essays on the Theory of Sexuality', in A. Richards (ed.) *On Sexuality*, trans. J. Strachey. Harmondsworth: Penguin.

Freud, S. (1986) 'On Dreams', in A. Freud (ed.) *The Essentials of Psychoanalysis*, trans. J. Strachey. Harmondsworth: Penguin.

Gasché, R. (1986) *The Tain of the Mirror*, Cambridge, MA and London: Harvard University Press.

Gatens, M. (1991) *Feminism and Philosophy: Perspectives on Difference and Equality*, Bloomington and Indianapolis: Indiana University Press.

Graff, G. (1979) *Literature Against Itself*, Chicago: University of Chicago Press.

Green, K. (1995) *The Woman of Reason: Feminism, Humanism and Political Thought*, Cambridge, MA and Oxford, UK: Polity Press.

Grimsley, R. (1961) *Rousseau and the Religious Quest*, Oxford: Clarendon Press.

Groethuysen, B. (1949) *Jean-Jacques Rousseau*, Paris: Gallimard.

Habermas, J. (1985) 'Modernity – An Incomplete Project', in H. Foster (ed.) *Postmodern Culture*, London and Sydney: Pluto Press.

Habermas, J. (1987) *The Philosophical Discourse of Modernity*, trans. Frederick Lawrence. Cambridge, MA: MIT Press.

Halley, J. E. (1991) 'Misreading Sodomy: A Critique of the Classification of "Homosexuals" in Federal Equal Protection Law', in J. Epstein and K. Straub (eds) *Body Guards: The Cultural Politics of Gender Ambiguity*, New York and London: Routledge.

Hart, K. (1989) *The Trespass of the Sign: Deconstruction, Theology and Philosophy*, Cambridge: Cambridge University Press.

Harvey, I. E. (1986) *Derrida and the Economy of Différance*, Bloomington: Indiana University Press.

Haverkamp, A. (ed.) (1995) *Deconstruction is/in America: A New Sense of the Political*, New York and London: New York University Press.

Huffer, L. (1995) 'Luce *et veritas*: Toward an Ethics of Performance', *Yale French Studies* 87: 20–41.

Hunter, D. G. (1994) 'Augustinian Pessimism? A New Look at Augustine's Teaching on Sex, Marriage and Celibacy', *Augustinian Studies* 25: 153–77.

Irigaray, L. (1985a) *Speculum of the Other Woman*, trans. G. C. Gill. Ithaca, NY: Cornell University Press.

Irigaray, L. (1985b) *This Sex which is Not One*, trans. C. Porter. Ithaca, NY: Cornell University Press.

Irigaray, L. (1991) *Marine Lover of Friedrich Nietzsche*, trans. G. C. Gill. New York: Columbia University Press.

Irigaray, L. (1993a) *An Ethics of Sexual Difference*, trans. C. Burke and G. C. Gill. Ithaca, New York: Cornell University Press.

216

Irigaray, L. (1993b) *Je, tu, nous: Toward a Culture of Difference*, trans. A. Martin. New York and London: Routledge.

Johnson, B. (1980) *The Critical Difference: Essays in the Contemporary Rhetoric of Reading*, Baltimore and London: The Johns Hopkins University Press.

Kant, I. (1929) *The Critique of Pure Reason*, trans. N. Kemp Smith. London: Macmillan.

Kirkman, N. and Grieve, M. (1986) 'The Ordination of Women: A Psychological Interpretation of the Objections', in M. A. Franklin (ed.) *The Force of the Feminine*, Sydney: Allen and Unwin.

Kofman, S. (1982a) *Le Respect des femmes – Kant et Rousseau*, Paris: Galilée.

Kofman, S. (1982b) 'The Economy of Respect: Kant and Respect for Women', *Social Research* 49, 2: 383–404.

Kofman, S. (1985) *The Enigma of Woman*, trans. C. Porter. Ithaca, New York: Cornell University Press.

Kofman, S. (1988) 'Rousseau's Phallocratic Ends', *Hypatia* 3, 3: 123–36.

Kofman, S. with Jaccard, R. (1986) 'Apprendre aux hommes à tenir parole – portrait de Sarah Kofman', *Le Monde Aujourd'hui*, 27–8 April, 7.

Lange, L. (1979) 'Rousseau on Women', in L. Clarke and L. Lange (eds) *The Sexism of Social and Political Theory: Women and Reproduction from Plato to Nietzsche*, Toronto: University of Toronto Press.

Le Dœuff, M. (1987) 'Operative Philosophy: Simone de Beauvoir and Existentialism', in E. Marks (ed.) *Critical Essays on Simone de Beauvoir*, Boston, MA: G. K. Hall & Co.

Le Dœuff, M. (1989) *The Philosophical Imaginary*, trans. C. Gordon. Stanford: Stanford University Press.

Le Dœuff, M. (1991) *Hipparchia's Choice: An Essay Concerning Women, Philosophy, etc.*, trans. T. Selous. Oxford, UK and Cambridge, MA: Basil Blackwell.

Le Dœuff, M. (1993a) 'Le Chromosome du crime: à propos de XY', in M. Riot-Sarcey (ed.) *Féminismes au présent (Futur Antérieur Supplément)*, Paris: L'Harmattan.

Le Dœuff, M. (1993b) 'Harsh Times', *New Left Review* 199, May–June: 127–39.

Léon, C. T. (1995) 'Beauvoir's Women: Eunuch or Male?', in M. A. Simons (ed.) *Feminist Interpretations of Simone de Beauvoir*, University Park, Pennsylvania: Pennsylvania State University Press.

Lerner, G. (1987) 'Women and History', in E. Marks (ed.) *Critical Essays on Simone de Beauvoir*, Boston, MA: G. K. Hall and Co.

Lloyd, G. (1984) *The Man of Reason: 'Male' and 'Female' in Western Philosophy*, London: Methuen.

Lloyd, G. (1993a) 'Preface to the Second Edition', in *The Man of Reason*, London: Routledge.

Lloyd, G. (1993b) 'Maleness, Metaphor, and the "Crisis" of Reason', in L. Anthony and C. Witt (eds) *A Mind of One's Own: Feminist Essays on Reason and Objectivity*, Boulder, CO: Westview Press.

McCarthy, T. (1991) *Ideals and Illusions: On Reconstruction and Deconstruction in Contemporary Critical Theory*, Cambridge, MA and and London: MIT Press.

McGowan, J. (1991) *Postmodernism and its Critics*, Ithaca and London: Cornell University Press.

Macherey, P. (1978) *A Theory of Literary Production*, trans. G. Wall. London: Routledge and Kegan Paul.

Mackenzie, C. (1986) 'Simone de Beauvoir: Philosophy and/or the Female Body', in C. Pateman and E. Gross (eds) *Feminist Challenges: Social and Political Theory*, Sydney: Allen and Unwin.

Man, P. de (1971) *Blindness and Insight: Essays in the Rhetoric of Contemporary Criticism*, Oxford: Oxford University Press.

Man, P. de (1979) *Allegories of Reading*, New Haven: Yale University Press.

Man, P. de (1982) 'The Return to Philology', *Times Literary Supplement*, 10 December 1982, 1355–6.

Martin, B. (1994) 'Extraordinary Homosexuals and the Fear of Being Ordinary', *differences A Journal of Feminist Cultural Studies* 6, 2 and 3: 100–25.

Miller, J. H. (1987) *The Ethics of Reading*, New York: Columbia University Press.

Miller, J. H. (1995) 'The Disputed Ground: Deconstruction and Literary Studies', in A. Haverkamp (ed.) *Deconstruction is/in America: A New Sense of the Political*, New York and London: New York University Press.

Moi, T. (1994) *Simone de Beauvoir: The Making of an Intellectual Woman*, Cambridge, MA and Oxford, UK: Blackwell.

Morris, M. (1981/2) 'Operative Reasoning: Michèle Le Dœuff, Philosophy and Feminism', *I and C* 9: 71–100.

Mortley, R. (1981) *Womanhood: The Feminine in Ancient Hellenism, Gnosticism, Christianity and Islam*, Sydney: Delacroix.

Mortley, R. (1991) *French Philosophers in Conversation*, London and New York: Routledge.

Nancy, J.-L. (1992) 'Elliptical Sense', in D. Wood (ed.) *Derrida: A Critical Reader*, Oxford, UK and Cambridge, MA: Blackwell Publishers.

Nicholson, L. (ed.) (1995) *Feminist Contentions: A Philosophical Exchange*, New York and London: Routledge.

Norris, C. (1987) *Derrida*, Cambridge, MA: Harvard University Press.

Norris, C. (1989) ''Philosophy as Not Just a "Kind of Writing": Derrida and the Claim of Reason', in R. W. Dasenbrock (ed.) *Redrawing the Lines*, Minneapolis: University of Minnesota Press.

Nye, A. (1995) *Philosophy and Feminism: At the Border*, New York: Twayne.

Okin, S. M. (1979) *Women in Western Political Thought*, Princeton, NJ: Princeton University Press.

Pagels, E. (1988) *Adam, Eve, and the Serpent*, New York: Random House.

Pateman, C. (1980) '"The Disorder of Women": Women, Love and the Sense of Justice', *Ethics* 91, October: 20–34.

Pateman, C. (1988) *The Sexual Contract*, Cambridge: Polity Press.

Philonenko, A. (1984) *Jean-Jacques Rousseau et la pensée du malheur – Le Traité du mal*, Paris: Vrin.

Plaskow, J. and Christ, C. P. (eds) (1989) *Weaving the Visions*, San Francisco: HarperCollins.

Plato (1961) 'The Republic', in E. Hamilton and H. Cairns (eds) *Plato: The Collected Dialogues*, Princeton: Princeton University Press.

Plaza, M. (1978) '"Phallomorphic Power" and the Psychology of "Woman"', *Ideology and Consciousness* 4, Autumn: 4–36.

Plotnitsky, A. (1994) *Complementarity*, Durham, NC and London: Duke University Press.

Power, K. (1992) 'Sed unam tamen: Augustine and his Concubine', *Augustinian Studies* 23: 49–76.

Radford Ruether, R. (1974) 'Misogynism and Virginal Feminism in the Fathers of the Church', in R. R. Ruether (ed.) *Religion and Sexism Images of Woman in the Jewish and Christian Traditions*, New York: Simon and Schuster.

Radford Ruether, R. (1989) 'Sexism and God Language', in J. Plaskow and C. P. Christ (eds) *Weaving the Visions*, San Francisco: HarperCollins.

Raymond, M. (1962) *Jean-Jacques Rousseau: La Quête de soi et la rêverie*, Paris: Librairie José Corti.

Rorty, R. (1982) 'Philosophy as a Kind of Writing', in *Consequences of Pragmatism*, Brighton, Sussex: Harvester Press.

Rorty, R. (1989) 'From Ironist Theory to Private Allusions: Derrida', in *Contingency, Irony and Solidarity*, Cambridge: Cambridge University Press.

Rorty, R. (1991a) 'Deconstruction and Circumvention', in *Essays on Heidegger and Others*, Cambridge: Cambridge University Press.

Rorty, R. (1991b) 'Two Meanings of "Logocentrism": A Reply to Norris', in *Essays on Heidegger and Others*, Cambridge: Cambridge University Press.

Rorty, R. (1991c) 'Is Derrida a Transcendental Philosopher?', in *Essays on Heidegger and Others*, Cambridge: Cambridge University Press.

Rousseau, J.-J. (1953) *The Confessions*, trans. J. M. Cohen. Harmondsworth: Penguin.

Rousseau, J.-J. (1960) 'Letter to M. D'Alembert on the Theatre', in *Politics and the Arts*, trans. A. Bloom, Glencoe, Illinois: Free Press of Glencoe.

Rousseau, J.-J. (1964a) 'Narcisse', in B. Gagnebin and M. Raymond (eds) *Œuvres complètes*, Paris: Gallimard (Bibliothèque de la Pléiade).

Rousseau, J.-J. (1964b) 'Lettres écrites de la montagne', in B. Gagnebin and M. Raymond (eds) *Œuvres complètes*, Paris: Gallimard (Bibliothèque de la Pléiade).

Rousseau, J.-J. (1966) 'Essay on the Origin of Languages', in J. H. Moran and A. Gode (eds) *On the Origin of Language*, Chicago and London: University of Chicago Press.

Rousseau, J.-J. (1967) *La Nouvelle Héloïse*, Paris: Garnier-Flammarion.

Rousseau, J.-J. (1969b) 'Lettre à Monsieur Franquières', in M. Raymond and B. Gagnebin (eds) *Jean-Jacques Rousseau – Œuvres complètes*, Paris: Gallimard (Bibliothèque de la Pléiade).

Rousseau, J.-J. (1979) *Reveries of the Solitary Walker*, trans. P. France. Harmondsworth: Penguin.

Rousseau, J.-J. (1987a) 'Discourse on the Sciences and Arts', in D. A. Cress (ed.) *The Basic Political Writings of Jean-Jacques Rousseau*, Indianapolis: Hackett Publishing Company.

Rousseau, J.-J. (1987b) 'Discourse on the Origin of Inequality of Man', in D. A. Cress (ed.) *The Basic Political Writings of Jean-Jacques Rousseau*, Indianapolis: Hackett Publishing Company.

Rousseau, J.-J. (1991) *Emile, or On Education*, trans. A. Bloom. Harmondsworth: Penguin.

Sartre, J.-P. (1958) *Being and Nothingness*, trans. H. E. Barnes. London: Methuen.

Schwartz, J. (1984) *The Sexual Politics of Jean-Jacques Rousseau*, Chicago: University of Chicago Press.

Searle, J. R. (1983) 'The Word Turned Upside Down', *The New York Review*, 27 October 1983, 74–9.

Sedgwick, E. K. (1990) *Epistemology of the Closet*, Berkeley: University of California Press.

Sedgwick, E. K. (1993a) 'Queer Performativity: Henry James' *The Art of the Novel*', *GLQ A Journal of Lesbian and Gay Studies* 1, 1: 1–16.

Sedgwick, E. K. (1993b) *Tendencies*, Durham, NC: Duke University Press.

Spivak, G. C. (1990) *The Post-Colonial Critic*, ed. S. Harasym, New York and London: Routledge.

Spivak, G. C. (1995) 'At the *Planchette* of Deconstruction is/in America', in A. Haverkamp (ed.) *Deconstruction is/in America: A New Sense of the Political*, New York and London: New York University Press.

Starobinski, J. (1988) *Jean-Jacques Rousseau, Transparency and Obstruction*, trans. A. Goldhammer. Chicago and London: University of Chicago Press.

Still, J. (1994) ''What Foucault Fails to Acknowledge': Feminists and *The History of Sexuality'*, *History of the Human Sciences* 7, 2: 150–7.

Stone, S. (1991) 'The *Empire* Strikes Back: A Posttranssexual Manifesto', in J. Epstein and. K. Straub (eds) *Body Guards: The Cultural Politics of Gender Ambiguity*, New York and London: Routledge.

Tavard, G. H. (1973) *Woman in Christian Tradition*, Notre Dame, Indiana: University of Notre Dame Press.

Trible, P. (1979) 'Eve and Adam: Genesis 2–3 Reread', in C. P. Christ and J. Plaskow (eds) *Womanspirit Rising*, San Francisco: Harper and Row.

Tuana, N. (1992) *Woman and the History of Philosophy*, New York: Paragon House.

Tuana, N. (1993) *The Less Noble Sex: Scientific, Religious and Philosophical Conceptions of Woman's Nature*, Bloomington and Indianapolis: Indiana University Press.

Verges, F. G. (1992) 'The Unbearable Lightness of Deconstruction', *Philosophy* 67: 386–93.

Vintges, K. (1995) '*The Second Sex* and Philosophy', in M. A. Simons (ed.) *Feminist Interpretations of Simone de Beauvoir*, University Park, PA: Pennsylvania State University Press.

Ward, J. K. (1995) 'Beauvoir's Two Senses of "Body" in *The Second Sex*', in M. A. Simons (ed.) *Feminist Interpretations of Simone de Beauvoir*, University Park, PA: Pennsylvania State University Press.

Welleck, R. (1983) 'Destroying English Studies', *The New Criterion*, December: 1–8.

Whitford, M. (1991) *Luce Irigaray – Philosophy in the Feminine*, London and New York: Routledge.

Wills, D. (1995) 'Jaded in America', in A. Haverkamp (ed.) *Deconstruction is/in America: A New Sense of the Political*, New York and London: New York University Press.

Wollstonecraft, M. (1975) *A Vindication of the Rights of Woman*, Harmondsworth: Penguin.

Zerilli, L. M. G. (1994) *Signifying Woman: Culture and Chaos in Rousseau, Burke and Mill*, Ithaca and London: Cornell University Press.

INDEX

221